The Animator's Motion Capture Guide

Organizing, Managing, and Editing

The Animator's Motion Capture Guide

Organizing, Managing, and Editing

Matthew Liverman

CHARLES RIVER MEDIA, INC.

Hingham, Massachusetts

Publisher: Jenifer Niles
Production: Publishers' Design and Production Services, Inc.
Cover Design: The Printed Image
Cover Images: © House of Moves 2003—Performance by Richard Dorton, © Red Eye Studio 2003,
               © Motion Analysis Corporation 2003.

CHARLES RIVER MEDIA, INC.
10 Downer Avenue
Hingham, Massachusetts 02043
781-740-0400
781-740-8816 (FAX)
info@charlesriver.com
www.charlesriver.com

This book is printed on acid-free paper.

Matthew Liverman. *The Animator's Motion Capture Guide: Organizing, Managing, and Editing.*
ISBN: 1-58450-291-6

All brand names and product names mentioned in this book are trademarks or service marks of their respective companies. Any omission or misuse (of any kind) of service marks or trademarks should not be regarded as intent to infringe on the property of others. The publisher recognizes and respects all marks used by companies, manufacturers, and developers as a means to distinguish their products.

Library of Congress Cataloging-in-Publication Data
Liverman, Matthew.
    The animator's motion capture guide : organizing, managing, and
editing / Matthew Liverman.—1st ed.
    p. cm.
  ISBN 1-58450-291-6 (pbk. : alk. paper)
  1. Computer animation.   2. Motion—Computer simulation   I. Title.
TR897.7.L5 2004
006.6'96—dc22
                2003024687

Printed in the United States of America
04 7 6 5 4 3 2 First Edition

CHARLES RIVER MEDIA titles are available for site license or bulk purchase by institutions, user groups, corporations, etc. For additional information, please contact the Special Sales Department at 781-740-0400.

This book is dedicated to everyone who strives to improve
themselves no matter what they are doing.

CONTENTS

ACKNOWLEDGMENTS

I would like to acknowledge and thank the following people and companies for their time, contributions, and support. This book would not have been possible without their tremendous help, and I am greatly indebted to them for taking time away from their pursuits to help me. Despite their generosity and help, it is important for me to point out that any and all mistakes made are mine and mine alone.

Animation Magazine, Auvis Studios, Annie Belanger, Paul Blagay, Rand Cabus, Charles River Media, Jon Damush, Mark Davis, Meg Dunkerley, Bill Galbreath, Giant Studios, Jeff Gibson, Johnathon Gilbreath, Jason Greenberg, John Haley, House of Moves, Tim Huntsman, Kaydara, Inc., Kinetic-Impulse, Alex Lindsay, Mary C. Liverman, Robert D. Liverman, LocoMotion Studios, Madcap Studios, Matt Madden, Rita Maloney, Mantis Motion Productions, Marilyn McDonald, Troy McFarland, Michael McGar, Gary Melzer, Chuck Mongelli, Motion Analysis Corporation, Jenifer Niles, Darek Oczak, Hajimi Ogata, Chris Olson, Alex Omlansky, Perspective Studios, Jarrod Phillips, Steve Pope, Annette Provost, Greg Pyros, Pyros Pictures, Inc., Red Eye Studio, Smashcut, Inc., Don Sood, Jerry Sood, Chad Stahelski, David J. Sturman, Texas State Technical College Waco, Tom Tolles, Wes Trager, Vicon Motion Systems, Johnathon Vought, Matt Warchola, Weta Digital, Richard Widgery, Z-UP Productions.

FOREWORD

Art imitates life. While this is certainly not always the case, the desire to do so is surely much more prevalent in the realm of 3D animation than in any other artistic medium. These days, of course we have the technology to assist artists and animators in the unenviable task of actually doing so. From high-end 3D graphics cards to some of the most sophisticated 3D animation software ever available, now more than ever, the ability exists for the artist to truly imitate life.

For many, this is welcome news. Artists and animators who for many years have been striving to find a balance between creating realistic animation as an art form and imbuing their animations with the flicker of life have the ability to replicate reality—a reality that only the most skilled animators can create on their own and that even moderately skilled artists can now achieve by using the right tools.

Motion capture (mocap) has become one of the key "weapons" in the arsenal of the 3D animators and artists. Best case for mocap is that it allows artists to focus 98% of their valuable time on elements of their art for which no technology currently exists for easy duplication, or on elements that animators desire to create from scratch and for which there is no realistic template. Worst case for motion capture is that the artists and animators get to start with 80% of the animation already complete, thus saving at least 20% of their time for other embellishments and polish of the animation.

This was not always true of mocap. In the early days of motion capture, many artists and animators often found motion capture data more difficult and onerous to work with than their own handcrafted animations. Plus, if the director of the mocap session had somehow instructed the performer to execute a move differently than the animator would have intended or the scene required, the animator would then be relegated to a hell of dealing with motion files that were very difficult to modify and implement. Because of this, many animators began to refer to mocap as "the Devil's rotoscope."

In 1990, Paul Verhoeven and Metrolight Studios decided to use mocap to animate a couple of shots for *Total Recall*. Because the technology was in such a nascent phase, not even the mocap service providers really understood how to make the data behave properly. Problems were plentiful and ranged from poorly captured data and bad camera calibration to severely limited ability to clean the resultant data. Nevertheless, the effects artists and animators persisted and were able to create a silk purse from a sow's ear, and they pulled off the shots, but not before most of the people involved had soured on the idea of mocap. It would take many years to overcome this early prejudice.

Luckily, video games were starting to move toward 3D technology and would simultaneously save the nascent mocap industry and push the mocap technology to new heights. Companies such as Acclaim Entertainment and Electronic Arts were embracing mocap as a viable time- and money-saving animation technique, and they pumped millions into the construction of new studios. Other game studios used mocap service bureaus and created a cottage industry built around the digitization of human motion and its use in the creation of the hottest game titles available.

Once game companies started using more mocap, several things became clear:

1. Mocap is a lot like shooting video or film, and similar preparations are necessary to obtain the desired results.
2. Mocap requires the absolute best talent available.
3. Most 3D animation software was ill-equipped to deal with motion-captured animations, making the data implementation difficult at best.
4. Most importantly, motion capture prepared for properly and used correctly was a huge time and money saver.

When House of Moves was founded over seven years ago, many FX and game companies had already used mocap with mixed results. Companies such as Electronic Arts were using mocap successfully both internally and at service bureaus. Companies such as Digital Domain used motion capture successfully on films like *Titanic* and in commercials for Nike® and Coke®. In spite of these successes, there were still a number of mocap service companies that consistently overstated the capability of mocap, thus disappointing and souring many potential users to its utility.

At House of Moves, we realized early on that to be successful with motion capture required the same key components of any good film or broadcast production, and that our expertise would have to reach beyond the "techie" world of 3D animation. Thus, we slowly began rebuilding the trust and confidence in motion capture technology. We also started to create tools like our Dominatrix™ plug-in for Maya®, our Diva™ processing software, and so forth to make it easy for animators to implement and modify the data. We have also worked side-by-side with the 3D software companies to help them understand the needs of mocap users.

These days, mocap is finding more and more use in film, and its popularity in games is greater than ever before. Companies such as SCEA, Electronic Arts, Acclaim, and many others own their own mocap gear and many of them use House of Moves' Diva software for processing. Motion capture has also been used successfully in films to create full-screen lead characters such as Gollum from the *Lord of the Rings* trilogy, who hold up next to live action actors as if they were all shot on the same live plates. There has even been talk of nominating certain mocap actors for Academy Awards®!

So, is motion capture for entertainment and games currently light-years ahead of its humble medical beginnings? Certainly. But, as Mr. Liverman will more thoroughly illustrate, none of the technology will save anyone from bad motion capture. All mocap is for naught unless one takes the time to prepare thoroughly, to organize, to pick the correct talent, and to choose the right service company. If one follows the counsel contained herein, the results will inevitably be immeasurably better.

—Jarrod Phillips
SVP Business Development
House of Moves Motion Capture Studios
www.moves.com

PREFACE

Character motion is one of the most critical elements in creating a believable look for a video game, animated project, or movie special effect. Good character motion can quickly take the viewer into the imaginary world and help sell the scene, while bad character motion can just as quickly ruin the believability of a game or scene. Without a doubt, motion capture gives you the most realistic synthetic motion possible, and for this reason many companies use motion capture as the source for many of their animations.

Only a few years ago, motion capture occupied a small, highly specialized niche in computer animation. With recent advances in technology, motion capture systems and the software used to animate motion capture data have become more affordable, sophisticated, user-friendly, and commercially available. The capability to deal with motion capture easily is quickly becoming one of many tools that computer animators must have in their toolbox. Jon Damush, the North and South American Business Development Manager for Games and Education at Vicon Motion Systems states that, "In the game world, projects are driven by time, and the amount of content that is needed on the new platforms is growing exponentially, while timelines are shrinking. A lot more work has to be done in the same amount of time and it's not practical to keyframe the large quantity of animations needed; that's where motion capture comes in. Motion capture is a tool to the animator's skill set."

So the question becomes, how does an animator get motion capture training? A select lucky few get their training while on the job, but most animators will be first exposed to motion capture while still in school and through this book. Several progressive schools have already started to integrate motion capture training into their animation programs. Texas State Technical College Waco (TSTC Waco) is one such school. Mark Davis, assistant department chair of digital media design at TSTC Waco, says, "A large number of game companies and animation houses don't own their own mocap equipment, but instead use a mocap service bureau. A student who understands the complexities and management issues that arise when using mocap, while possessing strong keyframing abilities, is more likely to acquire a job with a company that uses mocap or at a mocap service bureau." Vicon Motion Systems' Jon Damush says, "Vicon recognizes that schools are the source of animation talent, so we have focused to make our system available to them to train the next generation of animators. Schools don't need a large motion capture system for mass production purposes, they simply need a system that allows them to train their students and prove their point that motion capture is a valuable addition to their skill set."

As motion capture becomes more widely used and as more animators are trained to deal with it, it only makes sense that you and your company should have a plan in place for how to handle your projects that use motion capture. Your plan can simply address how to handle the motion capture on a single project or how to handle it consistently on several projects. This book is written from a motion coordinator's (lead animator's) point of view and gives my plan for how to handle motion capture, whether on a single project or multiple projects. It will provide you with a complete, start-to-finish plan for dealing with motion capture, hints on selecting a motion capture service bureau, how to cut costs, and how to streamline your process. It also gives you a motion capture terminology glossary and lists of motion capture service bureaus and motion capture performers.

1

AN INTRODUCTION TO MOTION CAPTURE

Where and when motion capture was first used is hard to say, because like most things it has been an evolving process. If you adopt a loose description of motion capture and define it simply as "the capturing of motion," then you could argue that photographing moving objects is a form of motion capture. In the late 1800s, photographers such as Eadweard Muybridge and Etienne-Jules Marey did this when they used photography to study human and animal locomotion.

Marey and Muybridge worked independently of each other, developing different techniques to study locomotion. One of Marey's techniques involved using a special camera, which he invented, that allowed several exposures to be captured on a glass plate and on strips of film that could pass through his camera automatically. Muybridge's approach consisted of using several cameras rigged to take successive pictures to capture a human or animal subject in motion. Muybridge later went on to entertain his audiences when he mounted his pictures in a modified children's toy called a zoetrope. Muybridge's zoetrope or, as he called it, zoogyroscope allowed several pictures to be fixed to a wheel; when the wheel revolved, the individual pictures appeared as an animated figure. Many believe that Muybridge's zoogyroscope and Marey's experiments with strips of film paved the way for the development of motion pictures.

Since motion capture as we know it today is mostly associated with the entertainment industry, an animation method called *roto-scoping* is more often credited with being the ancestor to modern day motion capture. Rotoscoping was used in the 1940s by Disney in the film *Snow White* and is a process where animators trace over film of actors acting out the scenes. Rotoscoping was not invented by Disney, however; it was invented many years earlier by a Disney competitor named Max Fleischer. Fleischer's studio later went on to gain notoriety as the creator of Betty Boop and Popeye, but along with his brothers, Dave and Joe, Fleischer invented roto-scoping around 1915 in an attempt to produce animation more efficiently and economically. David J. Sturman, is his paper *A Brief*

History of Motion Capture for Computer Character Animation, states that "rotoscoping can be thought of as a primitive form or precursor to motion capture, where the motion is 'captured' painstakingly by hand" (© 2003 IEEE).

According to Sturman, one of the very first examples of modern day motion capture, more specifically computer puppetry, came in the early 1960s when an electronic engineer, Lee Harrison III, created a system by which a person controlled the live movement of a character on a screen. He developed his system, which he called Scanimate, and by the late 1960s Scanimate was used heavily in television to create flying logos, but as computer technology developed, Harrison's system soon faded into obscurity.

It wasn't until the late 1970s and early 1980s that modern day motion capture evolved in much the same way as Marey and Muybridge's studies of locomotion. Several universities and companies worked independently and developed several different types of motion capture systems. Several articles written by David J. Sturman and Alberto Menache's book *Understanding Motion Capture for Computer Animation and Video Games* detail the early history of motion capture very well. Because motion capture systems were developed independently, the terminology used by the people involved also varied. The end result is that we now have several terms that basically describe the same things, and this can sometimes make motion capture more confusing than it needs to be. In the back of this book you will find a glossary that hopefully will make some of these terms more understandable.

Like the early photographic experiments, modern day motion capture was developed not only for entertainment purposes but also for the medical field, to help analyze human movement for the development of prosthetics, sports medicine, and joint mechanics. Harrison's Scanimate system could be categorized as a prosthetic system. Magnetic systems on the other hand did not develop until the early 1970s and optical systems not until the 1980s. By the late 1990s, however, motion capture had become the hot and exciting animation technology, being used in video games, movie special effects, TV commercials, and animated TV programs. Michael Gleicher and Nicola Ferrier state in their article, "Evaluating Video-Based Motion Capture":

> "Animation may seem to be an easy application of motion capture as precision is unimportant. Animation rarely cares about exact positions, as applications such as medical analysis might. Animation is more concerned with seemingly less precise things such as emotion, style or intent.

They went on to clarify that:

> Animation has direct needs for precision that stem from the sensitivities that viewers have in experiencing motion. For example, a viewer is likely to notice imprecision in a character's interaction with its world. A foot floating slightly above the floor, or sliding a small amount, or a hand not quite reaching the doorknob, are tiny imprecisions yet can completely destroy the illusion of realism."

Michael Gleicher and Nicola Ferrier, "Evaluating
Video-Based Motion Capture" (© 2003 IEEE).

Since motion capture was attracting a lot of attention in the entertainment industry, it wasn't surprising that soon a controversy developed. The question a lot of people in the animation industry were asking was "is motion capture animation?" The animation community was divided, with some animators insisting that motion capture was a technological process but not an art form, while others prophesizing that motion capture would revolutionize animation. Tom Sito, the president of the Motion Picture Screen Cartoonists Union (M.P.S.C.) Local 839, was quoted in the August 1999 issue of *Animation Magazine* as saying "it [motion capture] is by its nature a cheat." He did acknowledge that ". . . regardless of the arguments, performance animation artists [motion capture animators] would likely be welcomed into the animation union of which he is president."

This controversy reached a peak when, according to the August 1999 issue of *Animation Magazine*, Nelvanna/Medialab's animated TV show "Donkey Kong Country," which used motion capture in addition to keyframe animation, was rejected from qualifying for an Emmy award for best animated television series because The Academy of Television Arts and Sciences said it was not animation.

Writer Alex Lindsay summed up this controversy best in an April 2000 article he wrote for *3D Magazine*, "Thinking Inside the Box: Kaydara's Filmbox 2.0":

> "As motion capture has become more popular, many character animators have begun to think of it as the anti-Christ. They talk about its instabilities, lack of flare, and expense, but in reality, they see it as a threat to their livelihood. The issue these artists run up against is that motion capture provides a layer of detail that they don't. A character animator generally captures what we consciously notice about an individual. If they are an exceptional character animator, they will capture things that the average person would barely perceive. But what they don't capture is the information that neither the character animator nor the layperson ever consciously sees but routinely reacts to in their normal lives. . . .
>
> The other side of the debate is often filled with producers and mocap artists. They see motion capture as the messiah that will revolutionize the cost of production. While mocap is expensive in the beginning (system costs and internal development expenses are very high), the return, theoretically, is the ability to capture complex motion in or near real time, if done correctly, a motion-capture team can capture material in a single day that would traditionally take months and months to create. The problem is that it's never done "correctly." Motion capture still lies on the bleeding edge, and most who have experimented with it have experienced more of the bleeding than the edge. Shortcomings can include picking the wrong capture artists, spikes and warps in the data, improper direction of the capture artist, and changes to the scene after the motion capture. These issues often render mocap data completely useless. . . .
>
> The future, of course, is somewhere in the middle. The key is to capture all the little nuances and idiosyncrasies that the human body or animal structures may provide but still have the ability to adjust those motions easily and effectively long after the capture. Most likely, the person working with this data will be

neither a true character animator nor a mocap technician, but rather something in between."

(© 3D Magazine, CMP Media LLC, April 2000, pp. 45–47)

Much like the controversy that surrounded the validity of motion capture as animation, another argument soon arose, this time dividing the motion capture community. The argument was what term was the "best" term to define what we generically call motion capture. This argument arose because there are several different approaches and techniques used to capture a motion or a performance and there are several ways in which the captured data is used. Since these different systems are all lumped under the one generic term of "motion capture," some people feel that it does not properly define the work they do. *Animation Magazine*, in its August 1999 issue, quoted the president of Protozoa, Brad deGraf: "I dislike the term motion capture because it reinforces a shallow understanding, and trivializes the form. Performance animation is more broadly descriptive and inclusive. It implies a more active creative process and credits the deep heritage underlying the medium."

Whether it is called *motion capture*, *performance capture*, *performance animation*, *real-time animation*, or *digital puppetry* is really only a matter of how the data is being used and personal choice. People tend to use some of these term interchangeably, but they have subtle differences that make them unique. Some of these terms can also be considered subsets of another term, depending on your definition and point of view.

The following terms are defined according to my experiences, but it is safe to say that some people will not agree with these definitions. In this book, we will continue to use the generic term "motion capture" to describe the entire process, from collecting the data to using it as a baseline for animation.

Motion Capture (or Performance Capture): The process of obtaining and recording a three-dimensional representation of a live action performance or event by capturing an object's position and/or orientation in physical space. This three-dimensional representation is often used in the medical or entertainment industry.

Performance Animation: The motion performer's live action performance that is viewed as it is generated. The performer gets feedback to his performance as it happens, so it can be modified as it occurs.

Real-Time Animation: A live action performance that is presented on a character in real time. This includes animations that are performed, captured, and rendered in real time.

Digital Puppetry: A live action performance that uses several processes to create an animation and where the performer's controls do not necessarily correspond directly to the character's action. For example, a performer may use a joystick to drive the character's facial expression. Some of the processes a performer can use, among others, are real-time animation, performance animation, joysticks, sliders, digital gloves, pedals, and touch pads. Several performers also may act in unison during the performance, each controlling different parts of a single character.

TYPES OF MOTION CAPTURE SYSTEMS

As motion capture technology developed, several uniquely different types of motion capture systems evolved. Wes Trager's 1994, *A Practical Approach to Motion Capture: Acclaim's Optical Motion Capture System*, describes the four groups of motion capture input systems that existed at the time: acoustic, magnetic, optical, and prosthetic. The first three systems are easy to distinguish between, but the fourth, prosthetic, is more of a catchall group containing a few miscellaneous types of systems. My definitions of these systems are as follows:

Acoustic Motion Capture: Consists of transmitters attached to a subject that emit a sound. Audio receivers surrounding the subject then measure the time it takes for the sound emitted from the transmitters to reach the receivers, and from this they can triangulate the location in space of each transmitter. The transmitters are commonly placed on a person, at his joints, to capture his body movement.

Magnetic Motion Capture: A series of sensors that magnetically measure their relationship in space to a nearby transmitter. As with acoustic, these magnetic sensors are placed at the joints in order to capture the person's movement.

Optical Motion Capture: A series of reflective markers whose position in space is tracked by a number of digital cameras. In the case of human and animal captures, the markers are generally placed near the joints.

Prosthetic Motion Capture: An external structure attached to a limb or part of the body. Included in this structure is a series of encoders that measure the rotation and position of the performer's body as he moves, so that his motion can be analyzed. There are several different types of prosthetic motion capture input systems. Waldos, gloves, and some electromechanical suits are included in this group.

In addition to these four basic types of motion capture systems, there are other devices that sometimes are used and can be considered motion capture input systems. Some people may argue that armature devices are really a subset of prosthetic motion capture, while some feel there is a slight difference. Armature devices are generally not driven directly by the motion performer's performance as prosthetics are; instead, armatures are more commonly posed in positions, and then that pose is recorded as a keyframe. The animation is then built frame by frame from posing the armature.

Digital Armature Devices: Devices that consist of a series of rigid modules connected by joint sensors whose rotations are recorded digitally. The most common type of armatures are keyframe armatures.

As modern day motion capture has matured, acoustic systems have not proven to be a popular choice and have faded in obscurity; prosthetic devices continue to have only a small, specialized niche, while optical and magnetic systems have proven to be the more popular systems. All systems have their advantages and disadvantages. The main disadvantage to magnetic systems is that they require wires and a transmitter to be placed on the performer, which can hinder or prevent him from freely performing some motions. This is especially true if stunt or hard hitting motions are required. Optical systems do not have this problem, so they are the choice of most people in the entertainment industry in the United States. Optical systems, made by Vicon and Motion Analysis, are more widely used systems, while Giant Studios (formally Biomechanics) has its own unique optical system for its clients to use, but does not sell it commercially.

APPROACHES TO ANIMATING

Sometimes one of the most difficult decisions an artist or animator has to make is simply where to start. When a traditional cel animator or a computer animator begins an animation, there are three basic approaches he can use: *keyframing, straight ahead,* or the *combination* approach.

Straight Ahead Animating: A method of animating where the action is built in an evolving sequence of events one frame at a time. The animator starts at the beginning and moves one frame at a time until the animation is complete.

Keyframing/Pose to Pose/Pose Planning Animating: A method of animating where key poses showing extreme or important moments in time are done first. The space between the keyframes is then broken down further into smaller increments of time until the animation is complete.

The Combination Approach: A method of animating where the animator uses keyframes as guidelines to block out or get a rough estimation of the animation, then goes back and animates the motion using the straight ahead method. Many traditional animators feel that this gives them the best result, even though it is a more time-consuming way of working.

When dealing with motion capture data as the source of your animation, however, you don't need to decide where to start because that decision has already been made for you. Your approach started when the performance was captured during your capture session. All motion capture data begins as a straight ahead sequence of events, so your decision is not how to start, but rather how to best continue when you animate the existing data. Even though motion capture data starts off as a straight ahead process, the animator who will work with the data can use any one or several of the basic approaches and a few "advanced" approaches.

In addition to the three basic approaches, there are a few other approaches to animating that may be considered more advanced but are fairly common when animating motion capture data. *Nonlinear animation* and *procedural animation* can be used, depending on the software you are working with. Many people consider nonlinear animation a more expansive type of layered animation because the animator works with separate *clips* or *layers* of data. The confusion between what is layered and what is non-linear animation exists because some software packages use the terms interchangeably, and others use the term "layered" but include some tools that are really more non-linear tools.

Layered Animating: A method of animation that allows an animator to work on separate levels or "layers," which are independent of each other but when composited together blend to create a unique, new animation.

Non-Linear Animating: A method of animation that allows an animator to alter an animation or several animations from separate sources to create a new animation. The animator can blend, edit, scale, or reposition portions of an animation or several animations when creating the new one.

Procedural Animating: A method of animating in which the laws of physics or mathematics take over and dictate the look of the animation.

You will likely use several approaches, if not all of them, at one time or another while working with motion capture files. It is important to note that since motion capture data is captured as a straight ahead sequence, a keyframe is placed on every single frame. Technically there are keys between frames, too, so you should not approach editing motion capture the same way you would a fully keyframed animation. More than one animator has made the mistake of trying to delete large sections from motion capture data and then attempted to completely re-keyframe the deleted section, only to discover that this is a very time-consuming way to approach animating a motion capture file, not to mention that it defeats the purpose of capturing the motion to begin with. Because there is a keyframe placed on every frame, the straight ahead approach of animating can also be very time consuming; however, you may find this approach necessary in some situations. If you need to place a prop (such as a baseball bat) in a character's hand on every frame, there are quick techniques to get the bat close, but you may then choose to use the straight ahead approach and place the prop in the character's hand on each frame.

BASIC PRINCIPLES OF ANIMATION

Disney animators Frank Thomas and Ollie Johnston outlined what they called the 12 basic principles of animation, and nearly every book on animation since has mentioned these 12 principles or some variation of them. Animator Tony White's book *The Animator's Workbook* and animator and director Richard Williams' *The Animator's Survival Kit* are two good examples.

Whether you are using traditional animation techniques, computer animation, or motion capture, these principles should be kept in mind when animating a character. Taking these principles into account can help you achieve the look you are seeking for your animations.

Anticipation: Anticipation refers to movement in the opposite direction before the main action starts. The more simple the motion, generally the more simple the anticipation will be. An example of anticipation is when a human shifts backward, sinking his weight onto his back foot before pushing forward to run.

Arcs of motion: This refers to objects traveling on an arc through space as opposed to traveling on a straight line. For example, your hand does not move straight from front to back, but rather it travels on an arc as it swings.

Ease-in and ease-out: Sometimes called *slow-in* and *slow-out*, this refers to the change in speed as an object moves. Most objects start slow, accelerate to a constant speed, then slow to a stop. When an object accelerates until it reaches a constant speed, this is called ease-in. When an object decelerates until it stops, this is called ease-out. Remember, good animators know heavier objects need more time to ease-in and ease-out.

Exaggeration: Exaggeration refers to dramatizing a character's motions by pushing them past the extreme of natural movement. Generally, the more cartoon-like the character is, the more extreme the exaggeration can be and not look out of place for the character.

Follow through/overlapping action: Follow through is the opposite of anticipation: It occurs when the main action comes to a stop. Follow through or overlapping (in character animation) refers to secondary movement, such as limbs that stop after the source of the movement (usually the hips) has stopped. Secondary movements often move past the stopping point of the source and then settle back before coming to a rest. An example is when your arms continue to swing after your body has come to a stop after running.

Squash and stretch: Squash and stretch can be used to create a feeling of weight. A good example would be a ball bouncing. As it descends, the ball should stretch out to more of an oval shape, and as it hits the ground it squashes, then it stretches into an oval again as it leaves the ground before returning to a more round shape near the apex of the bounce.

Staging: Staging refers to presenting an idea or action clearly. How characters relate to each other, how a character moves, when actions happen in relation to other events, and how the scene is viewed all play a part in how clearly it is understood. Scenes that are too busy often overwhelm the viewer, and the idea is lost.

Timing: Timing refers to the pace in which actions occur. The character's personality and body type need to be taken into account when an animator is considering timing. Primary movement and secondary movements all need to be paced properly. Timing also refers to the pace that interaction between characters and props occurs.

Weight and balance: Having a character's weight balanced, distributed properly, and shifting correctly as the character moves is very important. When a human moves, his weight is shifted over the planted leg, and the passing leg is moved forward, finally hitting the ground in front of the character. A character's center of balance will also tip forward in the direction it is moving. The amount it tips depends on the speed of the movement (the character should tip more the faster he is moving).

Personality: Even if you take all of these principles into account, your character may still look somewhat "mechanical." Good animators are aware of this and are able to infuse their characters with *personality*. The principle of personality is of the utmost importance because it is the final measure of how people will respond to your character. It is an intangible quality that makes a person or character unique. Giving a character personality involves several factors:

- The physical appearance of the character
- The character's basic movements
- The character's actions
- The character's reactions to events or other characters
- The character's voice

As an animator, you have control of the character's basic movements, his actions, and his reactions, and if you are lucky, you will also have some say in the appearance of the character.

A good example of a live performer who uses his movements, actions, and reactions to brilliantly define his character's personality is Charlie Chaplin. Chaplin's movements and timing in his performances almost goes beyond physical boundaries. This means that it seems that Chaplin is sometimes able to defy the laws of gravity and force. Chaplin mastered the art of secondary motion, timing, and exaggeration to give his "Tramp" character an animated appearance. The other notable thing about Chaplin is that he is able to give the Tramp personality without ever speaking a word. A modern day athlete who also seems to defy the laws of gravity is Michael Jordan. This does not give him a personality, but Jordan's ability to make complex physical actions look easy and appear to defy physical laws makes him appear more than human.

MOTION CAPTURE AND THE PRINCIPLES OF ANIMATION

Even though these principles of animation are helpful to all three kinds of animators—traditional cel animators, computer animators, and motion capture animators—the motion capture animator will use these principles at different times throughout the animation process and in different ways than the other animators.

A good traditional cel animator and a good computer animator will consider these principles before they start an animation and throughout their animation process. However, when dealing with motion capture data, an animator will need to consider some principles during one phase of his animation process and others during the other phases. A motion capture animator has three distinct phases to his animation process: the preparation phase, the capture session phase, and the post capture phase.

The Preparation Phase

In the preparation phase, a motion capture animator needs to take these principles into account when developing the motion list, flowcharts and motion database:

- Ease-in/ease-out
- Exaggeration
- Follow through/overlapping action
- Staging
- Timing
- Personality

Ease-in/ease-out and follow through/overlapping action need to be considered when calculating the number of seconds a motion that will be shot at the capture session should take to complete. Many "twitch" games do not want to have long ease-in/ease-out or overlapping sections because quick user feedback is more desirable. In other words, the character needs to get back into a certain position quickly so that he can react to the next user input. A good example of a twitch game is basketball. Because it is fast paced, the characters need to respond quickly to user input and therefore do not have the time to gently ease-in or ease-out of many motions.

Exaggeration, timing, and personality go hand in hand, and all relate to the type of game or character the motion is for. A large heavy character may take longer to perform a motion and have more exaggeration in his performance. Keep in mind that if too much exaggeration is needed, it may be better to keyframe animate your motions. When exaggeration and timing are involved, you must consider user response time. In video games, user response time refers to the amount of time it takes a game's character to react after the user has given the character input. In other words, it is the amount of time it takes the character to react after a button is pressed. The character's personality affects the motions that he would perform, the amount of exaggeration needed, and the length of time during which he would execute them. Personality should be considered more in games that involve more character development. Sports video games generally don't consider personality as much as role playing games.

Staging mostly would be used when dealing with motions that are to be used in a cinematic sequence. The position of each character to the others and where the camera is located all need to be thought out before the capture session, not during it. Staging also is considered when capturing a multiple performer motion. An example would be a blocking motion for football: where does each person start, how much can he move side to side or front to back, where he will end in relation to the others, etc.

The Capture Session Phase

During the capture session phase, the motion coordinator and motion performer work together to contribute to the overall look of the motions captured. The performer needs to be able to execute the motion, and the motion coordinator needs to be able to direct the performer so that they can capture the motion they need to produce the final animation. During this capture session phase, several principles will occur naturally during a performance:

- Anticipation
- Arcs of motion
- Ease-in/ease-out

- Follow through/overlapping action
- Squash and stretch
- Timing
- Weight and balance

As stated before, all of these principles will occur naturally during a motion performance, but anticipation, ease-in/ease-out, overlapping motion, and timing can be coached slightly. Directing a motion performer to stop more quickly, run slower, settle faster, or crouch down more before jumping can help you capture the motion you are looking for. You need to remember, however, that there is a limit to controlling natural forces. With a few exceptions, arcs of motion, squash and stretch, and weight and balance occur naturally during motion and are mostly beyond human control.

Squash and stretch is an interesting and slightly frustrating principle when dealing with motion capture. The human body is flexible and squashes and stretches naturally, depending on what motion it is performing. When a baseball pitcher throws a ball, his arm actually stretches or elongates due to the elasticity of the muscles and tendons surrounding the joints. The body also naturally squashes or contracts on contact during a hard impact. A computer skeleton used in video games is a rigid skeleton and therefore does not squash or stretch. Because of this, difference adjustments to the captured data need to be made when fitting it to a skeleton. This slight variation to the captured data alters its authenticity to nature to a certain extent, but for animation purposes it is negligible.

The Post Capture Phase

It is during the post capture phase when the motion capture animator gets to use the principles and skills that most animators would consider truly animating. During this phase, a motion capture animator and a keyframe animator will consider all the principles. How a motion capture animator physically alters or changes an animation may be slightly different because motion capture data places a keyframe on every frame.

- Anticipation
- Arcs of motion
- Ease-in/ease-out
- Exaggeration
- Follow through/overlapping action
- Squash and stretch
- Staging
- Timing
- Weight and balance
- Personality

When animating over motion capture data, there are a couple things to keep in mind. Generally, if you have made a good decision about using motion capture and have captured the correct motions and the quality of the captured motions is good, then it is best to "animate" the data as little as possible. This does not mean you should be lazy, but if you have captured the motion you need, the majority of the post capture phase involves minor touch-ups to the data. You simply make the motions fit and blend together so that the user will have good response time. Other things might include making sure his arms don't pass through his torso or leg, or that the character is holding onto props when needed. Major changes in timing or exaggeration become difficult and are usually not good when dealing with motion capture.

By far the main thing that is unique about animations starting with motion capture data is that motion capture data provides the animator with quite a bit of baseline information, such as root movement and motion curves/paths. With the other forms of animation, the animator must truly build and control the timing and motion curves of the character from scratch, as opposed to enhancing an already existing performance.

CONCLUSION

- Motion capture in one form or another has been around for a long time.
- Motion capture has been used for both medical and entertainment purposes.
- Motion capture and its place as a legitimate animation technique is highly controversial.
- Many people still don't agree on what is the best term to describe what we generically describe as motion capture.
- There are several different types of motion capture input systems and devices.
- There are a few different approaches to animating that an animator might use.
- All animators should be aware of the basic principles of animation.
- Animators who deal with motion capture data should be aware of how the principles of animation apply to motion capture.

2

MOTION CAPTURE AND YOUR PROJECT

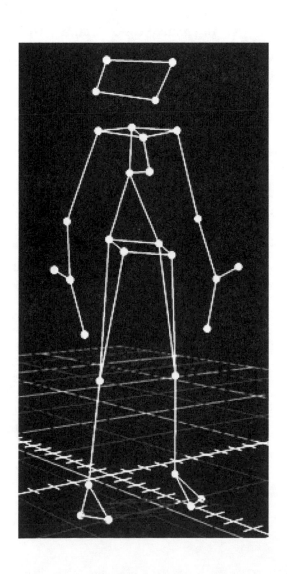

When you are considering whether or not to use motion capture as the baseline for your animations, you need to be realistic as to what to expect from motion capture. In the past, people have rushed into a decision to use motion capture before considering if it was truly the best approach for their projects. Motion capture will give you realistic-looking motion, but if your project needs very stylized, cartoon-like motions, motion capture may not be your best choice. When deciding, there are several factors that you need to consider. Some of these factors are more business or managerial considerations, while others are artistic or creative considerations. On some projects, the decision might be an easy one, and on other projects it may be more complicated. Regardless of the type of decision it is, all these factors need to be considered thoroughly if you are going to make the best decision for your project.

DECIDING IF MOTION CAPTURE IS RIGHT FOR YOUR PROJECT

First you need to decide which type of motion capture, if any, will work best for your project. As we talked about earlier, there are several different types of motion capture input systems. Most video game companies and special effects houses use optical motion capture, some use magnetic, and a select few use a combination of the two systems. Your choice of systems will affect the cost and possibly the quality of the motion data. Most likely your project will dictate which type of motion capture you should use. For example, if you are working on a non-linear project, you may decide to use a magnetic system; however, optical systems are often used on both non-linear and linear projects. If you need to capture facial motion, optical motion capture is your best bet, at least for the facial data. You may decide to use an optical system to capture the facial data and a magnetic system for the body motion. Keep in mind that projects that involve stunts and hard-hitting motions are more suited to optical motion capture.

Linear Project: A project that does not require any user input and where the animations have a predetermined outcome. An example of a linear project is a movie, TV commercial, or cinematic sequence in a video game.

Non-Linear Project: A project whose motions respond to commands from user input. A video game is an example of a non-linear project.

One of the most obvious issues to consider is the budget. Does your company or project have the money it will need, and are you willing to spend it on motion capture? It is impossible to say how much using motion capture will cost you because there are so many variables that will affect the cost. If you have used motion capture before and have an idea of the scope of your animation needs, simply contact a motion capture service bureau for a bid on the cost. In order for a motion studio to give an accurate bid, however, there is a lot of information you will need to provide them with. See Chapter 8, "Selecting a Motion Capture Studio," for more details on this. One reason that motion capture is considered so expensive by a lot of people is because it is a front-loaded expense. This means that the cost of a motion capture session usually comes at the beginning of a project. What a lot of people fail to consider is that, if done properly, motion capture can save money as the project progresses because it shortens the total time that animators need to work and generally requires a smaller team of animators than a project that keyframes all the animations from scratch. The most overlooked budgetary consideration is that it is common for video game projects that use motion capture to reuse the captured motion for many revisions of the game. This means that the cost of the initial capture should be averaged over the number of years the motion data will be used. Many sports games, for example, have a large major capture session and then use that motion data over the course of three or four years and produce three or four revisions of the game. They may have a small capture session every year to add or update some motions, but they get many years out of the initial capture data. Managers may feel a

$380,000 motion capture session is too expensive, but when compared to the overall cost of a project, sometimes around seven million dollars or more, the actual cost of the motion capture is minimal compared to the results. If the game is updated every year, this $380,000 expense can be averaged out over the three or four years that the motion will be able to be used. This does not even consider the number of platforms your game is being developed for. For example, if your game is being made for the Sony Playstation®2 and for Microsoft's Xbox™, both platforms will use the same captured data, so your company gets two platforms for the cost of one capture session.

If expense is the only factor keeping you from using motion capture for your project, or if you need only a small amount of motion, there are a couple of options you might consider. House of Moves and Red Eye Studio motion capture studios have library systems of stock motion capture files that you can buy. House of Moves' library consists of over 5,500 moves, broken into several different groups of motion. The generic group includes walks, runs, jogs, and other basic movements. It also has several different sports groups, a martial arts group, a medieval combat group, and a group of Special Forces–type motions. You can purchase individual motions or for a set price select as many motions from a group as you like. For example, if you need a few hockey motions for a demo, you can purchase the hockey group and select as many motions from it as you need. If you need some basic motions for an architectural walkthrough, you can purchase the use of the generic motion group.

Red Eye Studio also has an impressive library of moves. Its library motions are captured exclusively to be used in its library system. Some of the motion groups are the basic collection, modern military maneuvers, medieval warfare, and unarmed combat, to name a few. Red Eye's basic collection includes premade looping motions and transition motions, in addition to other basic movements. Each of Red Eye's groups consists of approximately 150 motions.

The price to use these motion libraries varies and may depend on a few things such as whether you are buying individual motions or buying the right to choose from a group of motions. It is possible that the file format you need the files delivered in will also affect the cost. The downside to using motions from a library such as this is that you may be limited by the way the motions were captured. This means that the motions may not be captured starting or ending with the character in the position you need him in, so be sure that this avenue fits your project best.

Another way to cut the cost of motion capture is to have cloud data delivered to you instead of skeletal data. There are some big drawbacks to this option, and it is not recommended unless you have experience working with motion capture data. *Cloud data*, also called marker data, is the motion capture data before it is fixed to a skeleton. Having the cloud data delivered to you requires the motion capture studio to do less processing, so generally it is cheaper. Before the markers are linked, cloud data can be difficult to comprehend; many studios link the markers during the capture session, so the figure is easier to see during playback. Figures 2.1 and 2.2 are examples of cloud data before and after the markers are linked.

Cloud Data: The position information of unlabeled markers in the motion capture software as they travel through time and space.

Skeletal Data: The movement of a skeleton as it travels through time and space after the marker data has been applied to it.

If you want cloud data delivered, you have the choice of getting the cleaned cloud data or raw data. Cleaned cloud data means that the motion capture studio did some clean-up to the data such as filling gaps and getting rid of spikes, phantom markers, and ghost trajectories, to name a few. If you get cleaned cloud data from the motion studio, it will need to be attached to your skeleton before your animators can begin editing. This task has been made easier with advances in some software packages, but unless you have experience with it, it is not recommended. You also

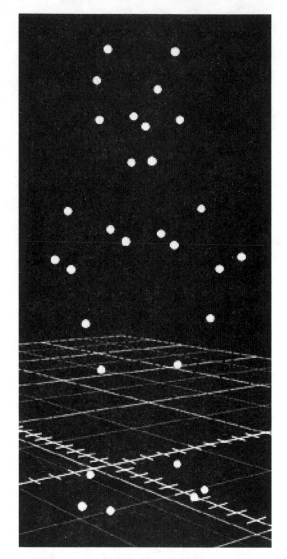

FIGURE 2.1   An example of cloud data without the markers linked. © 2003. Reprinted with permission from Kinetic-Impulse and Richard Widergy.

should keep in mind that if you have to do this extra step, it will add time to your animation schedule.

Cleaning: A generic phrase that includes several processes to get rid of irregularities in the motion capture data in order to improve its quality. Sometimes called *processing*.

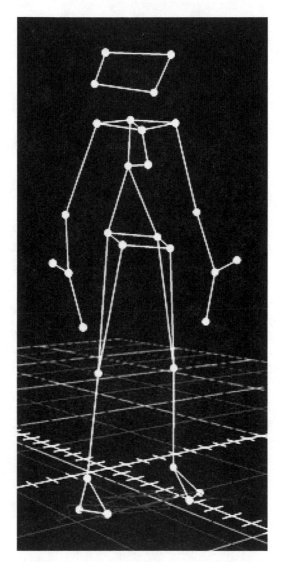

FIGURE 2.2   An example of cloud data with the markers linked. © 2003. Reprinted with permission from Kinetic-Impulse and Richard Widergy.

Getting the raw or uncleaned data will require you to do even more work to the data before editing can begin, and this is not recommended unless you have a lot of experience working with motion capture data that way. Again, some software packages have made cleaning motion data easier, but experience and familiarity with the tools is best. Raw data requires you to do all the cleaning and then fix it to a skeleton before you can even begin editing.

If your project has the budget for it, it is recommended that you get skeletal data from the motion studio. Motion studios have people with experience in cleaning data and fixing it to a skeleton, so it makes sense to have them take care of it. One way to help assure success is to let people do what they are good at.

Your project's timeline is also a major issue. Do you have the time to organize, execute, and animate the motion capture data properly? Again, this will depend on several factors, such as the number of motions you need to capture, the number of animators on the project, and the deadlines established. If your project requires a large number of motions to be animated (hundreds or even thousands) and has only a few animators and you have a short timeline, motion capture may be the only way for you to complete the project. A few animators can edit and animate hundreds of motions in a short period of time if you are well organized.

One area that needs to be worked out is estimating the number of days you need in the studio for your capture session, and this can be tricky because it involves several factors. The kind of motion you need to capture will affect how many capture days you need. If the motions you need to capture require a lot of special props, stunt motions, or complicated interaction of performers, then your capture will need more time than a capture session of basic motions. Whether your motions are basic or complicated ones, the number of attempts or versions it takes you to get the kind of motion you are looking for also matters. If it takes you seven attempts to get a simple walk motion, you will most likely not capture as many motions. Most motion capture studios use 100 basic motions a day as a baseline. This means 100 *finished* basic motions, so if it takes you seven attempts to capture a walk motion, this would count as only one finished motion. As the level of difficulty of your motions goes up, the baseline number of 100 finished motions per day goes down. More complicated motions generally take more prep time and may require more attempts to get what you need.

Your organization—or lack thereof—can also affect your capture. Obviously, if you waste time or spend extra time on set figuring out exactly what you need, you will not be able to capture as many motions. Experience also may play a factor. Generally, if your people have experience with motion capture sessions, they should be more efficient during a capture. With that said, there are still a lot of people who have experience capturing motion who are incredibly inefficient. If you need to capture 700 motions for your project and your motions are a mixture of basic with some complicated motions, it is recommended that you plan for at least a seven and a half or an eight day capture session in case you run into some complications or get behind schedule. This assumes that you are capturing all of your 700 motions during one capture session. If your project is composed of a higher number of complicated motions, more time should be scheduled. All motion capture studios help clients determine the level of difficulty of their motions. Keep in mind that scheduling more time than necessary is always better than not scheduling enough. If you finish early, you will most likely need to pay the studio for the days you did not use, but if you plan properly there should only be a half to one day of wasted time.

If your timeline allows or if you have several hundred or thousands of motions to capture, it is best to schedule at least two capture sessions, a primary and a secondary capture session. Not enough people realize the huge advantages to setting up primary and secondary capture sessions. If you schedule one large capture at the beginning of your project, you only have *one* chance to get everything right, so the likelihood that there will be missed or incorrectly captured motions goes up significantly. If that occurs, you will be stuck with the motions you captured. The other advantage to scheduling more than one capture session is that video game projects are dynamic processes and often change, so scheduling a secondary capture later in the project lets you capture motions to accommodate changes in the design of the game. Late changes made to the design are never good, but they do happen, so it is better to prepare for it.

Primary Capture Session: The main motion capture shoot, scheduled for capturing the bulk of the motions needed on a project.

Secondary Capture Session: A supplemental motion capture shoot, scheduled to capture any missed, changed, or cinematic motions needed on a project.

The look of your character also needs to be considered. Motion capture, if done properly, will give you very realistic human or animal motion, but if your project requires more dramatic or cartoon-like motion, the use of motion capture might not be right for your project. It is possible to get a motion performer who can act and add more personality to your character, but no matter what, the performer can only do so much because he is affected by the laws of physics. The overall look of the project also plays a part. Do the environment and background textures in your project fit with realistic motion of the characters? Again, if the overall look and feel of your project will not support realistic motion, then it may be better to consider another option for your animations. Sports video games are very good examples of projects that benefit from the use of motion capture. They generally seek realistic motion, have a small group of animators and a short timeline, and need thousands of animations.

You should also consider if motion capture can give you the motions you need. You need to know if the motions that you are seeking can be performed in the required amount of space or must be broken up to fit in. If you want to capture cinematic sequences for a movie or video game, can you capture the entire scene or break it down into pieces that can be captured in the amount of space available?

COMMON ERRORS WHEN CONSIDERING MOTION CAPTURE

There are several errors that people make when considering or using motion capture. These errors are often made by people who have never used motion capture before. It has been my experience that people who have used motion capture before but are not efficient with it also make many of these same errors.

Using motion capture makes the animator's job easier. Some people automatically assume that using motion capture will make the animator's job easier, but often the opposite is true. In the past, motion capture received a bad reputation from some animators because unrealistic expectations, lack of knowledge, and laziness actually made the animator's job harder instead of easier.

Using motion capture will save time. Again, the opposite often proves to be true. If not organized efficiently, dealing with large numbers of motion capture files can be a nightmare, and the time spent in post capture production greatly increases.

Using motion capture will save money. If handled properly, motion capture can be very cost effective, but if you try to "shoot from the hip" when organizing, cut too many corners, or aren't familiar with the details of your contract, using motion capture can easily cost you two to three times the money it should.

People underestimate the amount of planning that is needed prior to the capture session. Without the proper planning, working on a project that uses motion capture can be one headache after another. Planned properly, however, it can be an easy, straightforward process that is both efficient and effective.

People are unorganized during the capture session. Being unorganized during a capture session can easily have disastrous results. It is too easy to get behind schedule, run over time, capture motions improperly, or forget to capture important motions. Being organized will help assure those problems do not come up.

People underestimate the importance of using a good motion performer. The motion data captured directly reflects the movements of the motion performer, so you need to have a performer who is able to give you the exact motion you require. A great deal of care should be taken when selecting a motion performer.

People think they can fix bad motion data after the capture session. Whether the data is bad due to a bad performance or was poorly captured or processed, assuming you can fix it in the post capture stage is foolish. If you have to do damage control after the fact, it is always more difficult than doing it correctly the first time.

USING MOTION CAPTURE

In the recent past, some video game developers felt they could save money by purchasing their own motion capture system, thus avoiding the need to use a third-party motion capture service bureau. For the most part, this thinking is flawed. It is true that you can purchase an optical system and learn to use it fairly easily, but that does not mean your people will be proficient enough to capture large quantities of data for production. The main thing that sets the good service bureaus apart from the amateurs isn't the equipment as much as it is the people. The good ones have experienced people who deal with motion capture issues and problems every day and come up with ways to assure the problems don't occur again. Unless your company is willing to spend the money on a quality system and hire experienced people to work with the system, it is better to use a third-party service bureau for your motion capture needs.

Once you decide to use motion capture on your project, there is a lot of work to do if you want to try to assure your project is as effective and efficient as possible. Asking questions, planning, and organizing prior to a motion capture session are by far the best things that you can do. Lead Massive Technical Director for Weta Digital, Ltd., John Haley, says that "organization is key going in to a capture. Because you have a limited time to capture the best performance, having a well thought out plan is extremely important."

A good example of how the lack of organization and planning can have disastrous results was during the quest to be the first person to reach the South Pole. On November 2, 1902, British explorer Robert Falcon Scott and a small crew set out to reach the pole even though they had never driven sledge dogs or even skied before. It isn't surprising then that they were forced to turn back well short of the pole on December 30, 1902. The surprising part is that in 1911 Scott, with a new crew, made a second attempt.

At the same time that Scott was about to make his second attempt, there was a separate Norwegian team also trying to be the first to reach the pole. The Norwegians were led by explorer Roald Amundsen. Amundsen was an expert skier and a methodical planner and had spent years learning about polar clothing, travel, and dog handling from Eskimos. Amundsen used sledges pulled by dogs to haul the heavy supplies and save the men's strength. They also took three or four backups of crucial items and buried 10 extremely well-marked depots of food for the return trek. Amundsen even calculated how many dogs would be worn out from the journey and could be used as food. On December 14, 1911, Amundsen and four other men reached the South Pole. All the men and roughly one fifth of the dogs returned safely to their base camp on January 25, 1912.

Scott's second attempt didn't go nearly as well as the Norwegians. He originally had planned for a crew of four men, and the night before the trek he decided to take a fifth man along. Like the Norwegians, they had buried food and supplies for the return journey; however, the supplies were rationed for four men, not five. Their food depots were spread out further than the Norwegians, and the British team didn't mark their depot locations well. This meant that the depots would be difficult or impossible for the

British team to locate in bad weather. Because of his experience with dogs during his first attempt, Scott foolishly decided not to use dogs to pull the heavy sledges; instead, the men walked or skied while pulling them. The British team did reach the South Pole on January 17, 1912, a full thirty-five days after the Norwegians.

On their return, Scott and crew were exhausted from pulling the heavy sledges and hampered by bad weather. They had a hard time finding their food depots, and all five men died before they reached their base camp. Scott's last diary entry was on March 29, 1912.

Ironically and unbelievably, some feel Amundsen's achievement of being the first to reach the South Pole has been tainted by the Scott tragedy and because Amundsen, through his meticulous planning, made the expedition look too easy. Through his organization, planning, and experience, Amundsen made a trek—across approximately 700 miles of rough Arctic terrain, where whiteout blizzards are common, in temperatures ranging from 5 degrees Fahrenheit to 31 degrees below zero—look too easy.

This may seem like an extreme example of poor planning; however, the poor planning of a game's animations can also have disastrous results for your project. It can cost your company valuable time, man-hours, and money, and if you are developing the game for someone else, it can even cause you to lose the project. Many game companies even lay off people because the cost overruns on some projects hurt the company so badly. How would you like to be laid off because someone else didn't plan properly on his project?

How a company and its employees choose to approach a project speaks volumes about it and often leads to its success or failure. Some companies handle their business and money fairly loosely, while others have procedures and policies in place to try to help assure success. Are you and your company a Scott company or an Amundsen company?

A *Scott* company is characterized by:

- Shooting from the hip
- Reinventing the wheel with each new project

- Handling problems as they occur
- Needing to play catch up to finish

An *Amundsen* company is characterized by:

- Planning prior to start
- Having a system in place
- Anticipating possible problems *before* they happen
- Making it look easy

For some reason working with motion capture data either intimidates people or they try to handle it by "shooting from the hip" and more often than not underestimate the amount of work that needs to be done before a motion capture session can become a reality and the motion data is edited and ready to be implemented into their game. Regardless of the reasons, many companies seem to fall short in regard to how to best handle motion capture, instead choosing to handle it separately on each game and often not the same way from year to year. In other words they are constantly "reinventing the wheel" with each game instead of building on their past accomplishments and failures.

The problem with "being organized" is that most people feel they are organized but they don't seem to anticipate all the possible obstacles and consequences. Having a plan in place will help assure that your project's animations are handled in a uniform, thorough, professional, and timely manner.

A COORDINATED APPROACH

If your company has several projects that use motion capture data, it only make sense for you to have all your projects handled in a uniform way. Only by having a plan in place can a company ensure that its projects using motion capture are being handled efficiently and successfully. Instead, it seems most companies choose to handle each project separately and often not the same way from year to year. By not having a formal plan in place, a company needs to constantly reinvent the wheel with each game instead of building on its accomplishments and failures.

My plan for handling motion capture is loose enough to allow it to be adapted to different genres of video games, but also tight enough to assure that your animations are handled in a uniform, thorough, professional, and timely manner. It provides checks and balances to see that motions are not overlooked or captured improperly during the capture session and is broken down into three distinct stages: the pre-capture session preparation, the capture session, and the post capture session production.

The first stage entails doing all the legwork that should be done before the capture session happens. The second looks at what to do during the capture session, and the final piece examines what needs to be done during the editing process to get the motions into the hands of the programmers and into the game engine.

Handling motion capture properly through all its stages will save your company valuable time and money, whether you are integrating it into one game or developing a company plan for how to deal with it on many projects. Simply getting by and getting the job done does not address all the areas that should be covered. It is possible to ship a game that has poorly captured, edited, and organized animations; however, working on a game like that is a nightmare for the employees and costs the company more money overall.

Being organized helps you streamline and execute all steps, no matter how tedious, to help ensure that the animations in your game and future versions using those animations are easy to deal with, realistic looking, and completed on time and on budget. Many companies that capture motion only end up using 20–40% of the captured data, and that percentage is too small. If organized properly, your company should be able to use 80–90% of your captured data. It is worth noting, however, that even a good plan or systematic approach can fail if you do not have the proper people to implement and oversee it. Having the right people is just as important as having a good plan. You need people who will stick to the plan and see it through from the beginning of the project all the way to the end. Many video game projects have development times anywhere from nine months to several years, depending on their scope and how much reworking is done, so it is important to establish a proven plan and make sure it is carried out.

CONCLUSION

Deciding whether or not to use motion capture on your project can be a complicated decision. Business and creative questions need to be answered honestly in order to make the decision that is best for your project.

When Considering Motion Capture for Your Project

- Consider your budget.
- Consider your timeline.
- Consider the look of your character and the overall appearance of your game.
- Make sure the motions you seek can be captured properly.

Common Errors when Considering Motion Capture

- Assuming that using motion capture makes the animator's job easier.
- Assuming that using motion capture will save time.
- Assuming that using motion capture will save money.
- Underestimating the amount of planning involved.
- Being unorganized during the capture session.
- Underestimating the importance of using a good motion performer.
- Assuming that you can fix a bad performance, poorly captured, or processed data after the capture session.

Not being organized and having a plan can have disastrous consequences for your project. A coordinated approach to handling motion capture can help assure it is handled in a uniform, thorough, professional, and timely manner. Your plan should be loose enough to be adaptable to different projects, but also firm enough to see to it that not too many corners are cut. Your plan should provide checks and balances to see to it that your motion capture needs are handled properly. Even a good plan can fail without the right people to implement and oversee it.

3

THE MOTION LIST

SHOT 1

SHOT 2

SHOT 3

SHOT 4

The United States federal government is broken into three separate but equal branches and was set up that way so that each branch will act as a sort of "checks and balances" for each other. A good plan for organizing your animations should not only cover all aspects needed but should also provide some checks and balances to help assure no detail is overlooked. Developing a good motion list is only the first of three critical phases needed to fully plan a motion capture session. The three branches for organization in my plan are these:

1. The motion list
2. The flowcharts
3. The motion database

The first two phases, the motion list and flowcharts, are best developed together because each helps you see the flow of the motions from a different point of view. The third phase, the motion database, is developed later, but it makes sure you have not left out any details.

Some people might think that these steps are unnecessary or overkill, but it is not uncommon for a game's animations (motions) to be flowcharted by the animators after the capture session and only when they run into a problem. Unfortunately, by that time it is too late, and if there is a problem it is usually a serious one. If you don't flowchart your motions prior to the capture, and if you haven't scheduled a secondary capture session, you will be stuck with the motions that were captured or you will be forced to work harder to make up for the lack of planning by fully animating missed or incorrect motions. Many games have been made without checks and balances, but that does not mean that the motions are done well or the project runs as efficiently as it could.

If your company is hired to develop a game for a publisher, there is an added benefit to having a checks and balances system in place. Publishers pay out a lot of money to have a game made, and if your company has a system that proves to the publisher that you are doing all you can to help assure that its money is well spent and accounted for, then your company will be a better choice for them in the future over a company who does not have a system in place.

The majority of the motions captured for video games are what are called non-linear or user-controlled motions. Some games, however, are a mixture of both non-linear and linear motions.

Non-linear motions (user-controlled): Motions that require input from the user in order to be executed. In order to give the user an appropriate response time, these motions tend to be short in duration.

Linear motions (computer-controlled): Motions that do not require any input from a user in order to be executed. These motions can be used in cinematic scenes or in some cases in the game. When used during game play, these motions generally are used by the computer so that the animations flow together more naturally.

Since preparing and capturing linear and non-linear motions requires a different approach, it is highly recommended that you prepare separate motion lists for your linear and non-linear motions.

NON-LINEAR MOTIONS

As an animator, there is a fine balance that you should strive for in your game. You need to try to balance the response time that the designer envisions with realistic-looking motion; that's why it is important to work closely with the game designer. According to Tim Huntsman, lead game designer, "Appropriate response times should match the end-users expectation of what feels right, not necessarily what is right, for the animation as it appears in the game." So if you need a quicker response time but your motions take too long to execute and look good, then a compromise must be made. Non-linear motions have a tendency to make the flow of a game look mechanical, but only by getting the motions back to a core motion quickly can you give the user a quick response when he presses a button. As you can see, this is somewhat of a catch-22 situation: You want appropriate response time, but at the same time you want motions that flow together smoothly and realistically.

LINEAR MOTIONS

Some games are able to get around this delicate balance of "appropriate response time" and "realistic-looking" motion because the game is predominantly a cinematic-driven game. This means that a large portion of the motions used are linear in nature. Many companies show the linear motions from their cinematic sequences when they advertise their games on TV or during promotions because the motions flow together beautifully, but when you play the game, the in-game motions usually aren't nearly as good. Linear motions make a game look great, but control is taken away from the user. However, if done correctly, it is possible to add linear motions to your game without the appearance of sacrificing control.

A real nice example of in-game linear motions can be seen in Acclaim Entertainment's *ALL-STAR Baseball*™ series (2002, 2003, and 2004). In it, we included a motion called a Future Throw. A Future Throw is when the user chooses which base the fielder will throw the ball to before the batter even hits the pitch. When this happens, the fielder will field the ball and throw without pausing or getting back to a core motion. This makes the motions flow together seamlessly. If a Future Throw is not selected, the fielder will field the ball and then go into the core motion we called Ready Throw and idle there while waiting for the user to tell him what to do, whether to throw, run, and so on. The Future Throw adds a nice level of realism to the game because the fielders act more like real people and avoid the mechanical look of getting back to a core position. These linear motions are also used by the computer when the user is playing against it; this subtle trick makes the game look ultra-real because there aren't any odd stops or jerks in the motion when the computer is fielding. Cinematic motions, AI controlled game-play motions, AI controlled celebration motions, and fluff motions are all considered linear.

THE IN-GAME MOTION LIST

Once it is determined that you will use motion capture for your project, creating a motion list for the in-game motions you need to capture is the first step in organizing. Many motion capture studios request a *shot list* or *moves list* from potential clients in order to give them an accurate bid on the cost of their project, and it seems some people considered a motion list and a shot list the same thing. Depending on the information that you include, a motion list and a shot list can be the same thing, but there are differences. One of the major differences between a shot list and a motion list is that the shot list needs to have a brief description accompanying each motion to explain it in more detail. A description is needed so that the motion capture studio can make its best guess as to the complexity of the motion you want to capture. Our motion list is used only by people working on our project and as a starting point for organizing, so descriptions of each motion are not needed. The other major difference is that the motion list needs to have each motion broken down into thirds and include a starting position, main action, and end position.

Motion list: A record noting and breaking down all motions that will be captured during the capture session and the positions that each motion begins and ends in. It can also contain descriptions of each motion if needed.

Shot list: A record noting all motions that will be captured during the capture session, along with a description of each motion. Sometimes referred to as a *moves list*.

Creating a motion list for a non-linear project such as a video game requires you to think and break down each motion into thirds. The motion performance will be captured as a straight-ahead sequence of events, so the motion performer needs to know what position he needs to start in, what motion he is going to perform, and what position he needs to end in, so each motion on your motion list really requires three sections. We like to use the "/" or backslash to separate the sections of a motion.

Position he is starting in / Motion he is performing / Position he is ending in

There are, however, exceptions to having every motion broken down into three sections. When listing a core motion, it is not necessary to have a beginning or ending motion listed because the core motions are looping motions. Instead, you can just list core motions by themselves:

- Walk cycle
- Run cycle
- Jog cycle
- Crouch idle

Core motion: A motion that all other motions begin or end in and whose beginning and end frames are identical. Sometimes called a base motion, root position, or base position.

If your project requires you to capture transition motions, you need to list them in only two sections because they take the character directly from one core motion to another. Transitions are fairly self explanatory motions; however, you may want to list them in thirds in order to prevent confusion. Transitions are listed in two sections, as follows:

- Crouch idle / Walk cycle
- Prone idle / Crouch idle
- Prone idle / Run cycle

These same transitions, listed in thirds, are as follows:

- Crouch idle / transition to / Walk cycle
- Prone idle / transition to / Crouch idle
- Prone idle / transition to / Run cycle

Transition motions: Motions that take the game character from one core motion to another.

Like transition motions, motions that end with the character dying may require only two sections. Death motions may require three sections if you have a certain death position or pose that the motion performer needs to end in. Keep in mind that having a certain death position can create problems for the motion performer during the motion capture session. It may be difficult for him to end in a certain position if he is falling or being pulled backward by pulleys or has his momentum going in a certain direction, so you may want him to finish death motions in whatever position he ends in. The following are death motions in two sections:

- Crouch Idle / Shot in chest from front, falls to knees clutching chest, and dies
- Crouch Idle / Shot in front of head, spins around 180 degrees, and dies
- Crouch Idle / Shot in front of head, neck snaps back, falls straight down on back, and dies

If you need to list three sections for death motions:

- Crouch Idle / Shot in chest from front, falls to knees clutching chest / Face down position
- Crouch Idle / Shot in front of head, spins around 180 degrees / Face down position
- Crouch Idle / Shot in front of head, neck snaps back, falls straight down / On back position

Core Motions

The motions that all other motions begin and end in are called core motions. They are sometimes also referred to as base motions or in/out motions. Whatever label you give them, these motions are of the utmost importance because all the other motions in the game hinge on what they look like and how they move. It may help you to think of a core motion as the trunk of a tree; from that trunk motion there are many branches (or choices of motions) that the character can perform. After the character performs a motion, he needs to either get back to his starting trunk or transition to a different trunk before he can perform another motion. Core motions also "loop" with themselves, or begin and end with the same frame.

A simple example of a core motion would be if your project needs to have a motion where the character starts in a standing idle position and then does a shoulder roll to his right, ending in a crouched shooting position. In the motion list this motion would be listed as three separate motions: the stand idle motion is the core (in) motion, and the crouched shooting motion is the core (out) motion:

- Stand idle / Shoulder roll RIGHT / Crouched shooting

Listing motions this way helps make sure that you include every motion needed. There may be several motions on your motion list that appear to be identical; however, they have different core motions:

- Stand idle / Shoulder roll RIGHT / Crouched shooting
- Stand idle / Shoulder roll RIGHT / Prone shooting position

It is critical that the design staff all agree on the look of the core motions because hundreds of motions will start and end from them. Uninformed people usually don't understand how drastic a decision it can be to change a core motion after it has been captured. Trying to change a core motion can have several negative effects, from making the motions look choppy, to adding a lot more man-hours to the animator's schedule, to the worst possible case of needing to recapture motions.

Looping Motions

For game play reasons, core motions "loop" or "tile" with themselves. This means that they begin and end with the same frame, so when they are tiled or looped together with themselves, they flow together seamlessly.

Looping motions: Motions that have identical beginning and end frames. They are sometimes also called *tile motions*.

If we use the same simple motion example from before:

- Stand idle / Shoulder roll RIGHT / Crouched shooting

The motion stand idle is not only a core motion, but it is also a looping motion (its beginning frame is identical to its ending frame), and the crouched shooting motion will also loop with itself. There are two basic types of looping motions: cycle motions and idle motions. Cycles move the character through space, and idles do not propel the character.

Cycle motions: Looping motions that propel the character through space. Simple examples of cycling motions are runs, walks, jogs, and backpedaling.

Idle motions: Looping motions that are not locomotive; in other words they do not propel the character through space, but rather he remains almost stationary. Idle motions do not require any input from the user, so the character waits for input from either the user or the game.

If we again use our example from before, you will see that the core (in) motion and the core (out) motion are both idles, since neither one propels the character through space. The character will move through space while executing the shoulder roll to his right side, but when he ends in the core (out) he remains in place:

• Stand idle / Shoulder roll RIGHT / Crouched shooting

THE MOTION LIST PROCESS

As a general rule, we recommend that you compile the State Flowcharts first (see Chapter 4, "The Flowcharts") and then put the motion list and motion-set flowcharts together simultaneously.

There are a few factors that dictate which process you use to create your motion list. These include things such as time constraints, your knowledge of working with motion capture, and the kind of project you are working on. You should approach a project where you are asked to do patchwork differently than a project you build from the ground up. The three basic types of projects are these:

Re-shoot project: You may be asked to do a complete re-shoot of motion for the newest version of a game. If you are just recapturing the motions for an existing game where the motion flow and game design are already done, consider yourself lucky, because this is generally the easiest kind of project to work on.

Patchwork project: You may be asked to capture some motions for the newest version of a game, and the motions you will capture need to integrate with or replace the current game's motions. The complexity of this kind of project depends on how thoroughly the game was planned out before. A project like this can get complicated or can be very easy.

New project: You may be working on a first-generation game and need to build the entire game's motion list and flow from the beginning. This is generally the most difficult kind of project to work on; however, if it is done correctly, the future versions are very easy.

If you are working on a re-shoot project or a patchwork project, it is recommended that before you compile your motion list, you do some research first. Check the design documents, old motion lists, and flowcharts from the prior versions. Checking these will give you an idea of how the prior game's motions flowed together. If your version has the same game controls and design flow, then you may be able to reuse some of those lists or at a minimum get a baseline to work from. If your version has a unique design or different game controls, then you may need to start your list from scratch, but you may be able to get a feeling for the type of motions your game will need.

If you are working on a new project, you will have more work to do, but you also have the advantage of seeing that it is handled the right way from the beginning. Developing a thorough motion list should not be a one-time event handled by one person. Like most areas, it is a process that needs the input and cooperation of several people on the game. There have been a few games in the recent past where the motion list was compiled entirely by one person on the project. The list was then given to the motion coordinator just prior to the capture session, and he was expected to capture all the motions on the list. However, since he wasn't involved in the developmental process, it was almost impossible for him to make smart decisions during the capture or make sure every motion was captured. On every project where the motion list was compiled solely by one person, the list was incomplete, and important motions were not captured. If important motions are not captured, several detrimental things can happen:

- You may not have motions critical to the game or, if you do, they may not be able to be used. If you are lucky, the animators will be able to overcome this and keyframe or blend together the missing motions. However, it may force them to work harder, longer hours, and most people don't enjoy working harder to make up for someone else's oversights. You should also know that motions that are created because they were not captured tend not to look as smooth. If the motion that needs to be created is short in duration or a transition motion, it may look OK to create, but if it has a large range of motion, is longer in duration, or is a major motion, it most likely will not look as good as the captured motions.
- It may require you to make changes to the game's design to work with the motions that were captured. Changing a game's design because of improperly captured motion is never good and usually results in inconsistent and poor game play.
- It may force you to need a new capture session. A new capture session will obviously cost you more time and money. Depending on the number of motions that need to be recaptured, it could cause the game to go over budget or miss deadlines.
- The worst-case scenario would be that it could cause the project to be cancelled due to cost overruns or missed deadlines.

All the major areas—designers, programmers, and animators—need to be included in the process of developing a good motion list because the success of the motions and the look of the game depend on all areas working together. With that said, one person does need to be in charge of the process and actually compile the motion list. Generally, it should be the motion coordinator who is in charge; however, whoever it is needs to be the right person for the job. You don't want a motion coordinator who does not know the difference between offense and defense to be in charge of the motion in a sports game. Without a basic understanding of sports, it's not possible for this person to know what a particular motion should look like. This might sound like common sense, but it has actually happened. The person in charge of coordinating the motion needs to have certain skills in order to do the job effectively and efficiently:

- He needs to be a focused person and see a project through from beginning to end.
- He needs to be a good communicator.
- He needs to have good organizational skills.
- He needs to know the game controls and how they affect the motions needed.
- He must have a willingness to do all the necessary steps.
- He needs to have the time in his schedule to do the job properly.
- He needs to have knowledge of animation.

A motion coordinator must be the type of person who can see a project through from start to finish. A game's development cycle generally ranges anywhere from nine months to several years and can include thousands of motion files, so having someone who can stay focused over a number of months is crucial.

A good communicator isn't afraid to ask questions. People may wonder and ask, "Why are you asking so many questions? You're the one who is supposed to know this stuff." Simply explain to them that you do know what you are doing but what you don't know is what they are thinking and what their vision and expectations for the game and motion are. You can't assume that everyone is on the same page; you have to know they are. There is a quotation from former President Ronald Reagan that best sums this up: "Trust but verify."

Organizational skills are extremely important when trying to make sure every "t" is crossed and every "i" is dotted. The motion coordinator needs to be able to see the whole picture and still focus on the small details. The strength of your motion coordinator will either help or hinder your project drastically.

He needs to know the user controls and how they apply to the motions needed. This is an important issue because the user controls dictate the look and necessity of the core motions and how the motions will flow together.

He must be willing to do all the necessary steps, no matter how tedious, to see that every detail is handled. Preparing for a large motion capture session involves a lot of grunt work and can be very boring. The person needs to have a personality suited to this kind of work.

He needs to have the time in his schedule to organize the animations and capture session properly. People who have never been involved with preparing a motion capture session, and some people who have, underestimate the amount of time and planning that is needed. The motion coordinator should be in charge of the motion and not have a split responsibility.

A common mistake that some people make is in the belief that the person selected to be in charge of the process has to be the best animator. It is not necessary for him to be the best, but he needs to have managerial, organizational, and leadership skills in addition to the technical knowledge needed. Just because someone is the best at animating does not mean that he is the best manager and leader.

As was stated before, this is a group process, so the motion coordinator needs to talk with the design staff to find out what design direction they have in mind and what the user controls will be. Getting all of this background information may take several meetings, and I suggest asking a lot of questions and taking a lot of notes. Having brainstorming sessions like these is very important and accomplishes several things:

- It keeps creativity flowing and the ideas coming.
- It helps set a design direction for the game franchise.
- It provides checks and balances for the design staff.

In a creative environment, it is important to let people brainstorm. Brainstorming allows people to give input without the fear of judgment. It is important, however, to have a certain code of ethics while brainstorming. No idea should be labeled as stupid or dumb during the brainstorming session. When ideas are judged, people shut down creatively and stop offering ideas. Obviously there will be stronger ideas that get fleshed out more thoroughly while other ideas fall by the wayside, but there shouldn't be any judgment or condemnation of ideas.

The second benefit is that it also helps set a design direction for the game and for future versions of the game. Sometimes it is not possible to make the game you want in the first generation, but by knowing what you eventually want the game to be, you can move each new version toward that goal.

It also provides checks and balances for the designers by pointing out possible design weaknesses. Asking questions checks to see if everything has been considered. In doing so, the designers can come up with solutions to questions they may not have considered or had time to cover. Be wary of people who give answers like "Well, we'll figure that out when the time comes." This is a sure giveaway that they have not thought everything out, and it could come back and cause problems for you later. When developing a motion list, try to get the designers to agree on what we call absolutes in the game's design. Understanding the absolutes before starting on the motion list can save you a lot of time and energy.

Absolute: A commitment by the design staff about the design or the flow of the motions in the game.

An example of an absolute is when a designer says something such as "Characters with two-handed weapons will not need swim motions." Without judging if this is a good design or not, it lets you know that you don't need to worry about motions where the character is carrying a two-handed weapon blending into swimming motions. Absolutes are very easily seen in some sports games; for instance, pitcher motions do not need to blend into base stealing or batter motions. Being able to decide on the absolutes for a game is really a matter of asking the designers the right questions.

The Wish List

From the brainstorming meetings and the design document, the motion coordinator and the lead designer should compile a large "wish list" of motions. This wish list should include every motion that you would eventually like to have in the game. Because this wish list may be several hundred or even thousands of motions, it is best to organize them into sections. We found it easier to focus on one section at a time, complete it, and then move to another. Start with the motions that are critical to game play, then move to A.I. motions, fluff motions, celebrations, and such. When compiling the wish list and the flowcharts, there are a few questions you need to consider:

- Are there any absolutes that we know?
- What are the game controls?
- What do the core motions look like?
- What user-controlled motions do we want?
- What computer-controlled motions do we want, if any?

Knowing what the designers want the game controls to be is of extreme importance because it affects the flow of the motions. The game controls direct what position the character needs to begin in and end in, thus affecting the look of the core motions and the flow of all the motions.

Establishing the initial look of the core motions should also be done at this time. The physical look of the core motions may eventually change, but when the motions need to happen should not.

What this means is that the character might eventually be in a slightly different pose, but the timing of when the character needs to be in a pose should remain constant.

At this point, establishing a list of motions is somewhat easy, but it is a tedious process. Your list should include all motions needed, minus the cinematic sequences. It is important to include in-game computer-controlled motions, fluff motions, and any celebration motions on the wish list.

It may seem like a lot of extra work to come up with a motion list larger than the number of motions you will have time to get into the game, but working from a large wish list and then reducing it down to a realistic number of motions has several advantages.

It helps everyone involved in the motion list process to fully understand the design of the game. This point keeps coming up, but it is amazing how often a person you think is on the same page as you isn't. On one past project, we were surprised to find out in our fifth motion list meeting that one of the designers, who we thought understood the direction we were going, was really thinking we were talking about something else.

It helps make sure that every motion you need is considered and prioritized. This point is critical, too. Missed or wrong motions will make everyone's life harder, and there are too many things to keep track of to try to fly by the seat of your pants.

A large list also gives you the option to capture more motions, if you have the time and budget, during the capture session. It has been my experience that you should always take the extra motions to the capture session in case you get ahead of schedule and are able to capture more motions than originally planned.

If you are not able to capture additional motions at the capture session, having a wish list gives you an initial list of motions that can be added to future versions of your game. This means that your game is not only designed for one year, but it is designed for what it will eventually become in future versions. This initial plan for future motions may change, but it is always better to have a plan and alter it than to make it up as you go along.

Once the wish list and flowcharts are completed, the motion coordinator should schedule a meeting with the design staff, lead programmer, art lead, and anyone else who is interested. The feeling is that the more people who look at the list and ask questions the better, because you never know when they will think of something that you didn't. Just because someone is a first year artist or programmer doesn't mean that he might not be able to contribute to the motion flow of the game. This meeting is scheduled to achieve two goals:

1. To present the wish list and start reducing it down to a realistic number of motions for the capture session.
2. To get the other people to approve the motions. If everyone agrees on the direction the motions and the game design are going, then it reduces the likelihood of mistakes or surprises as the game progresses.

Reducing the wish list may again take several meetings, depending on the number of motions to be captured. You will generally get better results by having several short meetings than by having one long marathon meeting, because people's attention spans start to wander when confronted with a list of hundreds of motions and flowcharts.

Reducing the List

Next you need to reduce your wish list to a realistic number of motions that can be captured and implemented into your game. The easiest way to cut the list down is to prioritize and eliminate whole areas or states, such as doing away with swimming motions altogether. You may decide that having the character swim might be cool but isn't a priority, so you will save it for future versions. Before cutting too deep into your list, a very smart trick is to condense motions into what we call combination motions. Combination motions are usually two-in-one motions or three-in-one motions. This means that you will capture one longer motion, knowing that it will be broken into multiple motions once you get it back from the motion studio to put into the game. Done properly, this will allow you to capture more motions without any additional expense (for more details see Chapter 8, "Selecting a Motion Capture Studio," about the contract.

Combination motions: Motions that are captured together at the capture session as one movement but are then broken apart into individual motions to be used in the game by the animators.

Two-in-one motion: A motion that is captured as a single move during the capture session that will be broken into two separate motions by the animators in the post capture phase.

Three-in-one motion: A motion that is captured as a single move during the capture session that will be broken into three separate motions by the animators in the post capture phase.

For example, suppose you want to capture the following core motions and transitions:

- Stand idle
- Walk cycle
- Backpedal cycle
- Stand idle / Walk
- Stand idle / Backpedal
- Stand idle / Turn 90 degrees / Stand idle
- Walk / Stand idle
- Walk / Backpedal
- Backpedal / Stand idle
- Backpedal / Walk

These 10 motion can easily be combined into five motions, and doing so will free up five spaces on your list for other motions to be captured. Your combined motions list will look like this:

- Walk cycle
- Backpedal cycle
- Stand idle to walk / Walk to stand idle / Stand idle to turn 90 degrees to stand idle
- Backpedal to stand idle / Stand idle to backpedal
- Walk to backpedal / Backpedal to walk
- Space freed up for another motion
- Space freed up for another motion
- Space freed up for another motion
- Space freed up for another motion
- Space freed up for another motion

Depending on the size of the capture volume, it may be possible to combine this list even further or in another way. Notice that our stand idle motion is going to be captured at the same time the transition from backpedal to stand idle is shot. There are three important keys to combining motions.

1. Even though you are now capturing five motions at the capture session, you really want 10 motions made from these moves, so you need to have 10 unique motion names dedicated for these motions. The motion capture studio needs only the five names, but you and your animators need 10 names, so when they are broken up during the post capture process they are accounted for. An example of this is given in Chapter 5, "The Motion Database."

2. Only combine motions that can be performed in the allotted amount of time for each motion. If you exceed this number, it may actually cost you more money instead of saving, and this defeats the purpose of combining the motions (see Chapter 8 on the contract for more details).

3. You must also keep in mind whether or not the motion performer can execute the combined motions in the capture vol-

ume. If you are not sure, mark off an area the size of the capture volume with tape and have an animator perform the motions. It is important that he perform the motion at actual speed and stay within the volume. It would also be a good idea to time him and check the number of seconds it takes him to perform. Remember that your motion performer may be more athletically inclined than your animator, so if he comes close, your motion performer may be able to fully accomplish the motion during your capture session.

If after you have combined motions and cut major states you still need to reduce the number of motions on your list, cut into the fluff motions. Fluff motions are nice and give your game that little extra edge, but they aren't critical for game play.

Fluff motion: Any motion not critical for game play but used to enhance the visual look or feel of the game.

An example of a fluff motion would be when a character gets a drink, stokes a fire, urinates, or in the case of a sports game, when base coaches or coaches move. It could easily be argued that with the competitive nature of the gaming industry today, motions like these are a necessity and not just fluff. This may be true, but if you have to reduce your list, sacrifices need to be made. Other areas to consider are the number of death motions and celebration motions you have; see if you can do without some of them.

Before the motion capture session, all areas of production, design, programming, animation, and management need to give their approval or sign off on the final motion list. If someone has the wrong impression of which motions are being captured or how the motions will flow together, or if a major change to the gameplay is made after the capture session, this hurts the success of the capture, wastes money, or makes it almost impossible for the animator to deliver good motion on time.

EXCERPT FROM THE *CARRION* MOTION LIST

1. Alert walk / Alert walk / Alert walk

2. Alert jog / Alert jog / Alert jog

3. Alert run / Alert run / Alert run

4. Alert crouch walk / Alert crouch walk / Alert crouch walk

5. Alert stand / transition to / Alert walk

6. Alert stand / transition to / Alert jog

7. Alert stand / transition to / Alert run

8. Alert stand / Alert crouch / Alert stand

9. Alert stand / Alert crouch walk / Alert stand

10. Alert stand / Injured stand / Injured run

11. Alert stand / Reload weapon / Alert stand

12. Alert stand / Dive roll LEFT / Alert crouch

13. Alert stand / Dive roll RIGHT / Alert crouch

14. Alert stand / Call out with hand / Alert crouch

15. Alert stand / Butt of gun attack / Alert crouch

16. Alert stand / Weapon stuck flinch / Alert stand

17. Alert stand / Turn 180 / Alert stand

18. Alert stand / Turn 180 / Alert walk

19. Alert stand / Turn 180 / Alert jog

20. Alert stand / Turn 180 / Alert run

21. Alert stand / Turn 180 / Alert crouch / Turn 180 / Alert crouch

22. Alert crouch / transition to / Alert run

23. Alert crouch / Alert crouch walk / Alert crouch

24. Alert crouch / Turn 180 / Alert run

25. Alert crouch / Turn 180 / Alert crouch / Alert squat

You will notice in our excerpt from the *CARRION* motion list that each motion starts with a core motion, is followed by the actual motion being captured, and ends in another core motion. There are several idle motions, cycle motions, and transition motions, as well as combination motions. If you are experienced, you may realize this excerpt could be reduced even more. Number 11 and number 16 can probably be combined and captured as one motion.

THE CINEMATIC MOTION LIST

The linear motions for most games are usually composed of cinematic sequences and require a number of unique considerations when planning. Capturing motions to be used in a cinematic sequence is more like preparing a movie or play than the motion list for in-game motion. This is why we feel that linear motions should be handled separately and have their own motion list.

Generally, the linear or cinematic motion list won't need to be prepared until later in the project because the motions will be captured during a supplemental or secondary capture session. This also gives the designers more time to work out exactly what they need to convey in the cinematics and get the dialogue recorded. If your project is not going to have a secondary capture, then a lot of planning needs to be done so that the cinematic sequences are set prior to the capture. Major changes to what needs to be said or communicated that are made after the capture session may cause the motion you capture to be unusable. This issue comes up frequently with motion capture because some people in the video game industry change their minds late in the development cycle, or because they do not know what they really want before the capture session. This is one of the main reasons to schedule a secondary capture later in the project for the cinematic motions.

Developing a motion list for a linear project starts off like an in-game motion list, with preparation. After establishing the goal or message that each cinematic scene needs to convey, a script should be made. Depending on the complexity of your cinematic sequences, you may want to consider dialogue, movement, and blocking and then make storyboards illustrating your vision.

Storyboard Breakdown

The key elements needed when dealing with cinematic scenes are the script and storyboards. After the script and storyboards are complete, each scene needs to be analyzed and broken down for your motion list. As you go through the storyboards, you need to look at each shot in a scene to determine which characters need to be captured together, which characters do not need to be captured at all, and which characters can be captured independently. You also need to determine which shots need to be broken into pieces to fit into the capture volume instead of captured in their entirety. This means that some scenes may need to be shot in pieces and blended together later by the animators.

Storyboards in general do not need to be complex, detailed images, but rather they need to convey the characters, action, dialogue, and timing for each scene. Figure 3.1 is our example storyboard from our game *CARRION* and does not include the dialogue.

Shot number 1: Close-up on character A's face. He turns his head to see the silhouettes of three characters approaching (characters B, C, D). This shot is probably not worth capturing because animators can easily keyframe this one without much difficulty. Some people may not want to mix motions that are motion captured with keyframed motions, so for consistency they may want to capture this shot. If captured at all, character A can be captured independently of the background characters. Characters B and C should be captured together, but character D does not need to be captured with them. If shot number 1 is captured, it would be captured in two or three pieces.

Shot number 2: Character A folds his arms and looks at the other characters, character B has his arm on the shoulder of character C. Character D then enters the shot. Characters A and C are the primary characters and engage in conversation. Character B interacts with character C while character D does not move after he enters the shot. Characters A, B, and C should be captured together since they interact so tightly together. It is possible, how-

FIGURE 3.1 A simple storyboard example from *CARRION*. © 2003. Reprinted with permission from A. Omlandky.

ever, to capture character A independently and use character B's and C's movements to get character A's timing. Character D can be captured either separately or not at all; we recommend that character D not be captured for this shot.

Shot number 3: This shot is similar to shot number 1, in that it can be captured or it can be keyframed. There is character movement and dialogue but, other than timing, not any character interaction. The decision to keyframe or capture this shot may depend on the esthetic look that is sought, the timeline the animators would have, and the overall length of the shot.

Shot number 4: Characters A and C are seen walking together and talking. Characters B and D remain in the background. This shot can be captured in two pieces: background characters together, and characters A and C together. Since characters A and C don't directly interact, it may seem like they can be captured separately, but this is not recommended. When people walk or run together it is normal for their strides to be in sync, and we want their speed to be the same, so it is better to capture the characters together.

Since our example shots are fairly simple, no single motion had to be broken down in order to fit in the capture volume. We did split shots into pieces but not because the movement required was too large to fit in the volume. There are different ways to break down a shot, and how you decide to do it will depend on several factors. However you break it down, the most important issue to keep in mind is to do what is best for your project. Depending on the software your company uses and the skill of your animators, you may be able to capture some shots independently of each other and then have them pieced together after the capture session. Some animators prefer this way of working because they feel it gives them more control developing a shot; however, it may not be the most efficient way to work.

After each shot is broken down, you are now able to generate a motion list. Keep in mind that it is important that the filenaming convention you use for the cinematic sequences is structured so that the animators are able to find the pieces of each shot easily.

CONCLUSION

- A system of planning a motion capture session should provide checks and balances to help assure that no detail is overlooked.
- If your company is hired to develop a game for a publisher, there is an added benefit to having a checks and balances system: Your company will be a better choice for them in the future over a company that does not have a system in place if your system proves to them that your company is spending their money wisely.

- The majority of the motions captured for video games are called non-linear or user-controlled motions. Some games, however, are a mixture of both non-linear and linear motions.

- As an animator, there is a fine balance that you should strive for in your game. You should try to balance the response time that the designer envisions with realistic-looking motion.

- Some games are able to get this delicate balance of appropriate response time and realistic-looking motion because the game is predominantly a cinematic-driven game.

- There are differences between a shot list and a motion list.

- Creating a motion list for a non-linear project such as a video game requires you to break down each motion into thirds. Each motion listed should be broken into a beginning pose, captured motion, and end pose.

- Transition and death motions do not need to be broken down into thirds, but for the sake of clarity and consistency it is recommended.

- All major areas—game design, programming, and animation—need to be included during the process to develop a good motion list. When a motion list is developed by one person, problems always occur.

- If possible, establish some design absolutes before creating a motion list.

- Developing a large wish list of motion and then reducing it to get a realistic number of motions will help in creating a complete motion list.

- Capturing motions to be used in a cinematic sequence is more like preparing a movie or play than the motion list for in-game motion; this is why linear motions should be handled separately and have their own motion list.

- The key elements needed when dealing with cinematic scenes are the script and storyboards.

- After the script and storyboards are complete, each scene needs to be analyzed to determine which characters need to be captured together, which characters do not need to be captured at all, and which characters can be captured independently. You also need to determine which shots need to be broken into pieces to fit into the capture volume instead of captured in their entirety.

4

FLOWCHARTS AND MOTION DIAGRAMS

Batting Diagram (no contact made)

			Bad swing High BAT_0135 BAT_0136	Bad Inside swing High BAT_0145 BAT_0146		Wild Inside swing High BAT_0157
Wild Outside swing High BAT_0120	Bad Outside swing High BAT_0123 BAT_0124	High swing Outside BAT_0129 BAT_0130	High swing BAT_0137 BAT_0138	High swing Inside BAT_0147 BAT_0148		
Wild Outside swing BAT_0121	Bad Outside swing BAT_0125 BAT_0126	Outside swing BAT_0131 BAT_0132	Middle swing BAT_0139 BAT_0140	Inside swing BAT_0149 BAT_0150	Bad Inside swing BAT_0155 BAT_0156	Wild Inside swing BAT_0158
Wild Outside swing Low BAT_0122	Bad Outside swing Low BAT_0127 BAT_0128	Low swing Outside BAT_0133 BAT_0134	Low swing BAT_0141 BAT_0142	Low swing Inside BAT_0151 BAT_0152		Wild Inside swing Low BAT_0159
			Bad swing Low BAT_0143 BAT_0144	Bad Inside swing Low BAT_0153 BAT_0154		

As was mentioned in the Chapter 3, "The Motion List," the flowcharts are the second phase to our checks and balances system. Even though it is the second phase, some of the flowcharting is actually developed before the motion list phase, while some flowcharts are developed simultaneously with the motion list. When creating a video game, there are areas of development that happen in a linear fashion, meaning one must occur before another. For instance, the motion capture session must happen before you can start editing the motions. But there are some areas of development that happen simultaneously, such as the creation of the motion list and the motion set flowcharts. This is also true for the game designers. Design is a dynamic process, so minor and sometimes major changes to the game's design occur throughout the project.

Before you can begin flowcharting, however, the designers need to have a design document mapped out. Your project may require extensive flowcharting, or a minimal amount depending on the type of game it is and the scope of the project. It is important to note that the type of flowcharts we are talking about here are for the animators to get a feel for the flow and scope of the game. These flowcharts might not be user friendly for the designers or programmers because they may require more information on them. When working on a non-linear project such as a video game, there are two distinct stages of flowcharting. The first stage is a graphical representation of the main areas of the game. These main areas are part of the game's drive system, and we'll call them "greater states." The second stage of flowcharting breaks down these greater states into specific motions or motion sets. Breaking the flowcharts into two stages allows you to get an overview and understand the general idea of the game's structure and then develop the specific areas required.

GREATER STATE FLOWCHARTS

Flowcharting the greater states should be done before the motion list is developed. Flowcharting the greater states will give you an overall flow of the game and also help you group like motions together before a filenaming convention is set. Before you can start flowcharting, it is best to first establish the different states and to break out the key behaviors that are unique enough to be classified as a main group.

Greater States: The different emotional or mental states that influence the character. For example, if your game character is walking around casually, he is in a "relaxed" or "casual" state as opposed to an "agitated" or "attack" state. In a sports game, the different positions the players occupy can act as the states: pitcher, kicker, goalie, and so on.

Behaviors: A character's response to either an internal or external stimulus. A character's response to a stimulus is dictated by the game state he is in. For example, if your game character is walking casually down a sidewalk and gets shot, what does he do? Does he run away? Does he attack? Does he have one response to the being shot stimulus or does he have many responses?

The different states your game will have are obviously affected by both the genre of your game and the environments that it encompasses. You won't need a baseball double play motion if you're making a third-person shooter or an action/adventure, unless it's a special celebration type of move. Environments too have an effect on the states of your game. For example, your game may be an action/adventure game, but if you don't have water, you won't need swimming motions.

Flowcharting the states and behaviors should be done together with the game's lead designer. If your project has a design staff, it is even better to include the entire staff, to make sure everyone has input and so that everyone understands the design goal. How you work also depends on your design document. Some projects have a very developed design doc that explains every detail. Other projects tend to be rather loose and "design" as they go. We don't recommend this way of working. There have been many projects that have been in development for many years because the game has gone through multiple major design changes. Projects handled this way usually flounder and waste time, causing people to have to work extra long hours just to finish. Many times they even drop features and levels out of the game just to get the game finished. Dropping levels can totally disrupt the overall feel of a game, and when this happens the final product suffers.

Developing the flowcharts and motion list is a process, so it may take a few meetings to get all the questions answered and the absolutes worked out. Absolutes help to narrow the scope of the design needs. If there are unanswered question in the design doc, establishing absolutes can help you discover them. At your meeting with the designers, list the separate game states and absolutes as they are agreed upon. This will help give you a clear starting point for your motion list and flowcharts.

Another major question you should ask the designers and programmers when seeking absolutes is, "Do we need to capture transition motions? If not, how will they be handled?" This is a big issue and, depending on your project, it can have a huge impact on the look of the motions and on game play. As the person in charge of the animation (in our case the motion capture), you should be wary of programmers and designers who say you do not need to capture transitions.

If your transitional motions are handled by the game's engine, most likely they will be linear transitions. Short linear translations look OK sometimes, but if you have a slow motion playback option or longer transitions, then linear translations look awful. The engine will have the character take a straight line path from motion to motion, so the character's arm may cut through his torso or legs as he transitions from one motion to another. This not only looks bad, but it takes away the feeling of realism that many games try to instill.

A solution to linear transitions is to have the animators create the transitions. Depending on the complexity of the transition, this can be fairly easy, but others can be time consuming to create. The animators should be given more time in their schedule to create transitions, and from an artistic point of view, you may want to consider the overall look this will have. It may look strange to go from a captured motion to a created transition and then back to a captured motion. For some projects this will prove to be a non-issue, and the created transitions are great.

Even though you are trying to streamline your motion list and save money on the motion shoot, sometimes more is better. If you are able to capture the transitions, do it, so you aren't stuck if later you find out you need them. See Chapter 3 for information on combination motions if you want to capture transition motions.

The absolutes for *CARRION*:

- All biped motions need to be motion captured.
- All biped characters will use the same skeleton.
- All biped characters will share the same motion set. This means there aren't any unique motion sets for individual characters.
- We will need swimming motion.
- We will need climbing motion.
- We will need one-handed and two-handed weapon motions. This includes one-handed melee motions.
- We will need cinematic motion captured.

The designer of *CARRION*, Matt Warchola, designed the game to have the following major AI drive states (greater states):

- Death state
- Survival state
- Escape state
- Attack state

- Alert/Disturbed state
- Casual state
- Conditional idle state

We also agreed to have some special behavior modes grouped together for organizational purposes. In addition to the seven major states, *CARRION* has:

- Climb/Rappel behavior mode
- Swim behavior mode

These special behavior modes will act like states to help classify motions into specific groups. All swimming motions will be grouped together in one directory regardless of their actual greater drive states, and all climbing motions will be handled the same way. This means that if we have a motion where the character is shooting as he is rappelling, that motion will be grouped with the climb/rappel motions instead of with the attack state motions. These special behaviors are classified as special "modes" and are handled slightly differently by the AI system because they have unique responses to stimuli to consider.

Matt Warchola, the designer of *CARRION*, brilliantly designed the AI drive system to work as a "sliding scale" of greater states. This means that, depending on the stimuli, the game's character is moving either up or down between the seven main states. The character is always trying to reach level seven, but any time a negative stimulus is triggered, he will most likely drop down to one of the other levels. For example, if the character is hit with a flamethrower, there will be any number of behaviors that can occur, but if he actually catches on fire when he is hit by the flamethrower, he will go directly into the survival state, and his only concern will become trying to stay alive. If there is water nearby when he catches on fire, the character will seek it out; otherwise he will either do a stop-drop-and-roll animation or simply flail around on fire and die. Other possible responses to the catch-on-fire stimulus can easily be added to this type of design. War-chola says, "Behavior responses have been developed with a mod-ular approach in mind so that they can be plugged into and taken out of the game depending upon necessity. While this system is NOT intelligent in the truest sense (it does not learn new behav-iors), it is focused on simulating the transition in all characters from one mental state to another." If a negative stimulus comes in, the character will either remain at the level he is currently in or move down to any level lower than the one he is in, and possibly into one of the special behavior modes. Figure 4.1 shows the greater states in *CARRION* and how a character could move down if a negative stimulus comes in.

Unlike when the character moves down levels, as he moves up levels he moves up only one level at a time; in other words, he must reach level four before he can go to level five. If after a cer-tain amount of time a negative stimulus does not come in, the character can then move up another level. The character is always trying to move toward level seven. Warchola says, "Based upon the psychological principles found in Maslow's Hierarchy of Needs, this system applies consistent drive states and AI rules to every character in the game. An equilibrium point is built into the idle state [level seven] to produce a sliding continuum of character AI drives. Incoming stimuli may knock the character out of the idle state, but he will always try to return to a happy equilibrium." Fig-ure 4.2 illustrates the greater states (levels) and how the character moves up the chain.

We explained before that *CARRION* has special behavior modes and that these modes will be handled slightly differently by the AI system than the greater states. Since the responses to a stimulus are unique to the mode, each mode will have its own sliding scale contained within it. For example, if the character is in the greater state alert (level five) and he goes into swim mode, he will enter into swim mode alert. if the character then leaves swim mode, he leaves at the same level he is in. So the character could enter the swim mode at level six (casual), then go into swim mode attack (level four in the mode), then if he leaves the swim mode at that

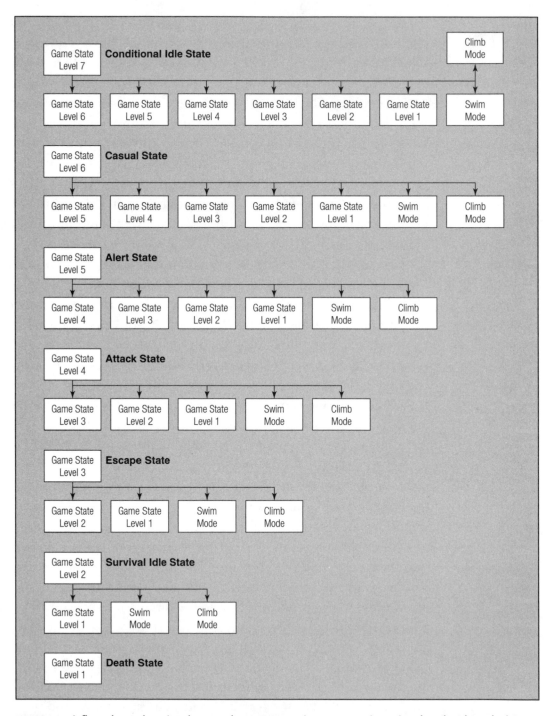

FIGURE 4.1 A flowchart showing how a character receives a negative stimulus that knocks him down to a different level or into one of the special behavior modes.

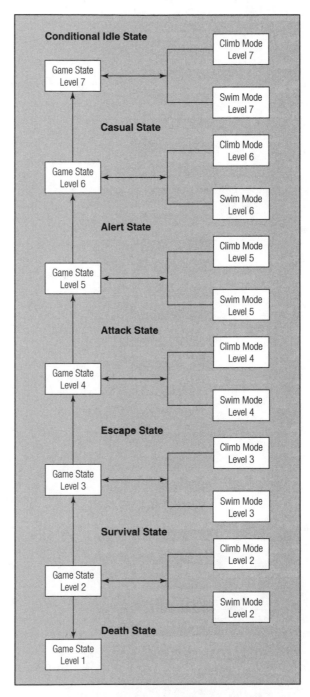

FIGURE 4.2   A flowchart showing how a character would move up through the greater states in an attempt to reach the equilibrium of level seven.

time, he would go back into the attack greater state, which is level four. Figure 4.3 illustrates the special behavior modes and how they fit into the greater states.

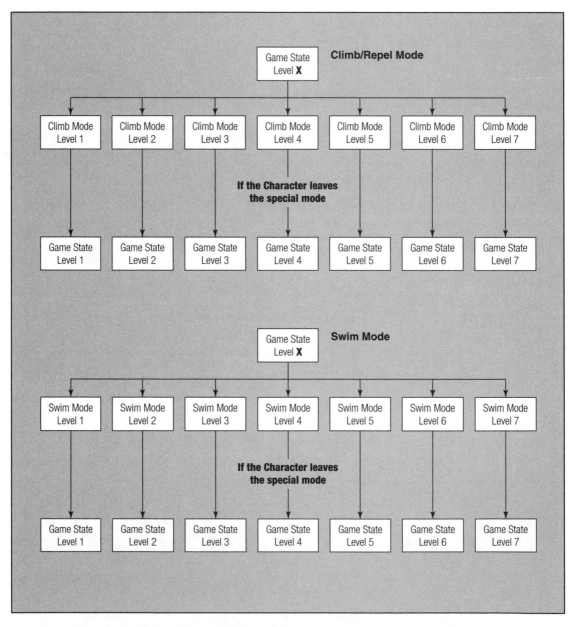

FIGURE 4.3   A flowchart showing how the special behavior modes work into the AI system.

MOTION SET FLOWCHARTS

After the overall flow of the game has been worked out, the next stage of flowcharting is to flowchart the more specific motions of each character or his motion set.

Motion Set: A group of movements made up of all the individual motions applied to a character or characters in a game.

Depending on the type of game you are working on, there may be a motion set that is considered to be "generic" and applied to multiple characters, or there may be "unique" motion sets for individual characters. An example of a generic motion set would be a run cycle, walk cycle, or shooting motion used by several characters; a unique motion set would be the position-specific motions that a baseball catcher would need but a first baseman or pitcher wouldn't use. If your game requires you to flowchart motion sets, they are developed at the same time as the motion list. We have already established that in *CARRION* we won't have any unique motion sets; instead, all the motions will have a large pool of motions that every character will be able to perform.

When we listed our absolutes, we did it to get the overall flow of the game, but the absolutes might not be specific enough to flowchart the motion sets. For example, one of our absolutes was "We will need climbing motions," but at that time we did not specify which kind of climbing motions we need. Do we need motions for a character climbing a ladder? If so, which kind of ladder? Will we have a rope ladder or a fixed ladder? When the character reaches the top of the ladder, how does he get off the ladder? Do the ladders end at floor level, or do they continue up through the floor? Do we need rope climbing motions? If so, is it a free hanging rope, or a rope against a cliff or wall? These are the specifics that need to be worked out with the lead designer before you can begin your motion set flowcharts.

Earlier we mentioned that your game's genre and environment will affect the greater states that you develop. Your game's controls, however, affect how your motion sets are grouped and need to fit together. Lead designer Tim Huntsman is one designer who firmly believes in seeing to it that the motion sets are developed in a way that allows the animations to flow together seamlessly. While working on *Legends of Wrestling*™ for Acclaim Entertainment, Huntsman developed what he calls the ISP system. This ISP system helps to group sets of like motions together and then establishes an intermediate start position (we called them core positions before) so that the characters can break into different motions seamlessly. Huntsman says, "The difficulty with a wrestling game is you have at least two characters interacting together—you need to have certain key positions earmarked such that they can break out of a move and transition to another without popping."

It has been my experience that working with a designer who pays attention to this detail in the design document is a luxury, so consider yourself lucky if you work on a project where the designer is helpful in developing and designing how the motion sets will flow. This point keeps coming up time and time again—how important teamwork and cooperation between the designers and animators are in creating a smooth-playing, cool-looking game.

There isn't really a right or wrong way to flowchart; it merely depends on what you are going to use the flowcharts for. The flowcharts that we have seen so far are used as a visual representation to help the motion coordinator and animators see to it that every motion is accounted for and included in the motion list. Flowcharts used by programmers are usually more detailed and show responses to stimuli. Figure 4.4 shows a more complex flowchart for making a baseball game.

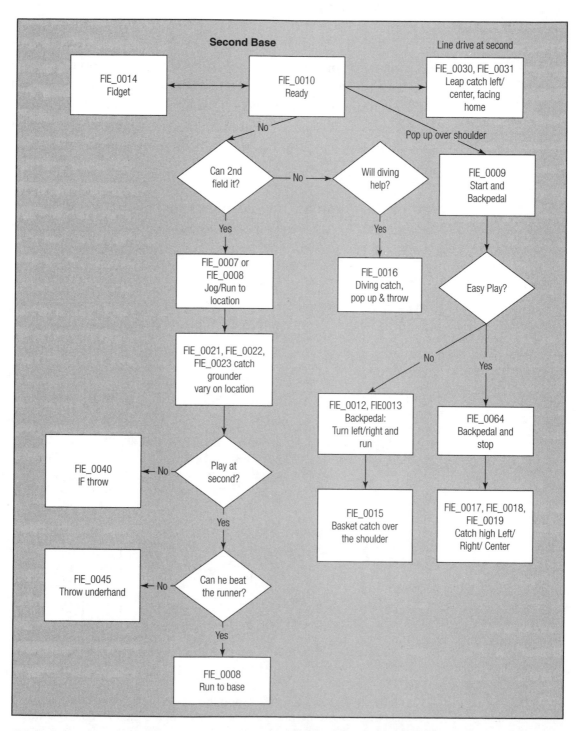

FIGURE 4.4   A more detailed flowchart used by game programmers for making a baseball game.

MOTION DIAGRAMS

Some areas of your project may best be represented in visual form by aids other than flowcharts; for a lack of a better term, we will call these motion diagrams. Like flowcharts, motion diagrams help the animators, designers, programmers, and others on the project get a visual representation of an area of motion. Figure 4.5 is a motion diagram of a baseball batter.

Motion Diagram: A visual aid other than flowcharts, graphs, and charts that is used to help visually represent the game states or motion sets.

Batting Diagram

							Minor avoid	Major avoid	Hit by pitch
Wild Outside swing High	Bad Outside swing High		Bad swing High	Bad Inside swing High		Wild Inside swing High	head	head	head
		High swing Outside	High swing	High swing Inside			chest	chest	chest
Wild Outside swing	Bad Outside swing	Outside swing	Middle swing	Inside swing	Bad Inside swing	Wild Inside swing	belt	belt	belt
		Low swing Outside	Low swing	Low swing Inside			knee	knee	knee
Wild Outside swing Low	Bad Outside swing Low		Bad swing Low	Bad Inside swing Low		Wild Inside swing Low	shin	shin	shin

FIGURE 4.5 A motion diagram illustrating the different possible responses a baseball batter has, depending on the location of the pitched ball. The gray area represents the strike zone.

Figure 4.6 is a further breakdown of the batter response. As you can see, if the batter swings at a pitch located in the wild outside column, there is only one possible motion that is triggered. If the batter swings at a pitch located in the strike zone and misses it, however, there are two possible swing-and-miss motions. If a batter swings at a pitch located in the wild outside column, he will have to lunge at the pitch, so the only follow through that is possible is a one-handed follow through. If a batter swings at a pitch in the strike zone, he will either follow through with one hand or two hands, depending on his swing style.

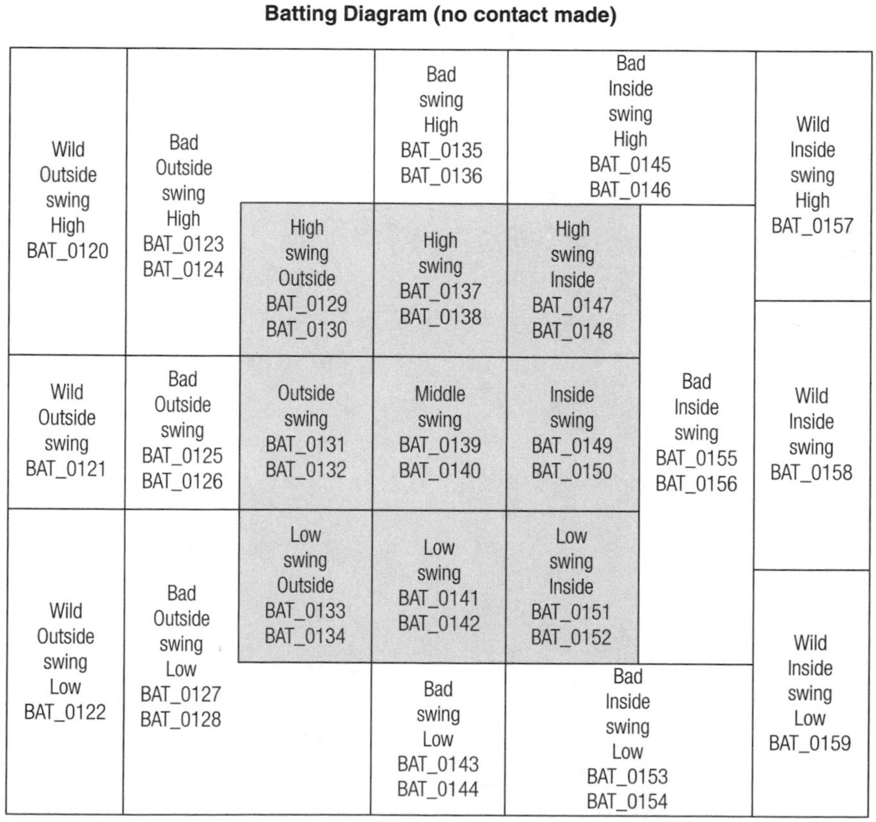

Batting Diagram (no contact made)

Wild Outside swing High BAT_0120	Bad Outside swing High BAT_0123 BAT_0124		Bad swing High BAT_0135 BAT_0136	Bad Inside swing High BAT_0145 BAT_0146	Wild Inside swing High BAT_0157
		High swing Outside BAT_0129 BAT_0130	High swing BAT_0137 BAT_0138	High swing Inside BAT_0147 BAT_0148	
Wild Outside swing BAT_0121	Bad Outside swing BAT_0125 BAT_0126	Outside swing BAT_0131 BAT_0132	Middle swing BAT_0139 BAT_0140	Inside swing BAT_0149 BAT_0150	Bad Inside swing BAT_0155 BAT_0156	Wild Inside swing BAT_0158
Wild Outside swing Low BAT_0122	Bad Outside swing Low BAT_0127 BAT_0128	Low swing Outside BAT_0133 BAT_0134	Low swing BAT_0141 BAT_0142	Low swing Inside BAT_0151 BAT_0152	
			Bad swing Low BAT_0143 BAT_0144	Bad Inside swing Low BAT_0153 BAT_0154	Wild Inside swing Low BAT_0159

FIGURE 4.6   A motion diagram showing the possible outcomes if the batter swings but does not make contact with the ball.

CONCLUSION

- Flowcharting is the second phase to our checks and balances system.
- The amount of flowcharting that the animators should do depends on how much work has been done by the designers in the design document.
- There are two distinct stages to flowcharting: the greater state flowcharts and the motion set flowcharts. This allows you to work from the general to the specific.
- Developing the greater state flowcharts before developing the motion list helps you get the overall feel for the scope of the animations.
- Developing the motion set flowcharts at the same time as the motion list allows you to check that the flow of your motions works the way the designers have envisioned and also helps you make sure you have not left any motions off the motion list.
- Motion sets may be made up of generic motions that multiple characters can use or unique motions that are specific to one character.
- Some motion sets may be best represented by motion diagrams instead of flowcharts.

5

THE MOTION DATABASE

SHOT 2

T he third and final phase to the checks and balances is the motion database. This phase often is left out when dealing with motion capture projects, but it is a crucial step in the process. Most people rely solely on a shot list, but the combination of a motion list and motion database is far more complete and inclusive. The motion list is merely a framework that the details are filled in on; it is a quick version for the designers, programmers, and others on the project to follow, and the more detailed information for each motion is included in the motion database. For this reason, it is much more useful to the motion coordinator and animators throughout the remainder of the project. You will need to prepare a shot list for the motion studio staff, but during the capture session and afterward you should work from the motion database.

The motion database: A record containing detailed information about every motion. It takes over for the motion list and is used by the animators until the completion of the project.

The motion database is used more than the motion list because it consists of more detailed information and is designed in a way that allows it to be used for several phases. It is very important, however, to have accurate, updated information in the database, so it must be constantly maintained.

Reasons for Using a Motion Database

- Acts as checks and balances for the motion list and flowcharts.
- Provides detailed information about each motion during the capture session.
- Provides an area to take notes on each motion during the capture session.
- Is used in the post capture phase by the motion coordinator to assign motions to animators.
- Provides the animators with the information they need to animate/edit the motion data.
- Helps the motion coordinator track the progress of the animators.

Microsoft Excel™ and FileMaker Pro™ are both excellent programs for creating a motion database, but the software you use isn't as important as the information your database contains. One factor that may determine your choice of software is that it must be able to integrate into your company's pipeline.

TYPES OF DATABASES

There are two basic types of databases and, depending on the needs of your project, you may need one or both of them. If you are making a video game, you will need an in-game database for all the motions that are in the actual game, but you may also need a cinematic database if your game has cinematic sequences or an introduction cinematic. In Chapter 3, "The Motion List," we talked about the importance of separating the cinematic sequences from the in-game motions on the motion list, and this is also true when creating a database. Some information included in an in-game database and in a cinematic database will be similar; however there are a number of details that are unique to cinematic sequences.

The In-Game Database

An in-game database needs to contain information and areas that are relevant during different phases of the capture process. This database will be used throughout the pre-capture phase, during the actual capture session, and during the post capture phase.

Basic Information Needed in an In-Game Database

1. The studio name
2. The project name
3. The motion studio name
4. The capture session date
5. The number of motion performers used for each motion captured

6. The number of props used during each motion

7. The motion performer's name who performed the motion

8. The props used during each motion

9. The name of the motion being captured

10. The priority given to each motion when it is processed

11. The name of the motion that the captured motion starts in (core in)

12. The name of the motion that the captured motion ends in (core out)

13. A complete description of the motion being captured

14. An area to take notes on each motion during the capture session

15. An area for the good takes of each motion

16. The total number of takes captured for each motion

17. An area to record the take that is selected to be processed

You may find that you want your database to contain even more information than the basic information suggested. Information such as the estimated number of seconds the motion should be performed in, the sample rate used to capture the motion, and the actual number of seconds the motion was executed in all may be useful during the capture session. Some other additional information may be used during the post capture phase, such as the time-code information from the capture session, the date the processed motion was delivered from the capture studio, the frame number the motion was blended in from, the frame number the motion was blended out to, the name of the animator the motion is assigned to, the date it was assigned to the animator, and the date the animator completed editing the motion.

Sample Rate: The amount of data captured per second. If you capture at 120Hz, you will get 120 frames per second. Sometimes referred to as *data rate* or *frame rate*.

If you like to stay "hands-on" during the entire process, you may find that the basic information is all that is needed. When our example database was designed, it was designed to be somewhat user friendly and not too crowded with information. We knew this database would be used over a number of months, so we didn't want it crammed with too much information. We also knew it would be used by the animators, and they tend to be more visual people, so we wanted it to be easy to follow. Figure 5.1 is one page from an in-game database that we created using FileMaker Pro™ and has been used successfully on several game projects.

MOTION DATABASE

		Motion name: DTH_0123_EXP_BLOWN_BACKWARDS.AMC
Studio name:	Quality Games Inc.	
Project name:	CARRION	Priority:
Motion studio:	GMC Studios	
Shoot date:	02-25-04	

Priority: Low   Good Take: Good Take: 2   Total Takes: 2   Final select: 2

# of performers: 1   # of props: 4

Performers names: Steve

○ Trampoline   ○ Stairs
◉ Pads
◉ Repelling harness
◉ 1 handed weapon
○ 2 handed weapon
○ Ladder
○ Saddle
○ Chair
○ Scaling wall
◉ Ropes

Blend in from: ALT_0010_crouch

Blend out to: DEATH

NOTES: frame # in   frame # out

Description:
Start in alert crouch, explosion in front of the character, blows him backwards, arms flailing, lands on his back. Dead on contact.

		Motion name: DTH_0124_EXP_BLOWN_FOREWARDS.AMC
Studio name:	Quality Games Inc.	
Project name:	CARRION	Priority:
Motion studio:	GMC Studios	
Shoot date:	02-25-04	

Priority: Low   Good Take: 1   Good Take: 3   Total Takes: 3   Final select: 1

# of characters: 1   # of props: 4

Characters names: Steve

○ Trampoline   ○ Stairs
◉ Pads
◉ Repelling harness
◉ 1 handed weapon
○ 2 handed weapon
○ Ladder
○ Saddle
○ Chair
○ Scaling wall
◉ Ropes

Blend in from: ALT_0010_crouch

Blend out to: DEATH

NOTES: frame # in   frame # out

Description:
Start in alert crouch, explosion in back of the character, blows him forewards, arms flailing, lands on his back. Dead on contact.

FIGURE 5.1   Our example motion database contains only the basic information, with the addition of areas to record the frame number the motion was blended in from and out to.

In this database example, you see that it contains only two captured motions per sheet. It was designed this way to make each sheet user friendly during the capture session. This layout allows you to locate information quickly and gives you enough room to fill in important information during the capture session. The one downside to this is that if there are a lot of motions to capture—a thousand or more—this layout makes the database binder quite large. See Chapter 11, "The Motion Capture Session," for more details about taking notes during the capture session.

Database Sheet Explanation

As we talked about earlier, your database sheet is useful during all three phases of production: preparation, the capture session, and post capture. Depending on the phase you are in, you will need to use different areas of the sheet. Figure 5.2 gives a breakdown of the different areas on the database sheet.

Areas to Be Filled in Prior to the Capture Session

During the preproduction phase, numbers 1–13 need to be filled in prior to the capture session. This helps you double check that your motion list and flowcharts are complete and accurate. It also helps you make sure all the special needs of each motion are covered before you arrive on the set.

- Numbers 1–4 are fairly self explanatory and are included to help identify the project the database sheet belongs to. Our example database requires us to fill in these areas only on the first sheet; it is then recorded on all the following sheets.
- Number 5 is an area to record the number of performers whose motion is being captured for that particular motion. Keep in mind that some motions may require two performers to interact, even though only one of them is being captured.
- Number 6 is the number of props used during the capture of the motion. Like the performers, these props can be either captured or non-captured props.

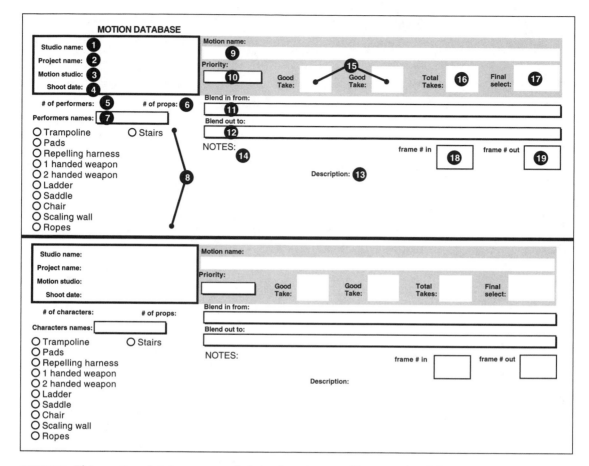

FIGURE 5.2   This motion database example is broken down to illustrate the different areas it contains.

- Number 7 is the name of the performers used to capture the motion.

- Number 8 is a list of the props that may be needed during the capture. In this database you can make a list of props and check the circle to the left of the prop to indicate if it is needed for that particular motion. White circles indicate it is not used, and black circles indicate it is needed. You can easily change the lists for different projects, so this database outline can be used for projects with specific needs.

- Number 9 is the name that you give to the motion being captured. Each motion name needs to be unique, so there should never be two or more motions with identical names. This part of the database has two purposes. The motion name is used at the motion capture session, but since this database is also used by the animators after the capture, this area tells the animator what name to call the animation when he is finished editing it.

- Number 10 is an area to indicate the priority given to the motion for processing and delivery. After the capture session, the motion capture studio needs to know in what order to process and deliver the motions to you. In this database, this area is a drop-down window, so all the priorities are in a list, and the appropriate one can be chosen for each motion. Some people use a numeric system to indicate priority, such as 1, 2, 3, or an alphabetical system, A, B, C. For clarity, a different approach is best. Using *urgent*, *high*, *medium*, and *low* priority is better. With a numeric or an alphabetic system there may be some confusion as to which motions are the highest and which are the lowest priority.

- Numbers 11 and 12, like the motion name, have two purposes. During the capture session they indicate what motion the captured motion should start and finish in. During the animation phase they also tell the animator which motions to use to blend with. In this database this area is a drop-down window, so all the core motions are listed, and it is simply a matter of choosing the appropriate one for each motion.

- Number 13 is the motion's description, and is one of the most important areas of the database. A good description is an area that many people leave out when they only use a shot list to prepare for a capture session. The description area is used during all three phases of the process, and because of this, an incomplete or bad motion description can cause a lot of problems. The description needs to be thorough enough for someone not familiar with the project to understand what is needed. If only one person can understand the description, then only one person really understands what needs to be captured, and this excludes everyone else from being able to contribute fully. If the director is called away from the capture session, it can continue without him if all the team members know and can reference what is needed.

An Example of a Bad Motion Description

Shot in the head, falls down dead.

Bad descriptions like this are common, but almost completely worthless during the capture session. A description like this gives only a vague overall description of the needed motion and is not nearly specific enough. It does not tell you from which direction the shot comes, how the performer's body should react when shot, which direction he needs to fall, or how his body is suppose to land.

An Example of a Better Motion Description

Character is shot in the head from behind, head snaps forward, arms go backward; he drops his gun and drops straight down to his knees, pauses, then falls straight forward on his face with his arm out to his side.

It is worth reiterating that with a complete description, a starting core motion, and an ending core motion, even someone not familiar with the project will be able to understand what is needed to be captured. This is a very important point. Every person attending the motion capture session needs to know what needs to be captured. The more sets of eyes you have knowing and watching each move, the better likelihood you have of being successful. This is especially important if the director needs to leave the set for some reason; the capture can continue under the guidance of one of the other crew members.

Areas to Be Filled in During the Capture Session

During the capture session phase, numbers 14–17 will need to be filled in. Taking notes and recording this information for each motion during the capture is an important step. These notes will help you avoid problems months later during the post capture phase. It also helps you remember all the unique problems or changes that occurred for each motion during the capture.

- Number 14 is an area of blank space set aside for taking notes on each motion during the capture session. After the capture session, these notes can be typed in that area of the database for future reference.

- Numbers 15–17 also are areas to record information during the capture session. Number 15 is for recording the number of takes that were good. Let's say we captured four variations of a particular motion, and we feel the first and fourth takes were the best. You would then put a number 1 in one box and a 4 in the other. In the total takes area—number 16—you would put a 4 because we captured four takes of the motion. Number 17 is the area to record the number of the take that you decide is the best one for processing.

Areas Used by the Animators for Editing During the Post Capture Phase

During the post capture phase, numbers 9 and 11–19 will be used by the animators to edit the motion files. During this time, the motion coordinator also will use these areas to make sure the motion data received from the motion studio is correct.

- Number 9 is the name that was given to the motion at the capture with a description added to it. By having the description added, the animator knows what filename to give to the motion after it is edited. By using the *CARRION* naming convention, the animator also knows by the filename which subdirectory the motion file is located in, so finding the files he needs to edit is easy.

- Number 10 is an area to indicate the priority given to the motion for processing and delivery, but it can also be used by the animator to tell him which motions need to be edited first. The priority a motion is processed in is not necessarily the same priority that it is edited in. The motion coordinator may change the priority before assigning the motions to the animators, and since the game-making process is constantly changing, the priority may even change after motions have been assigned. Remember that in our database this area is a drop-down window, so all the priorities are in a list and can easily be changed if needed.

- Numbers 11 and 12 have two purposes. During the capture session they told us which motion or position the performer should start and finish in. During the animation phase, they also tell the animator which motions to use to blend with. This area also is a drop-down window.

- Number 13 is the motion's description and can be used by the animator to help him better understand what the motion is supposed to be and look like. The description can also be used to double-check that the motion coordinator didn't make an error and select the wrong blend in or out motion.

- Number 14 is an area of blank space set aside for taking notes on each motion during the capture session. These notes are very important to the animator during the editing process. If the motion the animator is going to edit was captured as a combination motion (see Chapter 3), then the motion would be difficult to locate without the notes area. For example, let's say during our capture we captured three motions together. Motions ALT_0100.amc, ALT_0122.amc, and ALT_0123.amc were all captured at the same time and named ALT_0100.amc. When an animator tries to find motion ALT_0122.amc, he will not be able to find it unless he reads the notes area and sees that it was captured at the same time as motions ALT_0100.amc and ALT_0123.amc. He would then open motion file ALT_0100.amc and, using the motion description, select the portion that will be renamed ALT_0122.amc, edit it, and rename it. See Chapter 6, "Directory Structure and Filenaming Convention," for detailed information on filenames. Figure 5.3 is an example.

- Numbers 15, 16, and 17 also are areas where information was recorded during the capture session. In the post capture phase, these areas are used only if there is a problem with a captured

MOTION DATABASE

Studio name:	Quality Games Inc.
Project name:	CARRION
Motion studio:	GMC Studios
Shoot date:	02-25-04

Motion name:
ALT_0122_walk_to_crouch.AMC

Priority:
Low

| | Good Take: | | Good Take: | 2 | Total Takes: | 3 | Final select: | 2 |

# of performers: 1   # of props: 4

Performers names: Steve

Blend in from:
ALT_0100_walk

Blend out to:
ALT_0080_crouch

O Trampoline   O Stairs
● Pads
● Repelling harness
● 1 handed weapon
O 2 handed weapon
O Ladder
O Saddle
O Chair
O Scaling wall
● Ropes

NOTES: frame # in   frame # out
Captured with ALT_0100
and ALT_0123   Description:
                        alert walk / alert crouch / alert walk

---

Studio name:	Quality Games Inc.
Project name:	CARRION
Motion studio:	GMC Studios
Shoot date:	02-25-04

Motion name:
ALT_0123_crouch_to_walk.AMC

Priority:
Low

| | Good Take: | 1 | Good Take: | 2 | Total Takes: | 2 | Final select: | 1 |

# of characters: 1   # of props: 4

Characters names: Steve

Blend in from:
ALT_0080_crouch

Blend out to:
ALT_0100_walk

O Trampoline   O Stairs
● Pads
● Repelling harness
● 1 handed weapon
O 2 handed weapon
O Ladder
O Saddle
O Chair
O Scaling wall
● Ropes

NOTES: frame # in   frame # out
Captured with ALT_0100
and ALT_0122   Description:
                        alert walk / alert crouch / alert walk

FIGURE 5.3 An example of a combination motion, where the animator needs to read the notes area to find the motion he is seeking.

file and a new take needs to be processed and sent to you. Area number 16 also can be used to evaluate the difficulty you had in capturing a particular motion. If the total number of takes is large, then you know that move posed some problems during the capture or there were some technical difficulties at that time.

• Numbers 18 and 19 both need to be filled in by the animators as they edit the motion files. Number 18 is an area to record the frame number that is the same in the core-in motion and the captured motion. Number 19 is an area to record the frame number that is the same in the core-out motion and the captured motion. In other words, if we use frame number 15 of the core-in motion and blend it to the captured motion, then we would put a number 15 in the frame # in area. If we blend out to frame number 1 of the core-out motion, we would put a number 1 in the frame # out area. This is done because the programmers need to know which frame number of the motion they need to use to link or tile together with another motion.

In addition to areas 18 and 19, we highly recommend that you encourage your animators to take their own editing notes for each motion. These notes can be recorded right on the sheet or in a separate log. These notes can also prove helpful if a problem arises with a particular motion file.

Remember that this example database sheet was designed for in-game motions, in-game celebration motions, and in-game fluff motions. It is not adequate to be used for cinematic sequences because cinematic motions require more basic information.

The Cinematic Database

A database sheet for cinematic sequences needs to include the same basic information as the in-game database, but it also needs to contain some unique information in order for the motions to be captured properly.

Basic Information in a Cinematic Database that Is the Same as the In-Game Database

1. The studio name
2. The project name
3. The motion studio name
4. The capture session date
5. The number of motion performers used for each motion captured
6. The number of props used during each motion
7. The motion performer's name who performed the motion
8. The props used during each motion

9. The name of the motion being captured

10. The priority given to each motion when it is processed

11. The name of the motion that the captured motion starts in (core in)

12. The name of the motion that the captured motion ends in (core out)

13. A complete description of the motion being captured

14. An area to take notes on each motion during the capture session

15. An area for the good takes of each motion

16. The total number of takes captured for each motion

17. An area to record the take that is selected to be processed

In addition to these basic areas, a cinematic database also needs to include more detailed information about the overall scene.

Additional Basic Information in a Cinematic Database

- The location of the camera
- A description of the environment
- The dimensions of objects and props interacted with during the capture

The location of the rendering camera is important during a cinematic capture. By *rendering camera* we mean the camera angle used for the final render of the scene. During a capture session, the motion capture equipment itself uses several cameras to capture the data; these are important from the technical side, but the rendering camera is important from the artistic side. Having the rendering camera's location will help you frame the shot and also helps the performer know where his audience is. The performer might not look directly at the camera, but he still needs to know from which angle his performance needs to look good. During playback, it may be possible to watch the shot from the rendering camera's point of view and check the character's movement to make sure he stays in frame or that he is positioned properly through out the shot.

A description of the environment is very important when capturing cinematics. Distances, elevations, and weather conditions will all affect the performance and how you capture each shot. How far a character needs to move to interact with another character or to reach a doorway is important. This is made even more complicated if you are capturing a performer who is supposed to be a giant, with another performer who is supposed to be a dwarf. If two characters need to walk up a ramp, you should know how far they need to walk and what the grade of the ramp is. A steeper grade causes the body to lean forward more in an effort to maintain balance. All of this will affect the performance and the look of your captured motions. If you need to capture performers trudging through two feet of snow, you will want the performers to move differently than they would while walking down a sidewalk on a summer day. To get them to physically move differently, rather than just fake it, you may want to fill the capture volume with two feet of packing peanuts and have the performers wade through them to simulate the snow.

No matter what kind of capture you are doing, you must know the dimensions of the props and environmental objects that the performer needs to interact with. If he is shooting a gun, you need to know the size the gun will be in the rendered scene. Even the dimensions of objects such as doors that the performer needs to interact with need to be known. Is it a regular size door, or is it a huge castle door? If he reaches for the handle, is it three feet from the ground or five feet? If your performers are going to act out complex scenes, everything they interact with and the distances to get to them need to be known and included in your database. For example, let's say we have a character hiding behind a large crate that is the equivalent of three and a half feet high. The character then stands up and shoots his large weapon, which is fixed to his hip. If his hip measures three feet high, we have a problem because the weapon wouldn't be high enough to shoot over the crate, and because the weapon is fixed to his hip, he can't raise it to head height. All of these measurements need to be worked out prior to the capture session so that you don't capture motions that can't be used.

Prop: An inanimate object that serves as a means of support or assistance during a motion capture session.

How much information you need to include in your database also depends on the thoroughness of your storyboards and script. Make sure everything is covered, including dialogue. Also make sure that you have a complete description of the scene that each motion belongs to. For example, let's say you need to capture a character running away after a confrontation with another character. Could you capture the motion you needed? No, you couldn't, because you don't have enough information about the scene. What was said between the characters? Is the character running away angry? Scared? Is he being chased by the other character? Each of these would affect how the performer would run away. You should bring your script, storyboards, and database to the capture session, and all need to work together so that you can capture the motions properly.

Cinematic sequences in video games are used for several reasons: to set the theme of the game, as celebrations after a victory, as a transition to another part of the game, to pass information on to the user, or to introduce a character. Frequently, cinematic sequences tend to be a tight camera shot of two stationary characters standing face to face and talking. Occasionally they might shrug their shoulders or gesture with one hand during their exchange. Cinematics such as these may indeed convey the information, but they don't add to the esthetic look of the game.

Reasons Most Game Cinematic Sequences are Unsuccessful

- Some companies approach cinematic sequences as an afterthought instead of planning them out. They make the error of thinking that all they need to do is blend the in-game motions together to make the cinematic sequences they need. What they fail to remember is that in-game motions are short pieces that get back to a core motion (or position) quickly and are not always a realistic depiction of how a person would move or act in the real world. Real people don't worry about getting back to a generic core position and wait for input, they simply move. Most of the time, in-game motions strung together to create cinematic sequences simply look unrealistic.

- Some companies do not have the budget or manpower to have complicated cinematic sequences and try to conserve resources by making do with the motions they have. If the cinematic sequences are important enough to have in the game, they should be important enough to do correctly. Cutting corners on the cinematic sequences only cheapens the overall quality of the game.

- Some companies just don't know how to plan cinematic sequences.

Planning Cinematic Sequences

In Chapter 4, "Flowcharts and Motion Diagrams," we talked about working from the general to the specific, and the same holds true for planning cinematic sequences. One of the first jobs is to figure out the basic blocking of the characters and dialogue to help set the scene. If this is done by the game designer, make sure you sit down with him and figure out exactly what he is looking for in each scene. When blocking out the characters' movements, make sure you also take into account the capture volume size (including the height). As we mentioned in Chapter 3, if the movement required is over a large area, the scene may need to be broken up into smaller shots in order to be captured during the capture session, then pieced together afterward by the animators. Remember that you need to know the setting, environmental conditions, and any special requirements of each scene in order to capture each shot correctly.

Approach the scenes as if you are directing a movie or a play. Some movie directors are fairly loose with giving direction and let the actors explore their roles and give the performances they choose. Other directors like to control everything from how much wind blows, when rain starts or stops, if water will be calm or have ripples, and where shadows should be located. For game cinematics, this amount of control might be a bit too extreme, but the important point is that you plan and think through how best to communicate the idea or message of the sequences while still making them visually appealing. You might find that simplicity is best, but that shouldn't be an excuse not to plan the sequences.

If it's possible, act out and video tape each scene. Video taping from the position and angle you want the rendering camera to be in might help you better visualize the cinematic sequences and can even serve as storyboards for your motion performers. You also want to pay attention to the amount of time it takes to complete each scene. Remember that most motion capture studios charge by the second, so you need to know how long each scene lasts. Once you know the overall length of the scene, you can break the scenes down into the individual shots that you need.

Many game companies focus more on capturing a performer's body movement, or keyframing them, to the pace of the dialogue during the cinematic sequences than they do on lip-syncing facial movement to dialogue. This is understandable, given the timeline and budget most game companies have to work with. Working this way, however, places a lot of emphasis on the character's gestures because if the gestures are random or look out of place with the dialogue, the illusion of realism is lost. Understanding how gesture works with dialogue is important if you want your cinematic sequences to be appealing.

Gesture Along with Dialogue Can Help To:

- Define a character
- Set a scene
- Add to conversation
- Emphasize a point

Tom Chiarella points out in his book *Writing Dialogue* that there are several different types of physical gestures. He describes them as, Dramatic, Particular, and Incidental gesture. Dramatic gesture is used to emphasize the meaning of a conversation, for example when a crime boss rubs his cigar out as he explains he wants someone killed. Particular gesture is a gesture unique to an individual character and helps define him as an individual. A great example of this is in Akira Kurosawa's film *Seven Samurai*. The elder, stately samurai Kambei Shimada, played by Takashi Shimura, rubs his hand over his head when he is thinking. This gesture adds uniqueness and visual impact to his character. Incidental gestures are gestures that arise out of the setting or circumstances. A character may turn his head when a car honks, or he may be startled when a waiter drops a glass. You may want to script gestures into the characters you are capturing to help make your cinematics more believable and to better support the dialogue.

Depending on the complexity of your cinematics and the interaction of your characters, it may be important for you to select motion performers who meet the physical needs of your game's characters. We will use our same storyboards from Chapter 3 as an example. Shot number 2 is a fairly tight shot: Characters C and A are talking. Character C appears shorter, smaller, and older than character A. For this shot it isn't important that character A is played by a taller performer because we could use the old Hollywood trick and have character A stand on a platform for the shot if we wanted character C to be looking up at him. Character C could just as easily look over the top of character A's head as he delivers his lines. If, however, the shot required the characters to interact more, such as talking and then getting into a fight, the size difference would be more apparent. In that case, we may want to choose a smaller, older performer for character C and a larger, more muscular performer to play character A, so that they move more like the characters in the storyboard. Figure 5.4 illustrates the size of our characters.

Most motion capture studios recommend that you have your performers rehearse their moves prior to the capture session, but

FIGURE 5.4 An example of the size of characters A and C in relation to each other.

this is crucial for cinematic sequences. To get the best results possible from your capture, the performers need to get a feel for their characters, how the other performers work, and what you are looking for. Rehearsals are even more important if you need your performers to act to prerecorded dialogue. See Chapter 9, "Motion Performers, Stunt Coordination, and Directing," for more information on motion performers.

CONCLUSION

- The motion database is the third and final phase to our checks and balances system.

- The motion database contains more detailed information than the motion list and is used for the preparation phase, capture session phase, and post capture phase.

- There are two basic types of motion databases: an in-game database and a cinematic database.

- Because of its design, our example in-game database has areas that need to be filled in prior to the capture session, areas filled in during the capture, and areas used during the post capture phase.

- Having a thorough motion description is of major importance before the capture session occurs.

- A cinematic database needs to contain the same basic information as the in-game database, but it also needs to include some unique information.

- The main purposes of cinematic sequences in video games is to help set the theme of the game, create celebrations after a victory, act as a transition to another part of the game, pass information onto the user, and introduce a character.

- Many games have unsuccessful cinematic sequences because the company handles them as an afterthought instead of planning them out, they don't have the budget to capture motions specifically for them, or they simply don't know how to plan them.

- When planning cinematic sequences, work from the general to the specific. The better your feel for the entire scene, the easier it is to break it down into the individual shots.

- Approach the scenes as if you are directing a movie or play. This may help you communicate the message while still having visually appealing scenes.

- Don't overestimate the importance of gesture in cinematic sequences.

- Choose motion performers who are the best fit for your cinematic characters.

6

DIRECTORY STRUCTURE AND FILENAMING CONVENTION

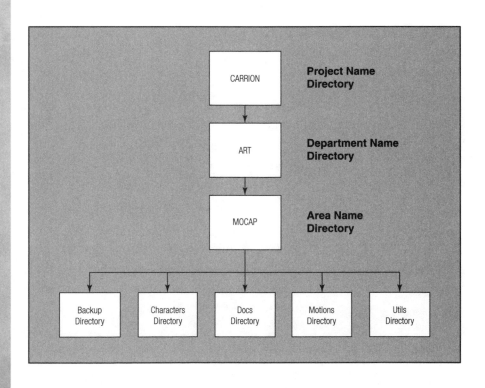

The directory structure and filenames that you choose need to be thought out and planned if you want them to be user friendly over the course of the project. It is common for files to be lost, copied over, or difficult to locate if there isn't a well thought out structure to the directories and filenames. Confusion is also compounded on large projects when you have to deal with thousands of individual motion capture files that need to be organized, blended together, animated, and then retrieved by the programmers. We have already seen how the motion list and flowcharts work together to complement each other, and in much the same way so should your directory structure and filenames. By working together, they will actually help prevent confusion and possible delays in your schedule. There are several advantages to having them planned out and working together.

- Doing so will make it easier for the animators to locate the motion files. Having the motion filenames coordinated with the directory they are located in makes finding the files very easy, thus increasing worker productivity.
- It makes tracking the motion files easier. The motion coordinator can track and locate motions easily and make sure the animators are still on schedule.
- It will help others who are not familiar with the project locate files. If you have employees join in the middle of a project or if others are asked to help out in a crunch, a simple organized structure allows them to ramp up easily, becoming productive more quickly. It will also make it easier for the programmers to locate the motion files they need, so that they can get them into the game.

DIRECTORY STRUCTURE

The main purpose of your directory structure is to have it organized in a way that helps everyone quickly and easily locate files. Because of this, the directory structure that you choose must not become a bottleneck or create a slowdown in the work flow. If there are too many subdirectories buried within the directories, it becomes time consuming and confusing to locate files. Confusion as to where to find files, compounded with the long hours of trying to meet deadlines, only adds frustration and stress to the animation staff. Whether you like to use shortcuts to get to certain directories or not, having a simple, clean directory structure is the key to being efficient.

Directory Structure: A series of folders and subfolders arranged for the purpose of organizing files.

As the motion coordinator, it is your responsibility to organize all areas relating to the motion for the game. This includes the motion capture files as well as the motion list, flowcharts, storyboards, skeletons, and plug-ins, and you should even have an area to back up old versions of files. The following directory structure examples include only the directories that affect the motion capture section of our game and do not include other areas of the project such as programming, design, work schedules, and so on, as seen in Figure 6.1.

```
CARRION/art/mocap/backup/
CARRION/art/mocap/characters/
CARRION/art/mocap/docs/
CARRION/art/mocap/motions/
CARRION/art/mocap/utils/
```

It is important to have the backup, characters, docs, motions, and utils directories all on the same level. This will give you access to all areas that need to be organized and also prevents you from having to dig through numerous subdirectories when trying to

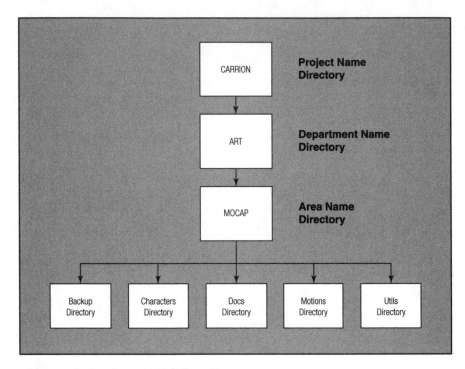

FIGURE 6.1 A simple, easy to follow directory structure.

work. Having an uncluttered area for the motion capture files and for the animators to navigate through is of the utmost importance.

The Backup Directory

Even if your company has an auto backup of your network system, it is a good idea to have an easily accessible backup directory. This backup directory is intended for certain key files and not for every single file; otherwise it may take up too much memory. This backup directory is just an area for you to place key files so that they are easily retrieved in an emergency. It is also important to make sure that your company's auto backup system is functioning properly. Once on a recent project we did not realize that the backup system was not working until we lost some files and tried to retrieve them from the backup. This Backup directory, as seen in Figure 6.2, is used as a backup area for old skeletons, models, cer-

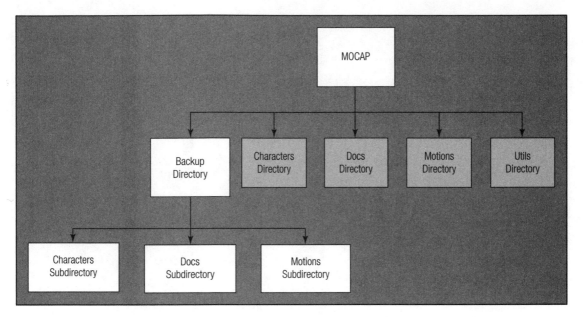

FIGURE 6.2   The Backup directory and its subdirectories.

tain motion capture files, motion documents, and so on, and is broken down into three subdirectories:

```
CARRION/art/mocap/Backup/characters/
CARRION/art/mocap/Backup/docs/
CARRION/art/mocap/Backup/motions/
```

The Backup/characters/ subdirectory will contain the old skeletons and character models. Sometimes you find you actually like an older version better than a new one, so it is best if they are kept accessible.

The Backup/docs/ subdirectory is where the old motion lists, flowcharts, storyboards, design document, and so on are kept. You may find that these documents also need to be referred to.

The Backup/motions/ subdirectory will contain old versions of the motion files. This subdirectory will be divided into numerous subdirectories in order to keep the motion files organized the same as they will be in CARRION/art/mocap/motions/finished/.

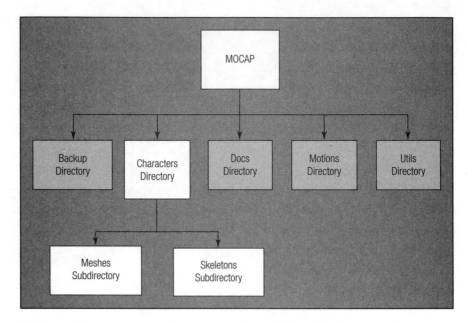

FIGURE 6.3 The Characters directory and its subdirectories.

The **Characters** Directory

The Characters directory is the folder that will contain the skeletons and character models used in your game. It can be broken into two main subdirectories: skeletons and meshes. You may find, however, that you want to copy the game skeleton into the motions directory so that the animators have easier access to it while editing the motion files (Figure 6.3).

```
CARRION/art/mocap/Characters/meshes/
CARRION/art/mocap/Characters/skeletons/
```

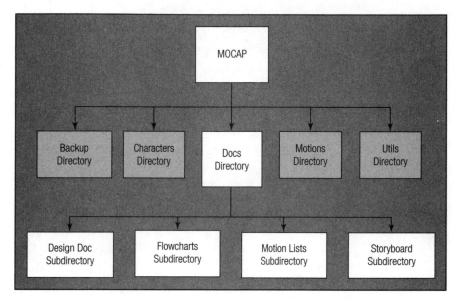

FIGURE 6.4   The Docs directory and its subdirectories.

The Documents (Docs) Directory

The Docs directory is where the documents created for your game are stored, and motion lists, flowcharts, design document, storyboards, etc. are kept. You may find during the course of the project that these documents may also need to be referred to and to be accessible by the entire team, especially if there is some confusion over a design element that relates to the motion flow (Figure 6.4).

```
CARRION/art/mocap/Docs/design_doc/
CARRION/art/mocap/Docs/flowcharts/
CARRION/art/mocap/Docs/motion_lists/
CARRION/art/mocap/Docs/storyboards/
```

The `motions` Directory

This directory is the largest and most complicated of all the directories and is where all the motion capture files will be located. The animators will be accessing this directory constantly during the animation process, either copying motion files to their local machines or working directly from it on the network. As seen in Figure 6.5, it is broken down into three major subdirectories:

```
CARRION/art/mocap/motions/finished/
CARRION/art/mocap/motions/raw/
CARRION/art/mocap/motions/working/
```

The `motions/finished/` subdirectory is where the finished motion capture files are kept. A finished motion is one that has already been animated and edited by the animators and is ready to be implemented into the game. This subdirectory will contain several subdirectories that reflect the different states that the character can go in during the game. For our game, *CARRION*, we divided the `finished` subdirectory into the following state subdirectories:

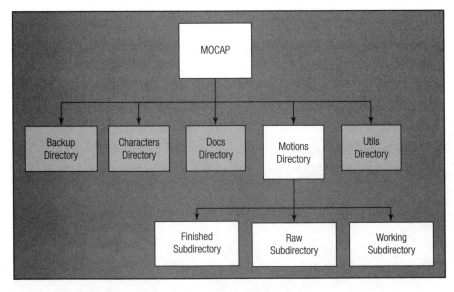

FIGURE 6.5   The `motions` directory and its subdirectories.

- Alert
- Attack
- Casual
- Climb
- Death
- Escape
- Survival
- Swim

Every motion file in *CARRION* will be categorized into one of the following game states. These states are shown in Figure 6.6, Figure 6.7, and Figure 6.8.

- The `motions/raw/` subdirectory is where the motion files that are delivered from the motion studio are kept. This subdirectory will have the same game state folders as the `motions/finished/` subdirectory.

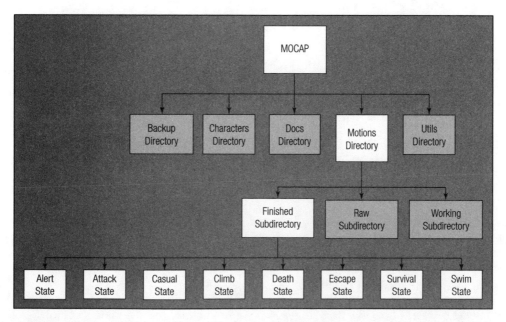

FIGURE 6.6 The `motions` directory, the `finished` subdirectory, and the individual game state folders contained within.

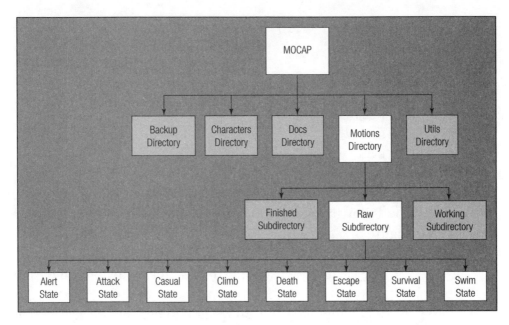

FIGURE 6.7 The motions directory, the raw subdirectory, and the individual game state folders contained within.

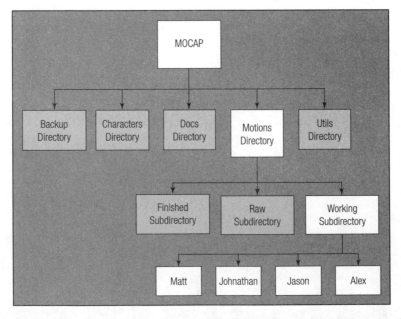

FIGURE 6.8 The motion directory, the working subdirectory, and the folders of individual animators who are working on the project. It is here that they will keep the motion files they are working on.

The `motions/working/` subdirectory is the folder where the animators who want to work from the project server will store the motion files they are working on. Once a motion file is finished, it is copied to the `CARRION/art/mocap/motions/finished/` subdirectory and placed in the appropriate subdirectory. This subdirectory can be broken into further subdirectories that correspond to the animator's names.

The Utilities (`Utils`) Directory

The `Utils` directory is the area for the utilities that the animators might need for the project, such as a motion inverter, importers, plug-ins, file converters, and so on. Depending on the software you use and the demands of your game engine, you might not need an area for special utilities on your project, or you may have so few special utilities that this directory does not need to be broken into further subdirectories. Figure 6.9 illustrates the `Utils` directory and its subdirectories.

```
CARRION/art/mocap/Utils/importers/
CARRION/art/mocap/Utils/inverter/
CARRION/art/mocap/Utils/plug-ins/
```

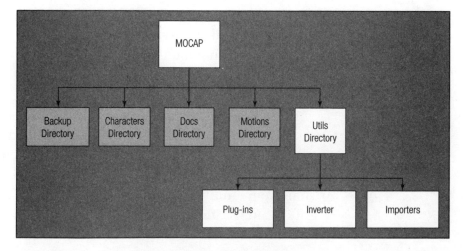

FIGURE 6.9 The `Utils` directory and its subdirectories.

On your network, setting up a directory structure with coordinated motion capture filenames that is easy and logical to follow is the most effective way to work because it allows everyone access to all the files. This does, however, assume that your company has a large enough network to support that much data.

If you are having your animators work entirely from their own workstations, you should still establish a universal directory structure for each animator to set up. The animators should be expected to follow the established naming convention and save the files into the appropriate directories. Doing this allows others to locate files easily in case the animator is sick or absent. If an animator feels it is too much of a burden to name and save files properly, get him off your project and replace him with someone who can act more professionally.

FILENAMING CONVENTION

Because there are a large number of motion files that require organization and monitoring when working with motion capture, there is a need to have a logical, easy-to-use naming convention that works in conjunction with your directory structure. One of the key elements that will separate a good filename from a bad one is that a good filename will work together with your directory structure. Keep in mind that the animators are not the only people who need to handle these files, so your naming convention needs to work for all areas of production.

There have been projects where it was the individual animator's responsibility to come up with a finished filename for the motions he edited. This is an incredibly inefficient way for a company to handle a naming convention. Filenames will not be consistent from animator to animator, and finding a given motion file easily is almost impossible. It is extremely difficult to track a finished motion file back to its source or even to verify that a motion file has been animated with a system like this. Whatever naming convention you decide to use, certain requirements should be met.

Filenames should meet these requirements:

- The name needs to be user friendly for the motion capture studio.
- The name needs to be user friendly for the animators.
- The name needs to work for the programming staff.
- The name should make it possible for each motion file to be tracked back to its source at the capture session.
- The filename needs to accommodate additional motions to be added in the future.
- The filename should correspond to the subdirectory in which it is located.

The difficult part is finding a naming convention that actually fulfills all of these principles and works for your project.

The *CARRION* Naming Convention

The filenaming convention we used for our example game, *CARRION*, addresses all these issues. This does not mean that it is the only naming convention you can use, but this same basic convention has been used on several games (sports genre as well), and it worked very efficiently and effectively. Our naming convention starts off as an eight-dot-three name for the motion capture session, and when the animators get the motion files back, they add a descriptor to the name so it is easier for them to work with, then the name is once again reduced to an eight-dot-three for the programmers to implement into the game. Handling the naming convention this way satisfies all groups who deal with the motion files and allows the file to still be tracked back to its source file.

Eight-dot-three filename: A filename that has only eight characters followed by a three character file extension.

An eight-dot-three makes it difficult to have a descriptive filename unless you use a complicated abbreviation system. The problem with a complicated abbreviation system is that everyone needs to know what the abbreviations mean or they won't be able to find the files efficiently. This becomes more of an issue when motion files are used over the course of several generations of a game and different people are assigned to work on it. A sheet decoding the abbreviations would need to be generated, but that kind of organization is rare in the game industry and slows down the editing process. The naming convention we used on *CARRION* uses a simple abbreviation system that is fairly easy to understand, and our abbreviations correspond to our directory structure.

- Example of a bad eight-dot-three filename:

  `CTSA001A.amc`

This filename is not good because it is hard to read, the abbreviation system is complicated, and it does not correspond to a directory structure.

The motion capture studio is going to be the first group to use the filenames that you choose, and most motion capture studios prefer that the filenames follow an eight-dot-three naming convention. Some studios may even insist that you follow an eight-dot-three format.

- Example of an eight-dot-three filename from *CARRION*:

  `ALT_0100.amc`

Many animators, including myself, prefer longer, more descriptive filenames so a file is easily identified in a list. The problem is that you can't be descriptive in eight characters, so we came up with a workaround. When the animators edit the motion file, they save it with a longer description attached to the name.

- Example of a filename from *CARRION* after it is edited by the animators:

`ALT_0100_shoulder_roll_right.amc`

Many programmers prefer the shorter filenames much like motion capture studios do. The problem is that the programmers handle the motion files after the animators do, so that means the filename will be shortened so the programmers can implement them into the game. A script can easily be written to truncate the filename back to the original eight-dot-three filename.

- Example of a filename from *CARRION* after it is truncated:
  `ALT_0100.amc`

The advantage to having the filename stay consistent through the entire process is that it can easily be tracked all the way back to the original capture data. If the programmers rename the file when putting it into the engine, or if the filename changes at any-time after the capture session, it makes tracking the motion more difficult or impossible. Tracking files is important if a file is corrupted or processed incorrectly or just to check to see if all motions are edited. It's not unheard of for the programmers to change filenames when implementing motion files into an engine. Paul Blagay, senior video game programmer, states that "as long as the filenames follow an eight-dot-three naming convention, there is no reason why filenames would need to be changed." Truncating the filename, rather than changing it, makes more sense.

The numeric portion of the filename is four digits long to allow for additional motions to be added in future versions of the game. Having four digits allows for 10,000 motions per prefix. In this example, the prefix we used is ALT. This means that there can be 10,000 unique names of motion files beginning with ALT.

- Examples of a filename range using the ALT prefix:
  `ALT_0000.amc—ALT_9999.amc`

Another advantage to using a four digit numeric is that the first number of the numeric can be used to keep track of the year the motion was captured. For example, let's say the first year that we captured motion for *CARRION* was in the year 2002, then we added motions in an updated version of the game in 2004. All the motions captured in the year 2002 will begin with the number 2, while motions captured in 2004, will begin with a 4.

- Examples of motion files captured in the year 2002:

  `ALT_2000.amc`

  `ALT_2001.amc`

  `ALT_2002.amc`

- Examples of motion files captured in the year 2004:

  `ALT_4000.amc`

  `ALT_4001.amc`

  `ALT_4002.amc`

Keep in mind that organizing your motions this way allows for 1,000 motions per year per prefix, instead of 10,000 total motions per prefix, but one thousand should be more than enough.

The filename you choose should also correspond to the subdirectory in which it is located. This makes it easy to locate files and for the animators to put files into their correct locations. If a file becomes misplaced, it is also easy to identify and find its correct location.

With the *CARRION* filenaming convention, we classify all the motion files and group them together by the type of motion they are. The motion files are grouped into the game state that the character is in when performing the motion. For example, if you have a motion where the character is climbing a ladder, that motion is classified as being in the climb state, so its prefix would be CLM. If another motion is of a character shooting his weapon, then doing a shoulder roll to his right, and ends shooting again, that motion is classified as an attack motion, and its prefix would be ATT. For sports games, the character's position can be used as the game state. In baseball for example, you would have batter motions, base runner motions, catcher motions, and so on. Other sports such as football, basketball, soccer, or hockey are not as easy to break down. Many motions can be executed no matter what position the character is playing. A motion like catching a football needs to be able to happen no matter which character is performing it; this makes it more difficult to classify into a position or state. For games with this problem, we recommend that motions unique to a position such as a quarterback or kicker have their own state, but motions such as catch motions that are not position specific should have their own state that is not a position. For example, some of the states might be QBC (for quarterback motions), KIC (for kicker motions), or CAT (for catch motions).

The directory names in *CARRION* were named the same as our game states: Alert, Attack, Casual, Climb, Death, Escape, Survival, and Swim. The prefix in our filenames, the first three characters, relates to the state the motion file is from. Our naming convention can be broken down into four basic levels:

- Prefix level
- Numeric level
- Descriptor level
- File extension level

The prefix level is a three-character abbreviation indicating which directory (and state) a motion file can be found in. For the Alert directory the abbreviation is ALT, for the Attack directory it is ATT, for Casual it is CAS, for Climb CLM, Death DTH, Escape ESC, Survival SUR, and Swim SWM. All the motion filenames will begin with one of these prefixes. The three-letter prefix is immediately followed by an underscore. Separating the various levels with an underscore makes the filenames easier to read when looking through a list of hundreds of motion files.

- Example:

  `ALT_0100_shoulder_roll_right.amc`

The numeric level follows the underscore after the prefix level. It is four digits in length, and no two motion files (in the same state) should have the same numeric. For example, only one motion in the ALT state will have the numeric sequence ALT_0100, but there can be an ATT_0100 motion or a CAS_0100 and so on. The four-digit numeric is followed either by an underscore and a description or by a dot and the file extension, depending on when in the process the file is being used.

- Example:

  `ALT_0100_shoulder_roll_right.amc`
  or
  `ALT_0100.amc`

The descriptor level is a brief explanation of what motion is being performed in the file. This description is given to the animator and then inserted into the naming convention during the animation process. It is added to make the file quicker to identify by the animators.

- Example:

  `ALT_0100_shoulder_roll_right.amc`

In order for the description to be more user friendly, it is important to be consistent with the words you choose and their order. If the action performed in the motion file is similar to another file, use the same terminology to describe them, and list the unique characteristic last. A good example would be when some motions will be captured moving to the right and to the left; use the same terminology to describe them and list the direction last in the description:

- Example:

  ```
  ALT_0100_shoulder_roll_right.amc
  ALT_0101_shoulder_roll_left.amc
  ```

Files named this way are very easy to find because the eye knows where to look to find the one difference in the names. This is especially helpful when you have an entire series of files that are similar but have one unique variable.

Within the descriptions you should also include underscores to separate the words to make them easier to read. Without underscores the descriptions run together, making them cumbersome and sometimes almost impossible to read.

- Examples of a difficult description to read:

  ```
  ALT_0100_shoulderrollright.amc
  ALT_0101_shoulderrollleft.amc
  ```

- Examples of an easier description to read:

  ```
  ALT_0100_shoulder_roll_right.amc
  ALT_0101_shoulder_roll_left.amc
  ```

The file extension level simply indicates what kind of file type the file is. In this case, our motion capture files are in the Acclaim Motion Capture (AMC) format. We could easily use BVH, FBX, ANI, or other file formats.

- Example:

  ```
  ALT_0100_shoulder_roll_right.amc
  ```

Remember that with our naming convention and directory structure, the name of a motion file will only change slightly throughout the course of the project. After the motion studio processes the motion files, they will send them back with our same eight-dot-three name, ALT_0100.amc. This motion is then put in the

Motions/raw/Alert/ subdirectory. When the animator edits the file, he will save the finished motion file with the descriptor level added: ALT_0100_shoulder_roll_right.amc. This finished motion file is then placed in the Motions/finished/Alert/ subdirectory for the programmers. The programmers retrieve the file they need, run the script to truncate it to ALT_0100.amc, and then implement it into the game engine.

Unix- and Linux-Based Organization Considerations

If your company uses the Unix or Linux operating system, you have more options when developing a naming convention. However, these systems also require that everyone involved follow the naming convention more strictly. Unix and Linux are case sensitive, so it is very important that the filename convention be followed strictly by the animators because typos and sloppiness can create a lot of problems in locating files. In order to prevent confusion, you should make sure that the prefix level and the description level of your filename use either all uppercase or all lowercase letters. Using all uppercase letters in the prefix and all lowercase in the description is a simple, clean, and easy approach. Mixing upper- and lowercase letters within a level makes them difficult to locate and read.

As the motion coordinator, if you want to do a quick list of only the Alert motion files (ALT) in a directory, you could do a simple list command such as LS ALT*.amc. However, if one of your animators uses lowercase letters when he should have used uppercase, his motion files will not be listed in your search.

In addition to making files harder to find, the mixing of uppercase and lowercase letters within a level can also make the filenames appear to "swim" when listed. Swimming is harder on the eyes because the filenames are listed closely together and undulate as you follow them across and down. This appearance of swimming is magnified even more as you scroll through a directory filled with thousands of motion files.

By having a well thought out plan, you can use this case-sensitivity to your advantage. By using a capitalization structure in the file extensions, you can assure that finished motion capture files can be found quickly. If the file extensions on working revisions are in lowercase letters (.amc) and the final version has an all uppercase extensions (.AMC), then it is easy to search for the final motions without listing the revisions.

- Example revision names:

  ALT_0100_shoulder_roll_right.amc

  ALT_0100_shoulder_roll_right_rev02.amc

  ALT_0100_shoulder_roll_right_rev03.amc

- An example finished motion name:

  ALT_0100_shoulder_roll_right.AMC

Conclusion

- Planning your directory structure and filenames as you develop your motion list is very important if you want the post capture process to work as efficiently as possible.
- Plan your directory structure to be easy to navigate through.
- Plan your directory structure and filenames to work together; this means that the filename will correspond to the subdirectory in which it is located.
- The filename should also correspond with the game states that the character is in when executing the motion.
- The filename needs to be user friendly for the motion studio, animators, and programmers to use.
- The filename needs to accommodate additional motions to be added in the future.

- The filename needs to be named in a way that allows it to be easily tracked all the way back to its original raw motion.
- If you are using a case-sensitive operating system, it is very important that everyone strictly follow the naming convention you establish. The naming convention you use should specify when to use upper- or lowercase letters in the filename.
- Using a case-sensitive operating systems can be used to your advantage when naming files.

MARKERS AND MARKER CONFIGURATION

Since you are using a third-party optical motion capture studio for your project, you don't really need to worry about markers and their placement. The motion studio is responsible for coming up with a marker configuration that will best suit the needs of your project. With that said, however, you do need to make sure that the motion studio has all the information it needs to best serve your needs. Greg Pyros, founder and owner of Pyros Pictures, Inc., says, "It is important for us to know what 3D software package our client is using and also how they are going to import the motion capture data into that package because it may change the marker configuration that we will use." Regardless of your project's needs and the motion studio you are using, it is a good idea to have some baseline knowledge of what markers are and what an example of a basic marker configuration can look like.

MARKERS

In the early days of motion capture, markers were sometimes referred to as *sensors*. More recently, however, the term sensor is used for dealing with magnetic motion capture systems, and the term marker is used when dealing with optical motion capture systems. It is important to note that a magnetic sensor is not the same thing as an optical marker. An optical marker is merely a reflective ball that the cameras are able to track through space; a magnetic sensor actually measures its spatial position and orientation in relation to a transmitter.

Marker: A retro-reflective sphere or hemisphere that is attached to the object that you wish to capture and whose location is tracked by the cameras.

The basic goal of marker placement is to position them on the performer to best capture the motion desired and in such a way that allows the markers to be seen by the cameras without hindering the performer from executing the moves. Markers are grouped together such that several markers are used to triangulate and capture the motion in a particular area of the body. Most clients want to capture the movement of the performer and not the secondary or overlapping movement of clothing or a cape, so the markers need to be attached as closely as possible to the performer's skeleton. If the markers are attached to loose or bulky clothing, the movement of the clothing will be captured, and the data won't be an accurate depiction of the performer's motion. For this reason, markers are often applied to a snug-fitting LYCRA® suit or attached directly to the performer's skin. Some studios prefer the performers to wear LYCRA shorts and shirts with the leg and arm markers attached to bands or directly to the skin, while other studios have full body suits for the performers to wear. Over the years, these full body suits have evolved from plain black suits to customized tight fitting suits with VELCRO® patches sewn on where the markers will be located. These newer suits also come in several different sizes and colors to accommodate the varying body sizes of performers.

The markers that capture the head movement are usually placed on a headband, LYCRA beanie, or some other type of hat. Sometimes they are attached to special glasses that the performer wears, so no headwear is necessary. If the performer you use has long hair, it should be worn up in a ponytail to prevent the hair from covering up the head, neck, and shoulder markers. Figure 7.1 shows a performer in one of the newer motion capture suits.

The hand and wrist markers are normally attached to Velcro bands, wristbands, or gloves like batting gloves or weightlifting gloves, but again this depends on the studio you are working with. In order to better capture the rotation of the performer's forearm, some studios may want the two wrist markers (on each wrist) to be attached to a small bar that holds them away from the wrist.

Some projects, such as football, may require the motion performers to wear protective equipment—a helmet and shoulder pads—during the capture, so markers located in these areas would

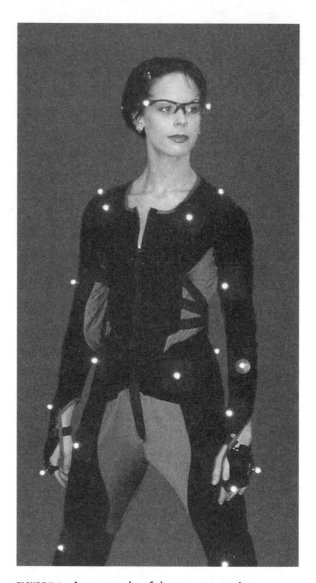

FIGURE 7.1 An example of the newer motion capture suits with Velcro patches. The performer is also wearing markered glasses to capture head movement. © 2003. Reprinted with permission from Motion Analysis Corporation.

need to be attached directly to the equipment instead of the performer. This generally does not pose a problem with data accuracy (by animation standards) because the in-game characters need to move as if they are wearing pads. Because the helmet and pads need to have markers attached to them, some studios have their own that are already markered up, but if you are going to use your own equipment, it is best if you send it to the motion studio well in advance of your capture day so that they can prepare and test it.

Markers can be attached to the performer in a couple of different ways. Many studios use Velcro or double-sided tape when attaching the markers to the performer's suit. In some cases they may also use additional tape to make sure the marker remains firmly in place. Tape or glue ordinarily is used to attach markers to shoes, since shoes are subject to a lot of stress and impact during a capture. When placing markers on the performer's skin, it is common to use spirit gum. When this is done, it is best to shave the area the marker is going to be attached to so that it can adhere directly to the skin. Whatever method is used to attach the markers to your performer, the main idea is that the markers be firmly attached and do not move around during the capture.

Body Markers

Most captures for video games now days are concerned mainly with capturing full body motion. Some games, however, are integrating finger motion and facial expressions from motion capture for added realism.

When optical motion capture was in its infancy, facial and digital captures were not possible, and body captures had technical limitations. The limitations of the cameras and hardware only allowed large 50mm markers to be used. With advances in technology, there are now several different sizes of body markers for a motion studio to use. Some optical systems have markers that come in 9, 12, 14, 20, 25, 35, and 50mm spheres. Giant Studios' motion capture system will even track tiny 5mm full body spheres. The capability of systems to track and use smaller markers is not the only recent improvement made in markers. If stunts or heavy impact motions are being performed, it is important that the markers don't injure the performer or break. Years ago, when we did captures for football games, we used to count the number of markers that would break and fly off the performers when they tackled or blocked each other. Even if we didn't see any markers come off, we had to check each performer after every take for loose or missing markers, and this slowed down the pace of our capture. Occasionally the performers would also complain about the markers hurting on impact. Some studios now use a softer or high action marker to help protect the performers and in an attempt to prevent the markers from breaking. Most markers consist of a ball and post that are two separate pieces; when they break, it is usually because the ball separates from the post, but soft markers are all one piece, and some are even made of cloth.

Chuck Mongelli, president of Perspective Studios, says, "All in all, marker setup is fairly simple unless your character or prop has a hierarchy above the base human. Obviously tails and braids fall under this additional setup, but when your props have a hierarchical structure, it can require some additional thought. An example of this would be a bicycle; an even further one is a bicycle with shock handlebars and seat." A basic body marker configuration will vary, depending on the studio and the kind of motion capture system it is using. Each motion studio has adopted a basic marker configuration that it feels works best with its system and that will best meet the needs of its clients. Mongelli says, "We have a marker configuration that is suitable for about 60% of the characters we see from our clients. We do, however, address marker setup every time, even if it is in-game motion for game development." With that said, basic body marker configurations usually consist of 38–50 markers as a starting point, but the studio may add more, depending on the complexity of the project. Wes Trager, former VP of Advanced Technologies for Acclaim Entertainment, states, "If you have three or four markers on a bone segment chances are you are going to see some of the markers with some of the cameras and therefore be able to determine where that bone segment is."

There are several factors that need to be considered when a studio is deciding the number and type of markers to use. Your skeleton, the software package you will be using, and the kind of motion you are seeking all play a role, along with several other technical issues. Issues such as the type of cameras being used, the number of cameras, the kind of camera lenses, and the size of the capture volume also must be considered. It is because of these issues that the motion studio is the best choice to handle the marker configuration for your character. You must, however, provide them with enough information about your project's needs and what your expectations are about the data that will be collected. If you want skeletal data and data from flowing clothing captured, the studio needs to know that well in advance of your capture. That type of information needs to be communicated to them during the bid phase, which is discussed in Chapter 8, "Selecting a Motion Capture Studio." Rand Cabus, Director of Sales and Marketing for Giant Studios, states, "It doesn't make sense if a client goes to a shoot and doesn't get the motion they need; we want the client to be happy with the motion captured so they can use as much of it as possible."

Marker Placement

Tom Tolles, House of Moves president, explains, "With an optical motion capture system there are three basic reasons for marker placement—to accurately define the position or orientation of a joint, for identification purposes such as distinguishing between left and right or between performers, and to help in reconstructing lost or missing data from other markers." This means that some markers are needed to help define the skeleton and its movements, while others are helpful in defining the performer's right side from his left, to distinguish one motion performer from another, or to help the studio retrace an occluded marker. These non-skeleton-critical markers are either asymmetrical markers or redundant markers.

Asymmetrical markers: Markers that are added to the marker configuration, or whose position in the configuration is changed to help identify a performer's orientation or distinguish one performer from another. These are also referred to as offset markers.

Redundant markers: Markers that are added to the marker configuration in order to help rebuild the position of markers occluded from the cameras during the capture. These are also called dummy markers.

When capturing motion, it is critical that the cameras are able to see the performer, so extra markers or redundant markers are especially helpful when the motion is such that markers become hidden from the camera's view. Motions where the performer is lying on the ground or has close interactions with another performer tend to occlude markers easily. When a marker does become occluded from the cameras, its position can be reconstructed using its last known position and its spatial relationship to the other markers. Figure 7.2 shows one possible marker configuration.

There is also another type of marker called a "virtual marker" that is sometimes needed. A virtual marker is not a physical object, but rather a mathematical equation mostly used to determine the true rotation point or center of a joint. Because markers are placed either on the skin or on clothing, their actual positions are not indicative of the true center of a joint, so if a client requests it, studios can calculate the position of a virtual marker at the center of the joint.

Virtual marker: A mathematical equation usually used to find the location of the actual joint center.

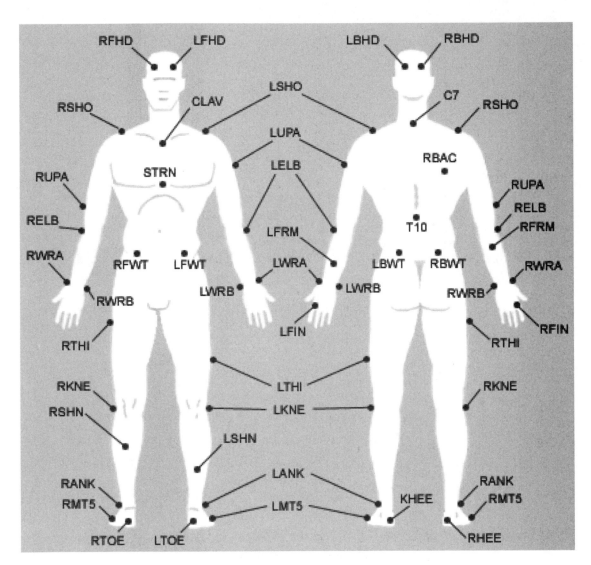

FIGURE 7.2   An example of a basic 41-marker full body configuration.

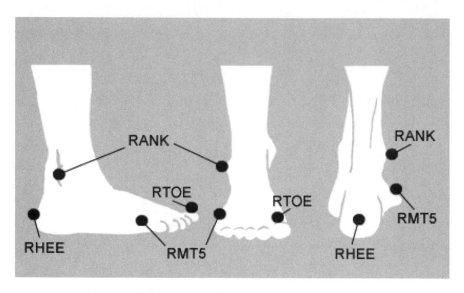

FIGURE 7.3   A close-up of the placement of the foot markers.

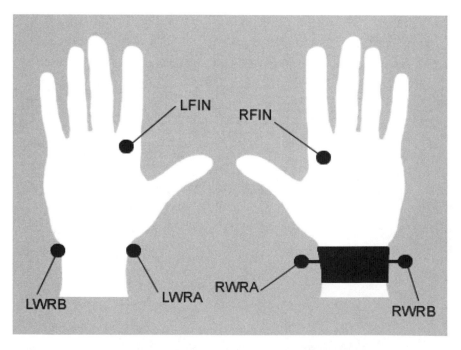

FIGURE 7.4   Two examples of how the wrist markers may be placed.

Facial Markers

With body captures, markers are placed on the head to capture the head's movement, but they do not capture facial expression. Generally, facial motion is captured during a separate capture; however, some studios capture both body and facial motion at the same time. Facial capture requires smaller markers to be used on the face, usually 3mm or 4mm hemispheres, and the number of markers used varies greatly, depending on the demands of your project. Facial captures use anywhere from 12 to well over one hundred markers. The markers are placed directly on the performer's face and are held into place with either double-sided tape or special glue.

Hand Markers

Like facial captures, digital or hand captures also differ from body captures. The smaller 3mm and 4mm spheres are used, and usually a special camera configuration and lenses are set up. The number of markers used on hand captures varies, but around 25 markers per hand is common. During body captures, wrist and hand markers are used to get the rotation of the forearm and to capture basic hand motion, but specific hand captures are generally set up for fine detail work, like the movement of individual digits. Red Eye Studio, a special effects studio that specializes in motion capture technology, is one company that successfully captures body, facial, and hand motion all at the same time. Using a total of 133 markers, they captured a guy playing the guitar. Chris Olsen, executive director for Red Eye Studio, says, "The guitar solo really raised the bar for full body motion capture, and we are thrilled with the precision and detail we are able to achieve on captures like this." Figure 7.5 is taken from Red Eye Studio's guitar capture.

FIGURE 7.5   Image of guitar capture at Red Eye Studio in which full body, facial, and hand motion were all captured simultaneously. © 2003. Reprinted with permission from Red Eye Studio.

Conclusion

Even though the motion studio is ultimately responsible for all marker concerns, it is your responsibility as the client to communicate to the motion studio what the needs of your project are. The more the motion studio knows about what you are trying to accomplish, the better it will be at addressing all your needs. You can't expect the motion studio to make assumptions as to what is best for your project. Some basic rules of thumb to keep in mind regarding markers:

- Marker placement is very important in order to collect the needed data.
- The closer the markers are to the source of the motion the better. This typically means the motion performer's skeleton.
- The markers need to be located so that the desired motion can be captured without hindering the motion performer's movement.
- The markers need to fit snugly on the performer so that they do not move around during the capture.
- The number of markers in a configuration and the size of the markers used depend on several issues. The type of motion capture system the studio uses, the type of cameras, the numbers of cameras, the lenses on the cameras, the capture volume size, and the specific demands of the project all have an effect.
- You need to communicate the demands of your project and what you expect to capture to the motion studio early in the process, so that it can make sure all of your concerns are addressed.

8

SELECTING A MOTION CAPTURE STUDIO

Service Description	Quantity/units	Cost	Total
Studio Setup	1.5 days	$4,500	$4,500
Stage Fee	8.5 days	$4,250	$8,750
Studio Capture	8.5 days	$51,000	$59,750
Prop Capture	8.5 days	included	
Motion Processing	24 days	$57,600	$117,350
Character Setup for MoCap	all characters	$3,200	$120,550
Performer Calibrations	2 per day	$5661	$126,211
Motion Modification	n/a		
Production Management	10 days	$8,000	$134,211
SUBTOTAL		**$134,211**	
Stunt Rigging/Props	2 days	$3,600	$3,600
Motion Performers	8.5 days	provided by client	
Stunt Coordination	2 days	$6,000	$9,600
Craft Services	8.5 days	$850	$10,450
Working Meals Client/Crew	8.5 days	$1,606	$12,056
Expendables	8.5 days	$297	$12,353
On-Site Data Verification	8.5 days	$12,750	$25,103
Video Support	8.5 days	$2,975	28,078
SUBTOTAL		**$28,078**	
		+$134,211	
CUSTOMER DISCOUNT		$21,860	
GRAND TOTAL		**$140,429**	

The process of working with a motion capture studio is broken down to three basic areas: the bid, pre-production meeting or phone call, and the contract. Because this is a process, it usually takes place over several weeks or months, and it is made infinitely more difficult if it is handled as a last minute thing by an unorganized or rushed client. Depending on the timeline of the project, it is common to have several meetings or conference calls to cover all the bases before the capture session.

There are a number of factors to consider when selecting a motion capture studio. Some of these factors may seem like small inconsequential issues, such as the location of the studio, the floor surface, or the studio personality, but others may be larger issues and seem like the only ones that matter, such as cost, quality of data, and deliverability. No matter what the issues are, you need to figure out which studio is the best for your project. Keep in mind that a large motion capture studio may serve your needs on one project but might not be right for the next, so shop around to match the needs of each project.

BASIC FEATURES AND SERVICES TO LOOK FOR IN A MOTION CAPTURE STUDIO

Cost: The cost is always a big issue. Obviously the cost of a motion capture session needs to be in your project's budget. After getting bids, look over the fine print carefully and make sure you understand the actual cost, not just an approximate cost.

Data quality: The quality of the data is also a major concern. Whether your project is large or small, the quality of the data delivered must be of a high level and acceptable. The problem is that there isn't a set standard as to what is acceptable quality. There are a few key things you can look for, however; check the character's feet when they are on the ground to see if they are skating or sliding. When your character is standing, his feet should be firmly on the ground and not moving around. Check the FCurves to see if all major spikes have been eliminated from the data, and make sure bones aren't flipped. It is also a good idea to play the motion in slow motion and look for irregularities.

Studio reputation: The reliability of the studio also needs to be considered. You need to make sure that the motion capture studio will be able to process and deliver your motion data to you on time. It won't do you any good to capture good motion data and have the studio fall behind on the delivery schedule, since this will inevitably affect your schedule also. Make sure a realistic schedule of delivery is put into the contract you sign.

Capture space: The studio's size or capture space needs to be big enough for a motion performer to perform the required motions. This means that if you need a run cycle or fast running motions, the performer needs to have room to get his speed up and slow down before entering and exiting the capture volume safely. This is important so that you can get consistent root movement and for the performer's safety.

Capture volume: The capture volume is the area in the studio where the markers can be seen by the cameras. This means that the performer's motion can only be captured when he is in the capture volume. Most studios have a small volume and a large volume marked off. A small capture volume is approximately $20' \times 20' \times 10'$, and large one is approximately $30' \times 25' \times 12'$. Of course the capture volume is limited by the number of cameras and the capture space available.

Cameras: A studio needs to have an adequate number of cameras to fully cover the capture volume. Most studios use between 8–16 cameras (sometimes more). The cameras also need to be positioned to help prevent marker occlusion and be out of the way so the motion performer can perform the requested moves. Keep in mind that the cameras' locations affect the motion performer's safety, and if they are in the way, they may become damaged.

Marker placement: Marker placement is very important and needs to be done in a way that gives the best possible data for joint rotation and won't hinder the motion performer's movement. If stunts are being performed, it is also important that the markers don't cause injury or break during a motion. Most studios have several marker configurations that they will use, depending on the problems that arise during a capture. Many studios alter markers in an attempt to make them stay together during impact or add more markers to the motion performer.

Props and equipment: Motion capture studios either have their own props, rigging, scaffolding, mats, and pads or they have access to them for a motion shoot. In order to get rigging that is safe for the motion performer, it is best to consult a professional stunt coordinator with a SAG card.

Floor surface: At a minimum, the floor surface should be clean (dust/dirt free and not concrete) so that the motion performer isn't in danger of injury. Most studios have a cushioned or rubberized floor. This also helps the performer prevent injury. Many studios will also customize the floor surface for you with dirt, Astroturf, wood, or ice, depending on the needs of your project.

Video tape: Motion capture studios videotape the capture session, and each take is slated and time coded. Some studios now use digital video capture. Taking video (digital or not) can be very important for making frame range selections after the shoot. The disadvantage to video is that it is usually taken from one angle, and it may be difficult to see whether the motion performer is fully in the volume or is in the position you need him in.

Playback systems: All motion capture studios have a way for the client to view the motion that was just captured. Just viewing the marker cloud data isn't good enough anymore, so most studios now are able to show you the motion on a skeleton with a mesh. It isn't always real time, but within a couple of minutes or so it is viewable. This is an awesome advantage because it allows you to see your motion from multiple angles, when video doesn't. Frame range selections aren't necessarily done at this time, but it gives the client a chance to select the best take for processing.

Liability insurance: A studio needs to make sure that it covers itself from possible liability in case an accident occurs during a capture session. This coverage should include the motion performers and staff working the capture session. As the client, you also need to make sure that you are covered in case of an accident.

A studio's personality: An active motion capture studio takes more of a role in helping the client meet its goals. An active studio will conduct motion performer auditions or will have good contacts with motion performers/talent, directors, stunt coordinators, and so on. An active studio may also revise shot lists at the half-day break and remind unorganized clients if they fall behind schedule. Active studios may also let the client know when they feel that what the client is attempting to do won't give them the results that they are looking for. This can be a sensitive issue, and even an active studio may need to play more of a passive role if the client is headstrong or not interested in help.

A passive motion capture studio may do some of the same things that an active studio does, such as performer/talent auditions and have good contacts with performers, but a passive studio tends to let the client do their own thing at the capture session, whether they are on schedule, ahead of schedule, or behind schedule.

Additional Features and Services a Motion Capture Studio May Provide

Catering and snacks: The larger motion capture studios have lunch catered for the client, performers, and motion studio staff working the capture session. This is done for convenience and to save capture time for the client. Snacks such as soda, candy, bagels, and donuts are also provided, but all of this is billed to you.

Client relations/entertainment: All businesses in the service industry need to build client relations, and a motion capture studio is not exempt. Some motion studios take their client to dinner at least one night during a capture session, and others will even arrange entertainment during the off-shoot time, such as movies or sporting events. However, this is a luxury that some of the larger studios sometimes provide and should not be expected. A lot of the time, it depends on its other commitments and schedule if they have the time to plan something.

CAPTURE SESSION BIDS

Here we discuss basic types of bids and the information you should provide to get an accurate bid.

Basic Types of Bids

Not all motion capture studios present a bid in the same way, so it may be difficult to figure out which bid is actually the most cost effective. Currently there are two main options for bids and one other minor option that has some interesting possibilities. The two major options are the flat rate bid, and the per-second bid.

The flat rate option is when the motion studio gives you a set fee for the motion that you want to capture. Based on your shot list, they approximate how many seconds of motion they think that you will need to capture, and based on that they give you a set fee for the capture. Sometimes included with this type of bid is a stage fee and other fees.

The per-second option is the way most bids are given; however, they are also the most complex. With this type of bid, the motion studio takes into consideration the number of seconds and the complexity of each motion and gives an estimate on the cost. This means that motions that are longer than the allotted number of seconds and motions that are more complex to capture and process will cost you more than simple, short motions. It is common with this type of bid to include a stage fee. You need to treat this kind of bid as an approximation and not a firm number; because of this, you need to make sure that you read and understand the contract thoroughly to prevent cost overruns (this will be covered later in this chapter).

The third option that has interesting possibilities is the remote bid. This type of bid is essentially a flat rate bid but with a twist. This remote bid option is when the client sends the motion capture studio a shot list and a videotape of the motions that it would like to capture, and the motion capture studio then captures the motions, processes them, and sends them back to the client. The client never has to travel to the motion capture studio, so a company in Korea can do a motion capture session in the United States (assuming there isn't a language barrier). Language barriers aside, working this way does impose some problems. It requires you to communicate your needs to the motion studio well in order for them to capture the motions you need. You can't expect them to be mind readers, so it is up to you to communicate what you need thoroughly. It also does not allow for on-set changes on your part, so you must have your shot list planned out very well. Marilyn McDonald, sales and marketing director for Mantis Motion Productions, says that these remote bids have worked very well for them, and in the near future they will be offering remote directing. With remote directing, the client will be able to view the capture session online as it is happening, communicate with the motion performer and studio staff, and actually direct the capture via the Internet. McDonald says, "Remote directing will allow our clients to be more actively involved in a remote capture and make changes or clarifications when needed."

Getting a Bid for Your Project

In order to give a bid, a motion capture studio will need certain information from you. Estimation bids can be made with very little information, but the more information you provide, the more accurate the bid should be. Some of the larger motion studios have a list of questions that they will provide to you to answer about your project before they give you a bid.

General information you may need to provide to get an accurate bid:

- When would you like to do the capture? Will there be a main and secondary capture?
- How many total motions need to be captured?
- How many motions require more than one motion performer? (This refers only to motions where more than one performer's motion is captured.) Sometimes more than one person interacts during a motion, even though only one of them is being captured. This is done so that the studio can determine how many capture suits, markers, marker sets, and so on it needs to prepare. Motions with multiple performers being captured are also generally billed a higher rate because of their complexity (see the actual bid or contract later in this chapter).
- Will the motion performer(s) need special equipment, such as football pads with markers on them? Are any special markers needed?
- Will prop motion be captured?
- How many motions require props to be captured?
- Is facial capture needed? Will it be done separately or during the body capture?
- What form does the final data need to be in? Cloud or skeletal data?
- Any additional processing needed—looping, blending, mirroring, and so on?
- If the motion studio is giving you a per-second bid, your motions need to be rated by their level of difficulty. Each motion capture studio handles its difficulty rating differently. Some studios may label them as standard and difficult or they may rate them as level 1, 2, 3 or A, B, C, and so on. In general the ratings are as follows:

- Level 1/standard motions: basic motions such as standing, sitting, walking, minor prop interaction, and basic punches/kicks. Smaller volume size and lower frequency may be used. Generally requires eight cameras.

- Level 2 motions: more difficult motions such as fast running, ballistic moves, major props (rigging, for instance), moderate occlusion, two-person captures, basic punching/kicking. Small and large volume sizes and higher frequency may be used. Generally requires 12 cameras.

- Level 3 motions: very difficult motions such as two or more performers with extended occlusion and/or contact (wrestling, hardcore fighting, numerous prop interaction, men on horseback, and so on). Small and huge volume sizes and higher frequency may be used. Generally requires 16+ cameras.

In addition to the capture information, it is common for studios to also charge for additional services. Studios break down what they charge for in different ways; some include a lot of information and break down exactly how much the client is charged and for what services, and other studios give a more generic bid, with minimal cost breakdowns. Examples of additional cost breakdowns may include:

- Stage fees
- Expendables
- Catering
- Motion processing
- Custom skeleton
- Performer calibrations
- Preproduction/studio set up
- Miscellaneous expenses/expendables
- Video support

All of these services (and more) would be included and usually itemized in the initial bid. Most motion capture studios also guarantee their bid for between 10 and 30 days.

It is best to get at least three motion studios to bid on your project and to let them know ahead of time that you are getting other bids. That way they may work with their numbers to give you the lowest bid they can. Getting bids and selecting a motion studio is a process, and some motion studios may lower their bid if they know that another studio has bid lower, while others give their lowest bid the first time. If you are still not sure which studio to choose after getting the bids, there are a couple of things you can do.

The most simple and easiest thing is to ask the studio for sample motions. They all have sample motions from shoots they have done in the past to show to potential clients. This might put your mind at ease if you are concerned about the quality of their data. Remember though that the sample motions that they show you will be representative of their best quality of data. You will want to ask them if the sample file is processed or raw data, and if possible ask to see both the raw and the processed data of the motions.

If you have the time in your schedule, you may want to try to set up a test shoot. Most studios will do a test shoot if they have the time in their schedule and if the project you are working on is a fairly large one. Have the motion studio capture a few motions that you select. If you are present during the test, you can see how the studio works and the quality of the data as it is captured. If you are unable to be present during the capture, you will at least have some specific motions to look over.

The following example bid is a fictitious bid for our game *CARRION* that shows what a per-second bid may consist of.

As you can see in this Bid, Generic Motion Capture Studios has its services itemized and separated in their bid. Some companies do this, and others provide less detailed information. The terminology that a studio may use on the bid may also change. One studio may charge for "stage fees" while another may charge for "studio setup." Essentially they are the same thing, so read the bids you receive and compare them line for line.

GENERIC MOTION CAPTURE STUDIOS

Bid proposal for Quality Games, Inc.
Adventure Game
January 5, 2004

Specs

- Production:
  Approximately 750 moves made up of 70% standard moves (walks, runs, turns, minor prop interaction) and 30% of which require rigging or stunt performers (rope climbing, falls, jumps, mini-tramp work, and so on). It is estimated that approximately 100 moves will be able to be captured per day. Additional time will be needed to set up for the moves requiring stunt work.
- **Characters:**
  There will be one character.
- **General Motions:**
  Approximately 750 moves, 70% standard moves and 30% requiring stunt rigging. Motion list has not been provided at this time.
- **Production Platform:**
  Motion capture files will be supplied to the client for their importing into their animation/game engine. We will deliver .amc files.

Service Description	Quantity/units	Cost	Total
Studio Setup	1.5 days	$4,500	$4,500
Stage Fee	8.5 days	$4,250	$8,750
Studio Capture	8.5 days	$51,000	$59,750
Prop Capture	8.5 days	included	
Motion Processing	24 days	$57,600	$117,350
Character Setup for MoCap	all characters	$3,200	$120,550
Performer Calibrations	2 per day	$5661	$126,211
Motion Modification	n/a		
Production Management	10 days	$8,000	$134,211
SUBTOTAL		**$134,211**	
Stunt Rigging/Props	2 days	$3,600	$3,600
Motion Performers	8.5 days	provided by client	
Stunt Coordination	2 days	$6,000	$9,600
Craft Services	8.5 days	$850	$10,450

GENERIC MOTION CAPTURE STUDIOS (*CONTINUED*)

Working Meals Client/Crew	8.5 days	$1,606	$12,056
Expendables	8.5 days	$297	$12,353
On-Site Data Verification	8.5 days	$12,750	$25,103
Video Support	8.5 days	$2,975	28,078
SUBTOTAL			**$28,078**
			+$134,211
CUSTOMER DISCOUNT			$21,860
GRAND TOTAL			**$140,429**

Production Summary

- Approximately 750 moves made up of approximately 70% standard moves (walks, runs, turns, minor prop interaction) and approximately 30% of which require rigging or stunt performers (rope climbing, falls, jumps, mini-tramp work, and so on).
- Processing time is based on the above complexity and formula and will be worked on by a team of two motion processors.
- Capture schedule would be over an eight and half-day period with an average of 100 moves to be captured per day, excluding the time required for stunt rigging and setup.
- There is only ONE main character and three minor characters to be captured.
- Capture schedule would be over an eight and half-day period.
- Average length of moves is :03 to :05 seconds.
- Moves list will be finalized by the client and sent to Generic Motion Capture Studios no less than two weeks prior to capture so that all arrangements can be finalized.
- Director for the session will be provided by the client.
- Motion performers provided by the client.
- Proposal is based on working on Generic Motion Capture Studios' stage with a volume height of 14 feet.
- Motion modification or enhancement is not included as part of this bid. However, if it is needed it will be billed at a daily rate of $1,200.
- Generic Motion Capture Studios will deliver .amc files.

Notes

- All moves are based on an average of 3–5 seconds.
- Single-performer "standard" motions over 5 seconds are billed at a rate of $25 per second.
- Single-performer "difficult" motions over 5 seconds are billed at a rate of $50 per second.
- Two-performer "standard" motions over 5 seconds are billed at a rate of $75 per second.
- Two-performer "difficult" motions over 5 seconds are billed at a rate of $125 per second.
- Motion modification/enhancements are considered any advanced editing for creating supplemental movement and fundamental changes to the captured motions and is often supervised. If needed, motion modification/enhancement will be billed at $1,200/day.
- If Generic Motion Capture Studios coordinates the talent, please add $1,200/day.
- Naturally, changes with minimal cost implications will be accommodated wherever possible; however, there are key points after which changes will have budgetary or scheduling repercussions. Other expenses, such as equipment rental, props, or performer auditions, will be billed separately at cost plus 15%.
- The payment schedule for this shoot will be as follows:
  10% of total cost to initiate preproduction
  15% of total cost deposit due on the first day of shooting
  25% of total cost due upon completion of shoot
  50% of total cost due on completion and sign off of data delivery

The information contained in this document is confidential and reflects **Generic Motion Capture Studios'** understanding of the project as it exists now. It does not in itself form a contract nor does it form an obligation prior to negotiation, and any additional information provided would allow **Generic Motion Capture Studios** to fine-tune these numbers. This estimation bid is good for 30 days from the submission date. Upon being awarded the project, final details will be included in **Generic Motion Capture Studios'** agreement contract.

Our bid from Generic Motion Capture Studios includes a $21,860 discount because we have done business with them before and have established a good working relationship. It is not uncommon for motion studios to give clients a discount, but it should not be expected.

Before deciding on a motion studio, remember to take into consideration travel expenses, motion performer expenses (if they aren't included in the bid), stunt coordination (if needed and not in the bid), prop expenses, food, and accommodations.

THE PREPRODUCTION MEETING OR CONFERENCE CALL

Once you decide to use a certain motion studio to do your capture, the motion studio will most likely want to set up a preproduction meeting. If your company and the motion studio are not able to meet face to face, a conference call will usually suffice. This meeting is to discuss all the issues in detail so that the studio can begin to prepare for the capture. Some of the information covered during this meeting will be the same information covered in the bid, but it is better to make sure needs have not changed too drastically and that all issues are spelled out in more detail. Because there are multiple issues to coordinate with the client, it is common to have several meetings or conference calls. This is done for two main reasons, first to double-check the information that they received in making the original bid and secondly to fill in other details and procedures. Even if the motion capture studio received a lot of detailed information about the shoot when making the original bid, a conference call/meeting should still be scheduled. Some motion studios even provide a preproduction check list for their clients prior to the conference call.

Even before a conference call is set up, some motion studios like to have the client's shot list. This way, the motion studio can check the client's rating of the motions (level 1, 2, and so on) and so the studio can look for any potential problems or details and prepare questions.

PREPRODUCTION MEETING CHECKLIST

The people who should be present during the preproduction call/meeting are (these titles depend on the studio and project):

Client:
- Producer
- Technical lead
- Lead animator/ motion coordinator

Motion Studio:
- Producer
- Production manager
- MoCap director
- QA artist

Information Covered on the Preproduction Check List:
- How many total motions need to be captured?
- How many motions require more than one motion performer? (This only refers to motions where more than one performer's motion is captured.)
- Will motion performer(s) need special equipment, such as football pads with markers on them? Any special marker needs?
- Will prop motion be captured?
- How many motions require props to be captured?
- Is facial capture needed? Will it be done separately or during the body capture?
- What form does the final data need to be in? Cloud or skeletal data?
- Any additional processing needed—looping, blending, mirroring, etc.?
- Difficulty rating for each motion.
  - Level 1/standard motions: basic motions such as standing, sitting, walking, minor prop interaction, basic punches/kicks.
  - Level 2 motions: more difficult motions such as fast running, ballistic moves, major props (rigging etc.), moderate occlusion, two person captures, basic punching/kicking.
  - Level 3 motions: very difficult motions such as two or more performers with extended occlusion (wrestling, hardcore fighting, numerous prop interaction, men on horseback, and so on).
- Are auditions for a motion performer needed, or is the client providing the performers? Who is coordinating the performers' travel, lodging, payment, and so on? Note: it is highly recommended by the motion studio

PREPRODUCTION MEETING CHECKLIST (*CONTINUED*)

that the client and the motion performer get together for at least one test rehearsal prior to the actual shoot.

Some studios call this test rehearsal a "pop" shoot because it takes place at the motion studio, so in addition to helping the performer and client, the motion studio actually captures some motion to help test the skeleton and pipeline.

- Once the motion performers are chosen, the motion capture studio needs the general body size of the performer (6' 0", 160 lbs.).
- Who is providing the shoes for the performer? If the motion studio is handling it, the performer's shoe size is needed. What kinds or type of shoes are needed?
- Date of the shoot. Are all the moves going to be shot at the same time, or will there be a main shoot and a secondary one?
- Location of shoot. Many motion studios will go on location as opposed to just shooting on their stage. If the shoot is at the studio, does the client need any special flooring? (Astroturf, dirt, and so on.)
- Who is providing the props? Are the props being captured? Are special props needed? Does the studio need to build them? Does the studio need to rent them?
- When does the motion studio need the client's skeleton (if they are providing one)?
- What is the skeletal posture?
- What is the skeletal structure?
- Will there be skeletal or motion scaling?
- Skeleton file type?
- Capture and delivery rate? (captured at 120Hz, delivered at 60Hz)
- Which axis/direction should the motion files follow?
- Animation files type? (.bvh, .amc, .ani, and so on.)
- What software will the client use?
- Is the client giving the motion studio a mesh? When does the motion studio need it?
- Are there any audio or video reference needs?
- How many of the client's people will be attending the shoot? (catering reasons)
- How many motion performers will be at the shoot? (catering reasons)
- Any special dietary needs from the client or performers?

What Constitutes a Capture Day? (Flexible)

- 8:15 am   Studio crew arrives:
                 Calibrate capture system
                 Prepare volume for the capture session
                 Prepare catering for the day
- 8:30 am   Motion performer(s) arrival
                 Performers are prepped for the day
                 Markers attached
                 Performer gets warmed up
- 9:00 am   Client arrives
                 Notifies motion studio of changes to shot list
- 9:30 am   Capture session begins
- 12:30–1:15   Break for lunch
                 Usually catered in studio or on location
                 Length of break determined by the client
- 1:30 p.m.   Capture session resumes
- 6:00 p.m.   Capture session wraps
                 Client and performers can leave
                 Motion studio crew has post-shoot meeting
                 Motion studio crew backs up captured data
- For capture sessions on weekend days, there will be an additional $45 per person fee. A minimum of four hours per day for capture and an additional 20% will be added to the daily expenses.

Job Responsibilities During the Shoot

- It is the client's responsibility to notify the motion studio's motion capture director of any changes/additions to the capture session each morning before shooting begins.
- It is the client's and the motion studio's motion capture director's responsibilities to co-direct the motion performer. The client is actively directing the performer and looking for the desired effect, while the motion studio's motion capture director is ensuring the motion is technically sound.
- It is the client's responsibility to select which take of each motion he would like processed for delivery. It is also his responsibility to communicate this to the motion studio's motion capture director.

PREPRODUCTION MEETING CHECKLIST (*CONTINUED*)

- It is the motion studio's motion capture director's responsibility to keep track of all takes, selected takes, and changes to the motion list on his trial notes.
- It is the client's and the motion studio's motion capture director's responsibility to communicate with each other to help ensure the trial notes are accurate.
- It is the QA artist/editor's responsibility to check the quality of each selected take on-set.

Job Responsibilities After the Shoot

- The motion studio will provide the selection process material to the client within two business day following the capture session. This material includes slated videotape reference with frame count, the master shot list (includes every take captured), and the select list (just the takes selected to be processed during the shoot).
- The client will then use the select list as an order form to make frame range requests, give priority order to each selected take, add any comments on processing, or choose a new select for a motion. Remember that if it is a select not originally chosen during the shoot, it was not QA'd on-set and may not be deliverable.
- Once the client has updated the select list, it is e-mailed to the motion capture studio so processing can begin.
- The processed motions will then be delivered to the client in sections or in bulk (the delivery deadline depends on the number of motions and the number of editors processing the data) via e-mail, FTP, or disk. Accompanying the processed motions is a ship list that lists all motion delivered at that time.

Data Problems

If problems occur with delivered data, the client contacts the motion studio's producer, who then investigates the issue. If it is an error on the motion studio's side, the motion is corrected and resent to the client. If the problem is on the client side (software peculiarity, pipeline issues), an extra charge may be incurred.

Final Data Delivery

Once all data is delivered and all problems are handled, the project is considered finalized. At that time, the motion studio will send the client a final cumulative ship list and a final invoice. The motion studio keeps all data archived, should the client need the data in the future (there is an additional charge for this service should it be needed).

Studio Credit

Screen credits for the motion studio's personnel are required. Immediately after completion or distribution, the client will provide the motion studio with suitable materials to be used for promotional purposes and press releases. These materials will include, but are not limited to, one broadcast quality copy of any rendered footage, imagery rendered to at least 300 dpi for print, and if it is a video game at least five copies of the finished game.

The motion studio may specify the type of document the motion list is to be (i.e. Microsoft Excel document, FileMaker Pro, etc.). They may even specify that the naming format of the motions be an eight-dot-three naming convention (i.e. `filename.bvh`, `filename.amc`) with a succinct, unique description.

THE CONTRACT

After the bid process and the conference call, the motion capture studio will send the contract to the client. The contract itself covers the same information that should have been already covered in the bid and conference call, in detail and legalese. The contract also specifies dates and deadlines, assigns liabilities, copyrights, and consequences for breaches of contract. It also singles out an individual who has the authority to act as a representative for each company, should problems arise.

GENERIC MOTION CAPTURE STUDIOS

Contract for Quality Games Inc.
Adventure Game *CARRION*
February 25, 2004

Agreement between **Generic Motion Capture Studios** and **Quality Games Inc.**

We are pleased to confirm this agreement entered into this twenty-fifth (25) day of February 2004, between Generic Motion Capture Studios, Inc. ("GMC Studios"), an Arizona corporation, 8700 Brodie Lane, Ste. 574, Sahuarita, Arizona 85629, and Quality Games, Inc. ("QGI"), a Texas corporation, 121 Malvern Dr., Austin, Texas 78745.

Per this agreement, GMC Studios hereby agrees to provide QGI with the following services in accordance with the detailed exhibits in connection with activities conducted by QGI for their game production. The following services in accordance with the detailed exhibits in connection with activities shall be referred to collectively as the "Work". The revised specifications and bid shall be submitted and mutually agreed upon.

QGI hereby engages GMC Studios, and GMC Studios accepts the engagement as follows:

1. **Deliverables (see Exhibit A for details)**

   Motion capture seven hundred and fifty (750) moves over an eight and one-half (8.5) day capture schedule with an additional one and a half (1.5) days for set up and stunt rigging. Seventy (70) percent of the seven hundred and fifty (750) moves are defined as "standard" moves (walks, runs, turns, minor prop interaction). The remaining thirty (30) percent of the moves are defined as moves requiring rigging or stunts. That thirty (30) percent is further defined as twenty (20) percent being slightly complex (i.e. climbing, kicking, acrobatics, etc.) and ten (10) percent being more complex (wire work, complex rigging, etc). It is estimated that approximately one hundred (100) moves will be able to be captured per day.

   See Exhibit A for a more detailed description of deliverables, services provided, and milestones to be met.

2. **Term**

   The term of this agreement shall remain in effect through the agreed upon delivery dates specified in Exhibit A of motion capture data to QGI.

3. **Payment**

   As full and complete consideration for all services provided by GMC Studios hereunder and all rights granted hereunder by GMC Studios, QGI will pay GMC Studios a minimum of one hundred and forty thousand, four hundred and twenty-nine dollars (US $140,429) for completion of the entire project. Final numbers may vary due to adjustments in the estimated prices for stunt materials and expendables, and any adjustments will be made with the final payment. The money will be distributed in the following manner:

$15,406.00 due upon awarding of the project.

$27,404.25 due upon the commencement of the motion capture session.

$27,404.25 due upon completion of the motion capture session.

$70,214.50 plus any approved overages and other adjustments due upon QGI's receipt and approval of the processed motion capture data in the form and format described in Exhibit A.

GMC Studios reserves the right to cease providing services if QGI is in default of any material provision of this agreement and such default is not cured within ten (10) days of written receipt by QGI of notice of such default.

Any additional services and considerations for such services will be described on separate attachments that will be approved to and made part of this agreement. Both parties prior to commencement of any additional services will approve such attachments. Any additional services relating to this contract shall be requested and delivered by the date determined and agreed upon by both parties.

4. **Warranties**

GMC Studios makes no warranty express or implied except as follows:

a. GMC Studios has the right to grant all rights granted herein, including but not limited to all necessary literary, artistic, and/or intellectual property rights, and is free to enter into and fully perform this agreement.

b. The exercise of rights granted herein will not infringe on any rights of any third party, including but not limited to copyright, trademark, unfair competition, contract, defamation, and privacy or publicity rights.

5. **Ownership**

a. Subject to QGI's payment to GMC Studios of all amounts payable to the extent that the Work includes material subject to copyright, GMC agrees that the Work shall be considered as a "work made for hire," as that term is defined in 101 of the Copyright Act of 1976 as amended, and that as a result, QGI shall own all copyright rights in the Work. If,

GENERIC MOTION CAPTURE STUDIOS (*CONTINUED*)

for any reason, the Work does not qualify as a work made for hire under applicable law, then GMC Studios hereby assigns and agrees to assign to QGI any and all of GMC Studios' right, title, and interest in and to the Work, including any and all copyrights, trade secrets, trademarks, and similar proprietary right therein, and QGI will have the right to use the same in perpetuity throughout the universe in any manner QGI determines without any further payment to GMC Studios whatsoever. GMC Studios will, from time to time, as may be requested by QGI, do any and all things that QGI shall reasonably request to establish or document QGI's exclusive ownership of any and all rights in the Work, including the execution of appropriate copyright applications or assignments. Notwithstanding the foregoing, QGI hereby grants and agrees to grant to GMC Studios an irrevocable, royalty-free, and non-transferable license to use and display selected portions of the Work solely for GMC Studios' own advertising, publicity, and/or promotions, subject to QGI's right to place reasonable restrictions on the portions of the Work to be used by GMC Studios and on the manner in which GMC Studios uses or displays the Work for such purposes.

b. Notwithstanding the foregoing, in the event that QGI fails to meet its payment obligations, the parties hereto understand and agree that the Work shall not be considered "work made for hire," and GMC Studios shall retain all right, title, and interest in and to the Work.

6. **Design Policy**

Should GMC Studios be responsible for providing any design for QGI's projects, design concepts will be based upon meetings and discussions with QGI. GMC Studios will establish one comprehensive design direction, based upon QGI's input to design ideas. Minor modifications to a presentation, if necessary, are considered part of the established budget. Overall design direction changes, after the initial design concept has been approved by QGI, will be considered alternatives to the original design for which QGI will be charged a fee in addition to the consideration set forth above in paragraph three (3).

7. **Indemnity**

a. QGI hereby agrees to indemnify, defend, and hold harmless GMC Studios and its officers, directors, shareholders, employees, agents, affiliates, successors, and assign against any and all actions, claims, demands, lawsuits, costs, and expenses (including reasonable attorney's fee) suffered, made, or incurred by GMC Studios arising out of

(i) the breach or alleged breach of any warranty, representation, undertaking, or agreement made or entered into hereunder by QGI; or (ii) the content of the literary or artistic materials by QGI to GMC Studios; or (iii) QGI's failure to have obtained all rights in the literary, dramatic, and musical material furnished to GMC Studios; or (iv) any claims or residuals, reuse, or other fees or compensation of any kind, however denominated, which are or become due in respect of any literary or artistic materials or any element thereof.

b. GMC Studios hereby agrees to indemnify, defend, and hold harmless QGI and its officers, directors, shareholders, employees, agents, affiliates, successors, and assigns any and all actions, claims, demands, lawsuits, costs, and expenses (including reasonable attorneys' fees) suffered, made, or incurred by QGI arising out of the breach or alleged breach of any warranty, representation, undertaking, or agreement made or entered into hereunder by GMC Studios.

8. **Time of Essence**

Time is of the essence of this agreement with respect to all obligations of GMC Studios hereunder. GMC Studios shall deliver to QGI each deliverable according to the Production and Delivery Schedule attached. QGI must give its approval in accordance with the Production and Delivery Schedule or it is understood that for each day's delay in approval, one or more days may have to be added to the final delivery date, depending on resources and commitments at the time of the delay. QGI will be liable for any overtime charges incurred to overcome such delays, and such charges will be approved in advance in writing by QGI.

Any changes or adjustments requested by the client on delivered, processed motions must be made within fifteen (15) business days after motion is delivered. All motions will be archived after sixty (60) days from final delivery of job, and a data retrieval fee will be charged to the client if data is needed after archiving.

9. **Changes and Change Orders**

Changes to the motion or the final skeleton will need to be evaluated at the time of the request to determine impact on schedule and/or budget.

The parties recognize that changes in the scope of work or deliverables may be desired from time to time. Proposed changes will be assessed to determine the impact (if any) on schedule and budget. Such changes shall be deemed to be immaterial and shall not affect the fixed price or due dates unless, within twenty-four (24) hours after QGI requests a change, GMC Studios

GENERIC MOTION CAPTURE STUDIOS (*CONTINUED*)

submits a Change Order to QGI that describes the requested change and the effect it would have (if any) on the price payable hereunder or the due date or both. QGI has twenty-four (24) hours to approve a Change Order. Notwithstanding the above, delays in approving schedules identified in this agreement for deliverables always affects budget and production schedules. GMC Studios will initiate a Change Order immediately upon the occurrence of delays in approval schedules. If QGI fails to approve a Change Order within twenty-four (24) hours after receiving it, GMC Studios will ignore the request for change and continue production as planned before the request was made.

10. **Representatives and Approvals**

QGI shall appoint a designated representative who shall have the authority to act on behalf of QGI with respect to all matters arising under this agreement, including the signing of Change Orders. The designated representative shall participate in all meetings to review deliverables; shall consolidate all review comments from QGI's organization; and shall have the authority to arbitrate and make final decisions on behalf of QGI. The signature of the designated representative shall constitute final approval of all deliverables, and if necessary, shall constitute official approval of Change Orders.

GMC Studios shall appoint a designated representative who shall have the authority to act on behalf of GMC Studios with respect to all matters arising under this agreement and shall be responsible for communication to all of GMC Studios' team members changes, deadlines, and comments from QGI.

Quality Games, Inc. Representative	GMC Studios' Representative
Matt Liverman	Annette Provost
QGI	GMC Studios
121 Malvern Dr.	8700 Brodie Lane Ste. 574
Austin, TX 78745	Sahuarita, Arizona 85629
Phone 555.555.1212	Phone 555.555.1212
Fax 555.555.1213	Fax 555.555.1213
mliverman@QGI.com	aprovost@gmcstudios.com

11. **Termination**

Either party may terminate this agreement in the event of a breach by the other party of a material obligation under this agreement if such a breach continues uncured for a period of ten (10) days after written notice. In the event of such termination by QGI, QGI shall have the option to pay GMC Studios for documented changes to date of termination. In the event of such termination by GMC Studios, QGI will have the right to receive all deliverables already paid for and will have the right to fair reimbursement for service paid for and not rendered.

12. **Non-Disclosure**

    a. Each party hereto agrees (i) to hold the other party's confidential information in strict confidence; (ii) not to disclose any confidential information of the other party, except to those employees, consultants, attorneys, accountants, and other advisors of the receiving party who have a need to know such information; (iii) to exercise at least the same care in protecting the other party's confidential information from disclosure as the receiving party uses with regard to its own confidential information; and (iv) not to use any confidential information of the other party for any purpose except in furtherance of the purposes of this agreement.

    b. For the purposes hereof, "confidential information" shall mean non-public information that the disclosing party designates as being confidential or that, under the circumstances surrounding the disclosure, ought to be treated as confidential. Confidential information shall include, but not be limited to, any information, idea, know-how, technology, invention, algorithm, process, technique, data, program, computer software, computer code and related documentation, proposal, prototype, design, work-in-process, future development, engineering, reengineering, financial data, information about costs and profits, projections, personal information, records, customer lists, contact persons, customer data, sales data, possible new business ventures and/or expansion plans or matters of a creative nature, or regarding any form of product produced, distributed or acquired by a party hereto or its affiliates. Confidential information shall not include information that (i) is now or hereafter becomes, through no act or omission of the receiving party, generally known or available in the computer graphics or software industry, or is now within or later enters the public domain through no act or omission of the receiving party; (ii) was acquired by the receiving party prior to receiving such information from the other hereto and without restriction as to use or disclosure; (iii) is hereafter rightfully furnished to the receiving party by a third party, without restriction as to use or disclosure; (iv) is required to be disclosed pursuant to law, provided the receiving party uses reasonable efforts to give the other party hereto reasonable notice of such required disclosure,

GENERIC MOTION CAPTURE STUDIOS (*CONTINUED*)

and cooperates in any attempts by such party to legally prevent such disclosure; or (v) is disclosed with the prior written consent of the other party.

13. **Force Majeure**

Neither QGI nor GMC Studios shall be liable, except to the extent provided for in this agreement, for any failure of performance hereunder due to causes beyond its control, including but not limited to acts of God (including, without limitation, fire, flood, or other catastrophes); malfunction or failure of the equipment, power, or facilities of GMC Studios; changes in the substance or application of any law, order, or regulation of any local, state, or federal government having jurisdiction over QGI or GMC Studios or any instrumentality of any one or more of said governments, provided such changes render QGI or GMC Studios performance impossible or inherently unprofitable; insurrections, riots, wars, strikes, lockouts, and work stoppages. Either party shall have the right to terminate this agreement in the event that a force majeure event affecting the other party continues in excess of thirty (30) consecutive days.

14. **Time Calculations**

For purposes of computing any time periods provided in this agreement, "business days" shall consist of weekdays (Monday through Friday), exclusive of holidays observed by the U.S. Postal Service. A period measured in "business days" shall end at 5:00 P.M. CST following the specified number of twenty-four (24) hour periods (excluding Saturday, Sunday, and holidays as specified above).

15. **Disputes**

The parties shall submit all disputes arising in connection with this agreement to a one-member panel in accordance with the rules of the American Arbitration Association. The prevailing party in arbitration shall be entitled to recover its reasonable attorney's fees and costs. The arbitrator's decision shall be final, binding, and nonappealable.

16. **Entire Agreement**

This agreement and the documents specifically referenced herein constitute the entire agreement among the parties with respect to the subject matter hereof and supersedes all prior agreements with respect thereto, and no statements, representations, warranties (express or implied), writings, understandings, or agreements of any party or of any representative of any party, in the negations leading to the execution and delivery of this agreement or at any other time, which are not expressed herein, shall be binding. This agreement may not be modified except by Change Order as provided herein or by a written amendment hereto executed and delivered to each party.

17. **Notices**

Notices and other communications with respect to this agreement shall be given by in-hand delivery, in which case a written receipt shall be provided by the recipient or by electronic facsimile transmission as follows:

If to GMC Studios, the transmission shall be sent to 555-555-1213 and shall include a cover sheet specifying Annette Provost or GMC Studios' current representative as the addressee.

If to QGI, the transmission shall be sent to 555-555-1213 and shall include a cover sheet specifying QGI's designated representative as the addressee.

18. **Governing Law**

This agreement shall be construed in accordance with the laws of the State of Arizona without regard to its conflicts of laws and principles. This agreement may be executed simultaneously in two or more counterparts, each of which shall be deemed an original, but all of which together shall constitute one and the same instrument. The headings contained in this agreement are for reference purposes only and shall not affect the meaning or interpretation of this agreement. Any action or proceeding arising under this agreement shall be adjudicated in the state or federal courts located in Tucson, Arizona, and each of the parties hereby submits itself to the exclusive venue of such courts for the purpose of any such action.

19. **Counterparts**

This agreement may be executed in two or more counterparts, each of which shall be deemed an original, but all of which together shall constitute one and the same document. Signatures and documents obtained by facsimile shall also be deemed to be originals.

IN WITNESS WHEREOF, the parties hereby execute this agreement as of the date first specified above.

GMC Studios, Inc.

By: _____

Print name: _____ Date: _____

GENERIC MOTION CAPTURE STUDIOS (*CONTINUED*)

Quality Games, Inc.

By: _____

Print name: _____ Date: _____

EXHIBIT A

Deliverables and Services

- Seven hundred fifty (750) moves with one (1) primary character and three (3) secondary characters to be captured during session which is tentatively scheduled for the week of February 20, 2002.
- Capture session to be held over an eight and one-half (8.5) day period with one and one-half (1.5) days additional for setup and rigging.
- Average length of moves is :03 to :05 seconds.
- Single-performer "standard" motions over 5 seconds are billed at a rate of $25 per second.
- Single-performer "difficult" motions over 5 seconds are billed at a rate of $50 per second.
- Two-performer "standard" motions over 5 seconds are billed at a rate of $75 per second.
- Two-performer "difficult" motions over 5 seconds are billed at a rate of $125 per second.
- Moves list will be finalized by the client and sent to GMC Studios no less than two weeks prior to the capture session so that all arrangements can be finalized.
- Director for the session will be provided by QGI.
- QGI to determine if capture session will be during weekdays or include weekends. Capture sessions on weekends will have an additional $45 fee per person with a minimum of four (4) hours per day for capture. There will also be an additional 20% added to the daily expenses.
- Motion performers provided by QGI. QGI agrees to be liable for any delays, cancellations, or postponements caused by the talent or service QGI provides.
- QGI will cover all lodging and travel expenses.

- GMC Studios will deliver .amc files.
- GMC Studios reserves all right, title, and interest in the technology created or developed by GMC Studios in producing the project. GMC Studios will have the right to use and permit others to see recorded excerpts or still photographs for GMC Studios' internal use and promotion of GMC Studios' business, provided that GMC Studios' obtains QGI's written consent, which shall not be unreasonably withheld or delayed. In addition, GMC Studios will receive a motion capture credit in the published game credits.

Production and Delivery Schedule

Week of February 5
- GMC Studios receives final move list, skeleton, model, prop list, and dimensions of props.
- GMC Studios contacts stunt coordinator to get list of requirements and needs for the capture session.
- QGI provides to GMC Studios a list of who will be directing and attending the capture session.
- GMC Studios to assist with accommodation needs.

Week of February 12
- Preproduction conference call occurs; moves list is covered and all questions answered.
- Skeleton and model to have been tested and sent back to QGI for final compatibility test.

Week of February 19
- GMC Studios prepares and sets up capture studio.
- Capture session begins.

Week of February 26
- GMC Studios' team begins processing capture data.

Week of March 19
- GMC Studios delivers final motion.

AREAS TO PAY PARTICULAR ATTENTION TO IN THE CONTRACT

Now that you have seen and read through all the legalese in a sample contract, there are two main areas that you are going to want to pay particular attention to so that the cost of your project does not run over the initial amount stated. These areas actually need to be addressed by you long before the contract phase, however. Check the contract and see that it reflects your needs.

The first area to pay attention to is the "average length" that the motion studio establishes for each motion. It is critical that you understand what this means. The motion capture studio is estimating what they think will be the average number of seconds that each motion will be. If they set a short average number of seconds per motion, then you can almost guarantee that the total cost of your project will be more than the initial amount. The number of seconds that the average is set at depends on the motions you are trying to capture. If the motions you need are very short in duration, then having a shorter average number is OK. However, a good length for video game motions is three to five seconds. Motions that are longer in duration than the average number are billed out at a higher rate than motions that stay within this average.

Make sure that the average that is set is *processed* seconds of motion and not *raw* seconds. It is standard that the average is processed seconds, but check with the motion studio to make sure that they use this standard.

Processed seconds: The number of seconds of motion that are cleaned and delivered after the capture session.

Raw seconds: The actual number of seconds of motion that were captured per motion. Sometimes called *captured seconds*.

Some motion capture studios may set the average at three seconds per motion, charge a higher rate for motions that go four seconds, and charge an even higher rate for the fifth second and above. This kind of sliding scale of costs can quickly add up if you have not been really careful with timing your motions ahead of time. Our sample bid does not include this kind of sliding scale; however, see Chapter 12, "Post Production," on frame range selections to learn how to select processed seconds.

An equally important area to pay attention to is the difficulty rating given to each of your motions. The reason for this is the more difficult a motion is to capture and process, the higher the rate it is billed at. Motions that are deemed "simple" or "standard" cost you less than those deemed "difficult." This proves to be the case in our sample contract.

- All moves are based on an average of 3–5 seconds.
- Single-performer "standard" motions over 5 seconds are billed at a rate of $25 per second.
- Single-performer "difficult" motions over 5 seconds are billed at a rate of $50 per second.
- Two-performer "standard" motions over 5 seconds are billed at a rate of $75 per second.
- Two-performer "difficult" motions over 5 seconds are billed at a rate of $125 per second.

It is important to note here that this is one of the main reasons why the Motion Coordinator should be included in the bid and contract process. Some companies feel that this type of contract negotiations are best handled by management, but without specific knowledge of setting a realistic "average" length for the motions, and the proper difficulty ratings for them, it would be impossible to make a smart decision. Having the average length for the motions set too low in this kind of bid will lead to cost overruns.

CONCLUSION

As you have seen, there are a lot of factors that go into deciding which motion capture studio is best for your project. Technical as well as contractual issues need to be thought out. Here are some things to keep in mind:

- There are a number of basic features and services to consider when looking at a motion capture studio.
- There are three major phases to the selection process: the bid, the conference call/meeting, and the contract.
- Always get at least three bids.
- There are a few different types of bids.
- There is some general information that you need to provide to a motion studio to get an accurate bid.
- More details are worked out during the conference call/meeting once a motion studio is decided on.
- All details are spelled out in writing when the contract is drawn up.
- There are a few areas in a bid and contract that you need to pay particular attention to. One of these main areas is to make sure the average length set for each motion is realistic to cover the majority of your motions.

MOTION PERFORMERS, STUNT COORDINATION, AND DIRECTING

A s the motion coordinator, your "animation" job really begins long before you get the motion capture data back from the motion capture studio. It begins with organizing and preparing and continues through the actual capturing of the motions, ending only after the post animating is complete.

There is an old motion capture saying: "garbage in, garbage out." This means that if you have not planned properly, get poorly captured motion data, or work with an inferior motion performer, then "garbage" is all that you are going to get. Lead massive technical director for Weta Digital Ltd., John Haley, says "Preparation, organization, flexibility, and the quality of your performer are the most important aspects going into a session." Assuming you have prepared properly and you are working with a quality motion capture studio, the only remaining variable is the motion performer.

Motion performer: Any person or animal whose performance is going to be captured, sometimes referred to as motion talent.

TYPES OF MOTION PERFORMERS

It is obvious that you will want to capture the best motion for your project, so avoid the temptation to suit up yourself or one of your friends as the motion performer unless your friend is proficient in the kind of motion you need to capture. Even if you are the best person to perform the motion, you need to decide if you are the director or the performer; you can't be both. As the director you need to observe the performance and critique it, which you can't do if you are performing. To obtain the best motion possible, select the highest caliber performer you can afford to use. Depending on the demands of your project, you may need several performers to get the desired motions. The four major types of motion performers are these:

- Animal performers
- Athletic performers
- Character performers
- Stunt performers

Animal Performers

Some projects may only need one motion performer, others may require multiple people to get the desired looked, and still others may need an animal performer to be captured.

If you need to capture animal motion, we recommend that you use a motion capture studio that has captured animal motion before. House of Moves and Perspective Studios have captured dogs, LocoMotion Studios a horse (several times), Motion Analysis Studios a lynx and an elephant, Red Eye Studio an iguana, and Madcap Studios in Australia has of course captured a kangaroo. Chuck Mongelli, president of Perspective Studios, when asked if his studio has ever done an animal capture, said "Our personal experience has included a dog capture; of course we capture Keith [his business partner] sometimes." Figure 9.1 shows Madcap Studios' Kangaroo capture.

There are some unique issues that arise with animal captures, such as how will the studio fix the markers on the animal? How will you get the animal to perform the required moves? Do you need a special capture volume and stage setup for the animal? How many hours can the animal perform in a day?

LocoMotion Studios had to deal with some unique obstacles the first time they captured a horse's motion. Michael Mcgar, LocoMotion Studios' president, says they first tried to fix the markers directly to the horse's coat, but the horse wasn't comfortable and would try to brush them off or bite them. The biting of the markers was a big safety concern for them because horses have sensitive digestive tracks and a swallowed marker could be fatal. They overcame this by constructing a custom designed "horse suit" to fit tightly to the horse, and then they could adhered the markers to

FIGURE 9.1 A kangaroo with markers attached at Madcap Studios in Australia. © 2003. Reprinted with permission from Madcap Studios.

the suit. The horse was comfortable with the suit, and they were able to capture some great motion data. Figure 9.2 is from one of LocoMotion Studios' horse captures.

If you need to capture animals, you will obviously need an animal trainer/handler, and you need to schedule several rehearsal sessions so that the animal can get uses to the motions and work out any potential problems before the actual capture. You do not want to waste time on your capture days trying to work out issues that could have been handled earlier. It is also important for you to communicate the capture volume size as well as the capture space

FIGURE 9.2 A horse and riders motion are both being captured by LocoMotion Studios. © 2003. Reprinted with permission from LocoMotion Studios.

size to the handler so that the rehearsals will be accurate. Many people overlook the importance of the size of the capture space. Whether animal or human, the performer needs to have enough room to get his speed up before entering the capture volume and enough room to slow down after leaving.

Athletic Motion Performers

If your project requires the motion performer to perform sports motion (such as a sports video game), you should get the highest caliber of athlete possible in that sport. A lot of video games use high school athletes, low-level college athletes, or their friends for their game's motion, and it shows. The higher the caliber of athlete, the better his motor coordination is and the better his chances are of performing the required motions in a small area. If he is a professional athlete, he must have good motor coordination to have achieved such a high level. Motion capture studios like to use as small a capture volume as possible (the smaller the volume, the better their quality of capture), so you need an athlete who has the skill and coordination to execute the motion is a small space. Other qualities to consider when choosing an athletic motion performer are these:

- Is the performer open to coaching, or does he only want to do it his way? This is important because there may be some differences between what is done in the real sport and what you need for your video game. A good example would be in a baseball game; the character gets into an unnatural core position after he throws the ball, whereas in the real world we wouldn't consider it.

- We have found that athletes who can break down a motion to its separate components are also good motion capture performers. These athletes also are generally good teachers or coaches because they don't just "do" an action, they also understand the kinesthetic reasons behind how and why they perform it the way they do.

- For a sports video game, you may want several motion performers to cover all the specific positions realistically, or you may want an athlete who can perform the moves of several positions. While capturing the motion for *Quarterback Club*™ *2002* (hereafter referred to as *QBC 2002*), we used athletes from several positions to help capture all the motion, but on *All-Star Baseball*™ *2002* (hereafter referred to as *ASB 2002*), we were able to used one good utility player for 80% of the motions.

- You may want an athlete who is good enough to mimic the unique mannerisms of marquee players.

- You may want an athlete who has been a motion performer before because he knows what to expect during the capture process. If he was a good performer once and hasn't been injured since, he is less of a potential risk.

To help your performer give his best performance, you may want to make the conditions during the capture as realistic as possible for the athlete. Some companies have brought in dirt and Astroturf for their captures, while others have gone on location to ice rinks, horse arenas, and track stadiums. In addition to the environment, we recommend that you allow the athlete to perform his sport as realistically as possible. While capturing the motion for *ASB 2002*, we had our performers throw and catch a real baseball for a majority of their motions. This made the motion studio staff a little nervous because if we broke a camera, they cost about $10,000 each to replace, but it was necessary to get the most realistic motion possible. If someone acts as if he is going to throw a ball but doesn't, he will "short arm the throw," which occurs because the human body will not elongate or extend through the motion if it is not exerting optimum force, and this will show up in the captured data. Some may argue that it isn't necessary because the animation tools are so easy that the animators can exaggerate the arm if needed. My question is why? If you can have the athlete perform it properly, you don't need the animators to worry about it later. It seems silly to assume that the animators will have the time and critical eye needed to make corrections when you could have captured it properly to begin with. A trick we used on *ASB 2002* was to have the performer throw a real baseball into a net (the kind used by football kickers). As long as our performer was accurate, no equipment would be damaged. Occasionally the performer threw the ball to one of our designers who was outside the capture volume.

Character Motion Performers

Selecting a "character" performer is essential for projects with cinematic sequences or CG characters that must have unique personalities. People with an acting background are the best choice for character motion performers because they should have an understanding of movement, timing, and body expression.

Another characteristic you may want to consider when selecting a character performer is the performer's body size. In the early days of motion capture, before technology allowed us to map motion easily to different skeletons, it was a huge concern to get a motion performer whose skeletal proportions were similar to the game's skeleton. Today the performer's body size really is only a concern when we consider the realistic look of his movements. If you have a character who is a giant, you may find it better to have a large, lumbering performer rather than a performer who is just acting like he is large and lumbering. People who are large and heavy naturally move differently from people who are not. Similarly, if you have a character that is old, select an elderly performer. While capturing the motion for the mascots in *ASB 2002*, we decided to use an overweight, clumsy guy as the motion performer, and this worked out very well for us because his motion mimicked a guy in a large, cumbersome mascot suit. If the mascot motions would have been a high priority, however, we would have preferred to have hired and captured a professional mascot's motions.

Stunt Motion Performers

Like a sports performer, a stunt performer needs to be good enough to perform the motions required in the amount of space available. Many motion capture studios have stunt performers they like to recommend, but we suggest you use only someone who has a Screen Actors Guild card (SAG card). A SAG card means that he is a working stuntman and not just someone who is willing to do stunts. You will probably also want a stuntman who "sells out the stunt." This means that, if you need him to take a hit (such as a football tackle), he does it; not selling out and overacting the hit is easily seen in the captured data. Other qualities to consider when choosing a stunt performer are these:

- If possible, use a stuntman who has done motion capture before. The experience of having worked with motion capture can help save you time and money. It is true that his fee may be more expensive than an inexperienced performer, but this is a nominal cost compared to the time that will be saved using someone who is experienced. An efficient, well-executed capture session will without a doubt save your company money.

- Professional stuntmen know what it is like to be on-set, so they are used to long, hard hours with periodic delays. This means they will be comfortable with the pace of a motion capture session and able to perform when required.

- When talking to a stuntman about price, ask about stunt adjustments on top of his scale rate. Stunt adjustments are standard in the movie industry and are common in motion capture performances. Think of a stunt adjustment as hazard pay: The more punishment he is asked to take, the more he gets paid. Stunt adjustments for motion capture projects, however, are slightly different than they are for a movie. Motion capture stunt adjustments may be based on the number of hard hits the stuntman has to endure or perform, as opposed to the complexity of one stunt. The rate is arbitrary and should be discussed prior to the capture date.

The Ultimate Motion Performer

If your project requires a well-rounded motion performer, it is in your best interest to find an all-purpose person who is qualified and good in all areas: athletic, character, and stunt performing. I am lucky to have worked with one such performer, Steve Pope, seen in Figure 9.3. Pope is a professional stuntman who has done work for television (*Third Watch, Homicide: Life on the Street, OZ*) and for movies (*Meet the Parents, Hannibal, Shaft, Bringing Out the Dead*). In addition to stunt work, Pope has been a motion performer and a stunt coordinator on several video games. His background also includes a bachelor of arts degree in theatre, varsity football, and

FIGURE 9.3 Professional stuntman and motion capture performer Steve Pope. © 2003. Reprinted with permission from Steve Pope.

varsity track at the University of Notre Dame. No matter what motion we needed him to perform, he did it and did it well. Pope is also receptive to coaching and is just an all around nice guy to have on-set.

One company that many motion capture studios call on when they need experienced performers and coordination is Smashcut, Inc. Smashcut is a full-service stunt action film company that specializes in providing performers and specialty talent for motion capture, motion pictures, television, commercials, video, and print. Smashcut is proud to be able to get involved in every part of the production process. They help design and choreograph all shot lists and scripts to better help the characters come to life. They employ the best of Hollywood's stunt coordinators, specialty riggers, and safety personnel to get the job done. Chad Stahelski, founder of

Smashcut, Inc., says "motion capture is a specialty within the industry and we pride ourselves on continuing to bring innovative movement to each character we capture."

PERFORMER AUDITIONS

Whether you are seeking animal, athletic, character, or stunt motions, it is important for you to be an active participant in choosing the motion performer. It is best if several people from your project also approve the performer so that you are sure he will meet the needs of your game. It can't be emphasized enough how important selecting the right person to be your performer is, since his movements are the basis on which all your game's motions are built. If you discover after your capture that the performer was not the right person, it will be too late. Most third-party motion capture studios will conduct and video tape performer auditions for their clients; however, it is best if you are present during the audition. Being present allows you to build a rapport with the potential performer, and you can find out little things about him such as whether he is willing to take direction, what his enthusiasm level for the project is, what communicating with him is like, or if he has any injuries, such as turf toe, that will show up in the capture data. Hip, foot, or leg injuries are a big deal if they cause the performer to favor one leg over the other as he moves. Cycle motions will appear to limp when looped if the performer favors one leg over another. This can sometimes be so subtle that during the capture it may be difficult to see, but the data doesn't lie. If an injury is there, you will see it in the captured data.

It is also recommended that you give him a realistic impression of what a motion capture session is really like; it is usually long, grueling hours of boring work for the performer. Some motions are more fun and creative, but it's mostly eight hours of tedious, short motion segments. You should also give him a feeling for the kinds of motions that would be requested of him so that he's not surprised later to find out that you want to hoist him up in the air by ropes and a pulley and drop him. Take note of whether the performer is right or left handed; for some projects this is not an issue, but for others it may make a big difference. Generally it is easy nowadays to flip motion from right to left, but it requires your skeleton to be symmetrical to do a good job, and some motions can't be flipped and work, so they need to be captured as either a right hander or a left hander.

When directing a motion capture session, it is good to work with performers who aren't afraid to give their opinion. That way you can talk about how they would naturally do the motion and decide if that is indeed how you need to capture it. Feedback from the performer is invaluable in capturing the most realistic motion possible. As the director, however, you are the one who needs to make the final decision of whether or not you need the performer to deviate from reality and perform the motion in a way that best suits your game.

MOTION PERFORMER SAFETY AND COMFORT

There probably isn't a worse case scenario than having a motion performer who gets injured during a capture session. Not only could it possibly hurt the performer's career, but it could also jeopardize your project. To help keep the performer safe and to get the best performance out of him, there are certain issues that you need to address.

One thing that most motion capture studios recommend, but few video game clients seem to follow, is to get together with the motion performer before the actual capture session for a rehearsal. Most companies underestimate the value of rehearsals when capturing in-game motions or they simply don't allow enough time for them in their schedule. When capturing cinematic motions, it would be a waste of time and money not to do rehearsals prior to the capture day. The performers need to work out their timing with dialogue and each other, especially if you have choreographed the performances. Regardless of the type of capture you are doing, having at least one rehearsal can only help improve your odds of success. Giant Studios recently wrapped up capturing motion for a major motion picture that required more than 20 motion performers. The scope of the project was so extensive that it required three stages, consisting of a primary capture stage, a secondary body and facial capture stage, and a calibration stage. Just organizing the motion performers was time consuming because they spent months in rehearsals prior to the capture.

Even better than having a rehearsal is doing a test shoot or a proof of principle shoot (POP shoot). A test shoot at the motion capture studio combines a rehearsal with testing the skeleton, marker setup, data quality, and the pipeline for data delivery. The studio gets to make sure all areas are covered, you get to see the quality of the data you can expect, and the performer gets to practice, learn the motion list, and know what will be expected of him. If the motion performer you are using is a first-time motion capture performer, a test shoot may also help him feel more comfortable in the studio and be more relaxed on the actual capture day.

This may sound silly, but the shoes the motion performer will use during the capture are very important. This is assuming that you want your performer to wear shoes. If your game character is barefoot, then you may want your performer barefoot during the capture, since humans move differently when in shoes. Dr. Robert D. Liverman, a retired exercise science professor from Illinois State University, says that "when you have shoes on and are running, you strike on the ball of the foot and roll onto the heel; when barefoot you stay on the ball of the foot more and not strike the heel. When barefoot, there is also a tendency to bend your knees more for cushion." Motion capture studios usually provide shoes for the performer because the shoes need to be fitted with markers. Where and how the markers are attached, however, may have a negative effect on his performance. Different types of shoes bend differently, and this can affect marker placement because you do not want the markers to hinder the performer's natural movement. Some studios glue the markers onto the shoes and reinforce them with tape, while others punch a hole through them to attach the markers. If they puncture holes in the shoes and insert a plastic strip to hold the marker in place, the performer's foot (especially toes) may be jammed against it when performing ballistic-type motions. After a few hours of jamming his toe into a piece of plastic, the discomfort could easily affect his performance. It is not uncommon for a motion performer to be limping at the end of the day because of sore toes, blisters, and cuts. Sometimes a motion studio will buy new shoes, and other times they have stock shoes for the performer to wear. Buying new shoes may cause a problem for the performer if the motions he needs to perform require ballistic, cutting moves, because new shoes sometimes aren't broken in enough to feel comfortable while moving quickly.

It is equally important to have the proper type of shoes for the performer. You do not want a football player trying to perform hard run cycles and ballistic cut moves to wear wrestling shoes. Wrestling shoes have very little if any padding, so hours or days of pounding and cutting may hurt his feet or knees and ultimately his performance. In this case, the performer may want turf shoes (especially if the capture is on Astroturf), or he may want cross trainer or court shoes that provide more lateral support.

A trick learned a number of years ago can overcome two of the three shoe issues. Ask the performer if he has a pair of shoes that he is comfortable wearing while performing the motions that you will require from him. If he does, offer to buy him a brand new pair or a pair of equal quality. Use his worn shoes for the capture session; this will make sure that the shoes he has are the right type and comfortable for him. The only concern for you then is how the motion studio is going to attach the markers. Talk to them and make sure that if they punch holes in the shoe there won't be a hard piece of plastic inserted.

The size and cleanliness of the capture space is also important to the motion performer's safety and performance. The capture space, or actual studio size, needs to be big enough for a performer to get his speed up before entering the capture volume and also big enough for him to stop after exiting. This is important so that the client can get a consistent root movement to make cycle motions, and it's important to the performer for his safety. I also have seen studios that had so much junk and trash scattered around that it was a potential danger to the motion performer. After running through the capture volume, the motion performer had to change directions to keep from running into junk, and the studio was lucky he wasn't injured.

Where the cameras are placed can also affect the motion performer's safety and performance. Studios need to have an adequate number of cameras, positioned properly, to cover the capture volume fully and help prevent occlusion; however, sometimes they get in the way. Most studios have their cameras mounted either on large tripods or high on the wall on trusses.

Tripods are very good for mobility, but they also cut down the overall capture space available. At times they get in the way of the performance and are dangerous. I have been to several capture sessions where tripods were either in the motion performer's way or the performer was afraid to execute the motion fully because he was afraid of hitting a tripod (remember, the cameras cost about $10,000 each). The camera wires are also a concern. When cameras are on tripods, the wires connecting the cameras are usually on the floor and pose a danger. Tripods and wires sometimes get in the way of the director and other people working the capture session, too, but my main concern with tripods is the safety of the performer and trying to reorganize a motion because we have to avoid a tripod.

Cameras mounted on a wall truss tend to be safer because they free up the capture space from being cluttered, and the camera wires are out of the way of the performers and staff. Cameras on trusses also tend to interfere a lot less with the execution of motions; only two times have I been worried about the cameras mounted on a truss affecting a motion I wanted to capture.

STUNT COORDINATION

For projects that require stunt work or hard ballistic motions such as football tackles, wrestling moves, and so on, the best way to help insure a motion performer's safety is to hire a professional stunt coordinator for the capture session. Like the stunt performer, this person should also have a SAG card. The stunt coordinator and the motion coordinator need to work closely together, not only so that the stunt performer is safe but also to ensure that the motion being captured will work.

Motion capture stunt coordinator Jeff Gibson, seen in Figure 9.4, is a professional stuntman and stunt coordinator and the sec-

FIGURE 9.4 Motion capture stunt coordinator, professional stuntman, and motion capture performer Jeff Gibson. © 2003. Reprinted with permission from Jeff Gibson.

ond unit director for the HBO series *The Wire* and comes highly recommended. He has worked on numerous movies (*Conspiracy Theory*, *Daredevil*, *Robocop III*, *Batman 2*, and *Batman 3*, to name just a few) and has also been working with motion capture for about nine years, so he has seen it evolve from its infancy. A stunt coordinator not only needs to be able to communicate with the stunt performers in a way they are used to, but he also has valuable knowledge about scaffolding, mats, pads, and riggings (i.e. pulleys, ropes, and harnesses) that are safe to use. Believe it or not, for the safety of the stuntman and for liability reasons, only certain approved pulleys can be used to lift humans. Because of his numerous years of motion capture work, Gibson also has several good tricks to help accomplish certain difficult motions.

Directing a Capture Session

As mentioned before, as the motion coordinator your animation job depends on capturing the correct motions at a high level of quality. As the motion coordinator, it is your job to have a full understanding of the motions that are needed, how they will interact with each other, and how they will need to be edited and animated to get them into the game. This is why the motion coordinator should direct the capture session.

If you are nervous about directing, however, you may consider hiring an independent director. An experienced director should be able to help you stay organized, keep the capture session on schedule, and raise pertinent questions about game design and motion flow. If you are thinking about hiring an independent director, however, you need to include him in your process as soon as possible so that issues can be addressed and talked about prior to the capture session. The director needs to be on the same page as you so that he can make informed decisions during the capturing that will affect how the motion data is handled once it is delivered by the motion studio. In addition to having the independent director run the capture session, you should have one or two of your own people assisting him and learning from him, so that future projects can be handled entirely with your own in-house staff. Here are a few things to keep in mind when considering an independent director:

- Check his references. Make sure he has really done the things he claims to have done.
- Ask what kind of motion capture shoots/sessions he has been involved in (i.e. sports video games, action games, cinematic, movies, etc.).
- Ask how large the capture sessions were that he has directed, the number of motions captured, the number of days the sessions lasted, and so on.
- Ask when the last time was that he directed a shoot. Motion capture technology has changed so much in a short period of time that the old way may not still be the best way. With that said, some of the "old school" tricks are still very useful and have not changed at all.

It is also recommended that you do not hire a director who has never been involved in the post capture process. A director needs to have good organizational and communicational skills, but he should also have experience with animating from motion capture data. Without some knowledge of how the motion files are to be animated and edited, it would be difficult for him to make smart decisions during the shoot. A common mistake made by directors who do not have animation experience is to recapture a motion if the motion performer looks down at the point he needs to stop. It is a natural human reaction to look for your mark when trying to execute in a given area, but it does not necessarily mean the motion needs to be recaptured. If the performer moved from the neck when he looked at his mark as opposed to from the waist, it is an easy fix for the animator to rotate the neck and head. If the performer bent from the waist, however, it may have changed the way he carried his entire body during the motion and may be enough to warrant capturing it again.

Paying Motion Performers

The motion performer's performance is crucial to the success of the animation that will result from it. Because of this, it has become my policy to pay the motion performer at the end of the last day he is performing. This way the performer gets immediate gratification for his efforts and will be more willing to work with you again. It can also be used to help motivate a performer whose enthusiasm is falling after several long days of difficult motions.

If the motion capture studio is responsible for paying the performers, have it written into the bid and contract that they will pay the performer the last day of the capture session. If the studio regularly pays the performers on time, they should not have a problem with this. If they do have a problem with it, simply explain to them that you just have the performer's best interests in mind.

If your company is responsible for paying the performers, have checks in hand and ready to give to them. I know of a company that delayed paying several motion performers for work they had done for over a year after the capture session. This type of behavior is not professional and will not foster a good working relationship with someone you may want to work with again. Taking care of your people is the best policy.

If you are not confident that your company will pay the motion performer in a timely manner, there is a way you can get it done. Ask the motion capture studio if they will pay the motion performers on the last day of capture and include the cost of the performers in the billing to your company. This way the motion performers are paid and happy and may be willing to work with you again. You must be aware, however, that having the performers paid this way will cost your company more money because it is common for the price to be marked up anywhere from 10% to 20% more by the motion studio. Then again, if your company pays in a timely manner, this would not be necessary.

The following pay ranges are from video game captures that I worked from September 1999 through November 2001, so they should be considered basic ranges:

- Pay scale for a motion performer can range between $300 and $1,000 per day.
- Pay scale for a stunt performer can range from $655 per day and up.
- Pay scale for a stunt coordinator can range between $650 and $1,000 per day.
- Pay scale for stunt adjustments can range between $600 and $1,000 per week.

Normally we pay a motion performer more per day if he worked a short capture (one to three days). If he worked a longer capture session (4 to 11 days), he gets a little less per day. Experienced stunt performers and performers who need to perform ballistic motions can usually demand higher pay.

You should also expect to pay any of the performer's travel expenses (plane ticket, rental car, gas and tolls, and such), food, and hotel, and on most captures I've been involved with we paid entertainment expenses such as movies or a beer with dinner. Every company has its own policy regulating how employees spend the company's money, but it is worth repeating: Taking care of your people (within reason) is the best policy.

CONCLUSION

- Choosing the right motion performer is critical for the success of your motions.
- Use as high a caliber of performer as possible.
- There are four basic types of performers: animal, athletic, character, and stunt.
- Animal captures introduce some unique issues.
- Have athletic performers perform their motions as realistically as possible; this includes the playing surface, such as dirt, turf, or ice.
- For character performers, people with acting backgrounds are generally best. However, you might choose them based on

physical appearance or age, since this also affects how people move.

- You should be an active participant in the performer auditions.
- No matter what kind of performers you are using, rehearsals prior to the capture date are important.
- Performer safety is of the utmost importance. For high impact or stunt captures, you should consider hiring a stunt coordinator and professional stuntmen.
- The performer's shoes are important because they affect his performance and safety.
- The client's capture director needs to have a full understanding of the motions needed for the game as well as good communication and organizational skills.
- If you are uncertain about directing a capture, you may want to hire an experienced independent director. If you hire an independent director, get him involved in your development process as early as possible.
- Make sure your motion performers are paid on the last day they are on-set.

10

FINAL PREPARATIONS BEFORE THE CAPTURE SESSION

Job Number: GMC123-456	DAILY SHOT LIST		
Capture Date: 02-29-04			
Client Name: Quality Games Inc.			
Project Name: CARRION Day 4			
Tape #: 04			
Crew Call 8:15 am			
Talent Call 8:30 am			
Client Call 9:00 am			
Lunch 12:30 PM			
Capture resumes 1:30 PM			
102 Moves Scheduled Today			
Alert Crouch & Alert Crouch Walk 1 Handed Weapons			
ALT_0005 Alert Crouch/ Alert Run/Alert Crouch			
ALT_0006 Alert Crouch/ Alert Crouch walk/ Alert Crouch			
ALT_0007 Alert Crouch/ injured stand			
ALT_0008 Alert Crouch/180/Alert Run			
ALT_0009 Alert Crouch/180/AlertCrouch/Alert Squat			
ALT_0010 Alert Crouch/investigate ground/Alert Crouch			
ALT_0011 Alert Crouch/Shoulder Roll RIGHT/Alert Crouch **Make rolls the same R/L			
ALT_0012 Alert Crouch/Shoulder Roll LEFT/Alert Crouch			
DTH_0020 Alert Crouch/Death crumple to the ground forward			
DTH_0021 Alert Crouch/Death Blown backwards violently convulsions before death			
DTH_0022 Alert Crouch/Death Blown Forwards violently head and arms snap back			
DTH_0023 Alert Crouch/Death Shot in the head from behind			
ALT_0013 Alert Crouch/ Alert Crouch walk/ Alert Crouch			
Alert Squat 1 Handed Weapon			
ALT_0300 Alert Squat/Alert Prone/Alert Squat			
ALT_0322 Alert Squat/ Behind corner, pop out 180 LEFT ALERT CROUCH, return			
ALT_0323 Alert Squat/ Behind corner, pop out 180 RIGHT ALERT CROUCH, return			
ALT_0324 Alert Squat/Fire wepon above head/Alert Squat			
Alert prone with 1 Handed Weapon			
ALT_0202 Alert Prone/ Roll RIGHT/Alert Prone			
ALT_0203 Alert Prone/ Roll LEFT/Alert Prone			
DTH_0030 Alert Prone/ Death try to get up off ground, fall to ground face first			
DTH_0031 Alert Prone/ Death rollover twitching and writhing before death			
DTH_0032 Alert Prone/ Death shot in the head			
ALT_0200 Alert Prone/ Crawl/Alert Prone			
Escape Motions with 1 Handed Weapon			
ESC_0018 Injured Stand /180/Injured Walk/Injured Run			
ESC_0019 Injured Stand /180/ Injured Run/Injured Stand			
ESC_0020 Injured Stand /180/ Injured Stand/Injured Walk/Injured Stand			
ESC_0004 Injured Run			
ESC_0007 Injured Run /Injured Walk			

E ven after organizing the motion list, flowcharts, and database, choosing a motion capture studio, going through the contract, and selecting motion performers and a stunt coordinator, there are still some little things you need to do before your capture session can be a success.

REFERENCE MATERIAL

It is a good idea to prepare some reference material for your motion performer. If you are doing a sports game, it would be a good idea to organize videotape of marquee players as references so that the performer can mimic their motions. This helps only if you organize the videotape so that locating the players is easy and is not time consuming during the capture session. Contact the motion studio ahead of time and request a television and VCR on the set so that your performer can watch a player and then mimic his motion immediately after.

If you are capturing motions to add to an already existing game, take screen grabs of the characters in the game when they are in the core positions so that the motion performer can see the exact pose he needs to try to begin and end in. If you are creating a new game, take digital or Polaroid photographs of a co-worker posed in the core positions; this will give the members of your project (designers and programmers) a chance to approve and agree on the look of the core positions prior to the capture.

A mesh of the game's character is also another good reference for the motion performer. If the motion studio that you are working with has a real-time playback system, it is a good idea to have a mesh of your game's actual character instead of a generic character for the playback. This way your motion performer can get a feeling for what your character looks like and how his movements affect the character. For instance, you might have a character with extra-long arms; by seeing his movements on the character, your motion performer will have a better idea of how to customize his movement for the character's physical build.

PROPS

Having the proper props for the motion performer is very important. Most motion studios have a wide variety of different props that their clients can use, and in many cases these props are very good. There are times, however, when you need to consider buying or making your own props for your project. When you are considering props, there are four major areas you need to take into account: scale, weight, safety, and occlusion.

The scale or size of the props is important for capturing realistic motions and motions that will require less post capture altering. Having the performer's hands in the correct place on weapons or when reaching for door knobs or hitting the right mark for fight scenes needs to be considered before the capture session. Otherwise you may add more hours to your post capture process.

The weight of the prop also affects the performer's performance. If the character in your game is supposed to be carrying a heavy chain-fed machine gun, it is best if you have a prop gun that is the proper size and somewhat heavy in order for his body to move properly while carrying it. When a person carries a heavy weight, his posture and movements change; if the weight is extreme, his body will also try to counterbalance the weight. Weight also changes the degree and type of anticipation he will have before performing any movement, so unless your character is heroic or you want more generic-looking motions, then giving the motion performer a heavier prop when necessary will give you better-looking motions.

We have already discussed in Chapter 9, "Motion Performers, Stunt Coordination, and Directing," the importance of performer safety, but you will need to consider it when dealing with the props, too. If you decide to make customized props that are heavier or more realistic for the performer, you need to make sure that the prop will not endanger him when he is performing the motions. If you are having him perform stunt motions, you need to calculate whether he will land on the prop and injure himself. Because of issues like this, it is recommended that you hire a stunt coordinator for your capture session and that he approve any customized props prior to the capture session.

During a capture session, marker occlusion is an issue that all optical motion capture studios must consider, so keep in mind that customized props may need to be constructed in a way that helps prevent the markers from being occluded from the cameras. This is one of the main reasons that motion studios like to build the customized props for their clients. If you want to build your props yourself, you will need to complete them in time to get them to the capture studio prior to your capture session so that the motion studio staff can approve them.

There are also some props that require an orientation consideration. This means that you need to make sure that they are held in the same way every time they are used. A baseball bat is a good example. If you are capturing the bat's motion in addition to the characters motion, you need to make sure that the performer holds the bat with it facing the same direction on every take. This is easily done by marking the bat with tape and making sure the performer lines his hands up on the tape the same way every time. If you have never worked with motion capture files, you may not see the relevance in this, but in the post capture process, the motion files will need to be blended together. If the orientation of a prop is not consistent, when the files are blended together, the prop will spin around in an attempt to solve for the different orientations. This can be very problematic, depending on the number of separate motion files that are affected and the deadlines involved. Animators can fairly easily reanimate simple prop motion, but this is time consuming and not necessary if you just plan for it prior to the capture session.

THE CAPTURE SESSION TEAM

If you are using a local motion studio, this issue may not be as important, but if you need to travel to the motion studio, this is a very important issue for getting the most value out of your motion capture session. To get the most out of your motion capture session, it is important to take only the necessary people to the capture. Most companies nowadays are concerned with budgets, so only people who are working on the capture session should attend. A manager who wants to watch the session should not take the place of an animator or designer who is needed to help make the capture a success. It does not matter if you are a manager or not; if you go to the capture, then you need to help.

In order to capture the motions the way you need them, it is recommended that you have at least two people, but it is ideal to have three or more people from your company attend and work the capture session. It is common for problems and obstacles to arise, and having the people present who can best solve them will save you time. If every time an issue arises you had to call your company and track down the person who can help you, you would waste valuable, expensive capture time. The best team to take would be composed of the motion coordinator (lead animator), the lead designer, and another animator or designer who does not have motion capture experience. With this team, the motion coordinator or lead designer can direct the capture and get assistance from the other, and the junior animator can help out and get experience so that one day he can organize and direct a capture.

If you are using a local motion studio and travel expenses are not a concern, have several junior motion animators and designers help with the capture on different days so that you can get more employees with motion capture experience. Getting people experience without immediately making them responsible for the success of the capture is the best way to help assure that you will always have experienced people at your company. Being exposed to a well-run capture session and experiencing some of the obstacles that can occur are the best ways to get employees experience and to help assure that future capture sessions are as cost effective as they can be.

If the motion studio has a real-time playback system or one that allows you to view a character performing a motion just after it was captured, that makes taking two people to the capture a possibility. One person experienced in motion capture and one other person familiar with your project's needs can easily make an organized capture a success. Having a good playback system will allow you to view each motion quickly from multiple angles and decide if it is acceptable or not. This may be a real money-saving approach that a company can use if travel and lodging expenses are a concern, but the downside to this is that other designers or animators do not get the experience of working a capture.

THE DAILY SHOT LIST

One of the confusing things about working with motion capture is that sometimes a term has a couple of different meanings, and sometimes there are multiple names for the same thing. An example of this would be the terms "capture session" and "shoot." They mean the same thing but, depending on which motion studio you are dealing with, either term may be used. The term "shot list" is slightly different from "daily shot list," and "motion list" is different from "motion database," but they too are often confused with one another. In Chapter 3, "The Motion List," we talked about the motion list, and our motion list did not include descriptions of each motion, but our motion database did.

Most motion capture studios need a shot list from you before giving you a bid. They are in essence asking you for your motion list, but they need to have brief descriptions included for each motion. In other words, this shot list is a cross between our motion list and our motion database. Remember, the shot list should not be confused with the daily shot list.

Daily shot list: A record containing the names of the motions and the order in which you want them captured on a given day.

When planning your daily shot list, it is important to consider several factors, but even if you plan perfectly, your daily shot list will continually change as your capture session progresses. Even though it will change, it is still important to make an initial daily shot list because it will help you make sure that you plan your time properly and stay on schedule. Generally, if you are working with an experienced motion studio, you can estimate capturing around 100 finished motions per day if they are basic moves. You can easily capture around 120 motions in a day if you are efficient with your time and you don't need multiple takes for each motion. If your project contains more complex motions, that number drops to about 60–80 motions, and in projects that contain a lot of stunt motions or motions that require a lot of preparation work it drops to between 20 and 40 motions per day. This also assumes that you are efficient with your time and do not spend too much time between takes or motions. Figure on 50 motions being finished before your lunch break, and reevaluate your schedule when you break. You may shoot multiple takes of a particular motion, but at the end of the day you should have around 100 individual finished motions.

If you are very lucky, the motion capture studio may create your daily shot lists for you. This is an extreme luxury and should not be considered the norm. Most motion capture studios leave this type of organization up to you, but a proactive studio may create them for you. Figure 10.1 is an example of a daily shot list prepared by the motion capture studio.

One disadvantage to having your daily shot list created by the motion capture studio is they may not consider all the factors that should be considered when planning this list. The following factors need to be considered when planning your daily shot lists:

- Priority of the motion
- Complexity of the motion
- Time of day
- Motions groupings
- Motion performer fatigue
- Motion performers' schedules

Job Number: GMC123-456	DAILY SHOT LIST		
Capture Date: 02-29-04			
Client Name: Quality Games Inc.			
Project Name: CARRION Day 4			
Tape #: 04			
Crew Call 8:15 am			
Talent Call 8:30 am			
Client Call 9:00 am			
Lunch 12:30 PM			
Capture resumes 1:30 PM			
102 Moves Scheduled Today			
Alert Crouch & Alert Crouch Walk 1 Handed Weapons			
ALT_0005 Alert Crouch/ Alert Run/Alert Crouch			
ALT_0006 Alert Crouch/ Alert Crouch walk/ Alert Crouch			
ALT_0007 Alert Crouch/ injured stand			
ALT_0008 Alert Crouch/180/Alert Run			
ALT_0009 Alert Crouch/180/AlertCrouch/Alert Squat			
ALT_0010 Alert Crouch/investigate ground/Alert Crouch			
ALT_0011 Alert Crouch/Shoulder Roll RIGHT/Alert Crouch **Make rolls the same R/L			
ALT_0012 Alert Crouch/Shoulder Roll LEFT/Alert Crouch			
DTH_0020 Alert Crouch/Death crumple to the ground forward			
DTH_0021 Alert Crouch/Death Blown backwards violently convulsions before death			
DTH_0022 Alert Crouch/Death Blown Forwards violently head and arms snap back			
DTH_0023 Alert Crouch/Death Shot in the head from behind			
ALT_0013 Alert Crouch/ Alert Crouch walk/ Alert Crouch			
Alert Squat 1 Handed Weapon			
ALT_0300 Alert Squat/Alert Prone/Alert Squat			
ALT_0322 Alert Squat/ Behind corner, pop out 180 LEFT ALERT CROUCH, return			
ALT_0323 Alert Squat/ Behind corner, pop out 180 RIGHT ALERT CROUCH, return			
ALT_0324 Alert Squat/Fire wepon above head/Alert Squat			
Alert prone with 1 Handed Weapon			
ALT_0202 Alert Prone/ Roll RIGHT/Alert Prone			
ALT_0203 Alert Prone/ Roll LEFT/Alert Prone			
DTH_0030 Alert Prone/ Death try to get up off ground, fall to ground face first			
DTH_0031 Alert Prone/ Death rollover twitching and writhing before death			
DTH_0032 Alert Prone/ Death shot in the head			
ALT_0200 Alert Prone/ Crawl/Alert Prone			
Escape Motions with 1 Handed Weapon			
ESC_0018 Injured Stand /180/Injured Walk/Injured Run			
ESC_0019 Injured Stand /180/ Injured Run/Injured Stand			
ESC_0020 Injured Stand /180/ Injured Stand/Injured Walk/Injured Stand			
ESC_0004 Injured Run			
ESC_0007 Injured Run /Injured Walk			

FIGURE 10.1   A daily shot list prepared by GMC Studios for our game *CARRION*.

You have already given your motions a priority in order for them to be processed, and that same priority can be used when organizing your daily shot lists. Motions that are needed for the game should be captured before fluff motions; in case you get behind schedule, you will capture the important motions.

The complexity or difficulty of each motion also needs to be considered. It is not smart to have a stunt performer performing difficult stunt moves first. If he gets hurt, you won't be able to use him for the remainder of your motions. Instead, have him perform the bulk of your motions first, saving the difficult stunts for later in the week.

The time of day should be considered along with the difficulty of the motion. Early in the morning, it is not smart to have the performer trying hard ballistic motions. Instead, give him some time to loosen up and stretch. Do this even if he has had time to stretch prior to starting the capture session. Something as harmless sounding as a pulled muscle can be catastrophic to your capture, not to mention to the performer. Another bad time to schedule ballistic motions is right after the lunch break. It isn't easy getting tackled, performing stunts, or trying to perform hard running motions on a full stomach. Remember that the performer's comfort will affect the quality of his performance.

It is generally better to group similar motions together. This is done for a couple of reasons. First, it helps you make sure you haven't forgotten to capture a motion. Secondly, it is easier for the motion performer to get the feel for a particular motion group, giving a more consistent performance.

Performer fatigue should also be accounted for. Many motions take a toll on the performer's body, either from pounding or from hard stopping, and you need to be sensitive to this. If your performer looks tired or isn't executing as well as he was earlier in the day or in previous day, ask him if he is tired. If he is, schedule a day of light or easier motions; you may even want to give him a later check-in time the next morning so that he can get some more rest. Sometimes motions that don't seem to be fatiguing can be after a half-day of them, so pay attention to his energy level. Diet may play a part in his performance, so ask your performer if there are any special dietary needs he has. For instance, he may be a vegetarian; if so, when the motion studio has lunch catered, make sure they provide a vegetarian dish.

The coordinating of the performers also needs to be planned for in the daily shot list. Your project may involve several performers, some of whom need to interact together during the capture. For example, if you are capturing a sports game, you may need offensive and defensive players blocking each other or boxing each other out, so both performers need to be at the studio on the same day and at the same time. For the *Quarterback Club™ 2004* motion shoot, we captured five sport performers and two stunt performers motion for the game. Only three of them were on the set at any one time, so we needed to schedule their travel to coincide with our daily shot list. A capture like this not only puts pressure on you to capture all the needed motions, but it also has the added pressure of capturing certain motions on specific days; otherwise the performer will not be available.

MISCELLANEOUS ISSUES

There is also some backup information that you should make sure you have available while on-set during the capture. Be sure to take work phone numbers (including extensions) and mobile and home phone numbers of managers or other team members from your company who are not attending the capture, in case you need to have them answer a question or help you solve a problem. Not being able to communicate with the right people when you need them can cause delays or force you to make an uninformed decision that affects the quality of your project. Just because you are the one at the capture session does not mean that you have the answers to all the questions or problems, so you shouldn't feel bad to use your other team members as a resource if you need to. Unfortunately, this kind of situation happens more often than you might think. Something as simple as having contact numbers on hand can save you a lot of headaches during the capture and help you capture the motion your project needs. At a capture session, it is better to have too much information and not need it than to need more information than you have.

The final issues to check before your capture session are to double-check your travel itinerary and the itinerary of the motion performers, along with checking that the motion studio has all the props and supplies you need for your capture. If you mailed props, had the studio build props, or shipped supplies, make sure they have arrived prior to your capture. Most likely it wasn't your job to schedule the travel, but you are the one it affects if it is not handled correctly, so make sure the performers' travel times are correct and that they know where they are going and when they need to be there. The less they have to worry about, the better, so pick them up or arrange for someone from the studio to be waiting for them.

CONCLUSION

- Always bring reference material for yourself and your performers. This will better help them understand your needs and help get them into character or mimic the performance you are requesting.

- Make sure your props are taken care of and will best suit your needs.

- Consider the props' weight, orientation, and size and how it affects the performer's safety.

- There are several factors to consider when planning your daily shot lists: priority of motion, complexity of the motion, time of day, motion groupings, performer fatigue, and performer schedules.

- Make sure you have contact phone numbers for all the people not attending the capture that you may need to communicate with.

- If you are traveling, double-check your itinerary and travel plans.

11

THE MOTION CAPTURE SESSION

Job Number: GMC123-456

CAPTURE SESSION TRIAL NOTES

Capture Date: 02-28-04
Client Name: Quality Games Inc.
Project Name: CARRION Day 3
Tape #: 03

M#	props	Motion Name	T#	timecode	Notes
DTH_0200		Death (eaten on ground)	1	00:05:31:00	TEMP MARKER ON RIGHT HIP starting on mats; **good**
			2	00:08:32:00	starts on mats; jeff pulls him; might be okay but not sure so we are going again
			3	00:12:28:00	starting on mats; moved them in the capture volume more; **keep**
ALT_0375		Alert stance/damage shot in back	1	00:22:29:00	TEMP MARKER ON RIGHT HIP starting on mats; 1-not much action 2-same as first one 3-better; **keep 3rd**
ALT_0376		Alert stance/damage (upper body backwards)	1	00:26:11:00	TEMP MARKER ON RIGHT HIP starting on mats; 1-not much action; 2-good **keep 2nd**
ALT_0377		Alert stance/damage (upper body forwards)	1	00:27:49:00	TEMP MARKER ON RIGHT HIP starting on mats; bends forward 1-good; **keep**
ALT_0378		Alert stance/damage (shot in back-snap torso forward, arms back)	1	00:31:52:00	TEMP MARKER ON RIGHT HIP starting on mats; jeff pulls him forward to the ground; then back up to alert stance; 1-didn't get up to alert stance; 2-good **keep 2nd**
ALT_0379		Alert stance/damage (fly forward; face first. Land on chest)	1	00:35:10:00	TEMP MARKER ON RIGHT HIP starting on mats; jeff pulls him forward; then back up to alert stance; **keep**
ALT_0380		Alert stance/damage shot in back	1	00:36:59:00	TEMP MARKER ON RIGHT HIP starting on mats; good action; **keep**
ALT_0381		Alert stance/damage (upper body backwards)	1	00:40:42:00	TEMP MARKER ON RIGHT HIP starting on mats; 1-not broad action; 2-bigger action-put hand in air; 3-good **keep 3rd**

If you have never been to a motion capture session, it can seem overwhelming. This is especially true if you are unorganized, but after reading this book that won't be the case. This chapter covers what you can expect during a capture session and some tips and trick to help you capture motions that will be easily blended together seamlessly.

GMC Studios, the motion capture studio that we used for our game *CARRION*, included in their preproduction meeting what their typical capture day consists of (see Chapter 8, "Selecting a Motion Capture Studio"). This is not a firm schedule for a capture day and can be altered within reason to suit the client's scheduling needs. Remember that it is common for most motion studios to charge more per day if you want to capture on weekend days. As you can see, a full capture day is around a 10-hour day for the motion studio crew, with about seven and a half hours of that actual capture time. This too may be different, depending on the studio you are working with, so you need to ask how many capture hours a day consists of when inquiring about a bid. The motion performer also has a long day and is performing motions for seven and a half hours, so it is not surprising that fatigue will affect your daily shot list.

WHAT A TYPICAL CAPTURE DAY MAY CONSIST OF

8:15 a.m.   Studio crew arrives.
- Calibrate capture system
- Prepare capture volume for the capture session
- Prepare catering for the day

8:30 a.m.   Motion performer(s) arrives.
- Performers are prepped for the day
- Markers attached
- Performer gets warmed up

9:00 a.m.   Client arrives.
- Notifies motion studio of changes to daily shot list

9:30 a.m.   Capture session begins.

12:30–1:15   Break for lunch.
- Usually catered in studio or on location
- Length of break determined by the client

1:30 p.m.   Capture session resumes.

6:00 p.m.   Capture session wraps.
- Client and performers can leave
- Motion studio crew has post-shoot meeting
- Motion studio crew backs up captured data

Even though the motion studio allows you to arrive later than the motion performer, it is better if you arrive at the same time. If you and the performer have traveled to do the capture, it is recommended that you chauffeur the performer to and from the capture. This way you can make sure he is on time, and you can assess how he is feeling that morning so that if needed you can rearrange your daily shot list. Another nice thing about this type of arrangement is that it gives you time to build more of a rapport with the performer.

After introductions with the motion studio staff on the first morning of your capture, one of the first things you need to do is learn the motion studio's shoot terminology. If this was not covered during the preproduction phone call, you should do it before starting your capture session.

The additional noise on a motion capture set is a funny thing. At a lot of motion capture sessions, it is so quiet that you can almost hear a pin drop, but a capture session is not the same as a movie set. Sound is not being recorded, except maybe on the session videotape, so coaching the performer as he is doing the motions is highly recommended. This of course assumes that coaching is needed and depends on the individual motion. Playing music, as long as it isn't too loud, is also a good idea to lighten the atmosphere during a capture. As long as the additional talking or music isn't distracting to the motion performer and doesn't hinder the director and motion studio staff from communicating effectively, it is perfectly acceptable.

Even though you are hoping for a more relaxed atmosphere, you do not want your capture session to be open to anyone who wants to wander in. For the most part you should have a closed set; this is mostly for the performer's comfort, but also to protect the confidentiality of your project and to set something of a professional working environment. Your performer may be distracted by people wandering in and out, and he may be self-conscious about performing in front of others not on the project. It is common for motion studios to give tours to potential clients and to bring a guest or two into a capture session briefly. When this happens, they are usually quiet and unobtrusive, and they don't stay long. If this proves to be too much of a hindrance to your capture, just ask them if you can have a closed set, and they will happily comply.

If your capture session is a multiple-day capture, the first half-day of your capture may be used as preparation time for you and the studio to make sure you have everything you need to progress along smoothly over the course of the capture. We talked in Chapter 2, "Motion Capture and Your Project," about estimating the number of days you will need to capture your motions. In our example game, *CARRION*, we want to capture 700 in-game motions and 50 cinematic motions, with an estimate of 100 motions captured per day, so it would be logical to schedule a seven and a half-day capture. Doing this, however, does not take into account any on-set preparation, getting behind schedule, or stunt motions that generally take more time than standard motions. For these reasons, we scheduled an eight and a half-day capture to get the 750 motions we needed. The first half-day is a prep day with only a few motions captured. Motions such as walks, the core positions, jogs, and runs are generally the best motions to capture first. Also, simple motions such as turns and transitions between core motions should also be captured at this time.

Simple motions are good to start with to help the motion performer get used to what he needs to do. Simple motions also tend to go quickly, so you can capture multiple motions and get ahead of your schedule on the first day.

Remember that it is common for the motion studio to charge you a stage fee for every day of your capture. This fee reserves their studio for you, so you pay whether you use it or not. If you schedule a seven-day capture and finish your capture in six days, you still pay the stage fee for the unused seventh day. By the same token, if you only schedule six days and need an additional day or two, the studio might already be reserved for another client and not be available.

Another area that you may want to handle during this half-day prep time, if you have not already thought of it, is to modify or alter the physique of the motion performer to best represent your game character. During the *Turok*™ *Evolution*™ motion shoot, we added foam pads under the motion performer's arms so that he could not rest his arms all the way down close to his torso. We decided to do this because the game's characters were more heroic in build and had disproportionately thicker torsos. By padding our performer, we saved time in the post-animation process because our animators didn't have to spend time pulling the characters arms out of his torso. When House of Moves was hired to capture motion for the movie *Mighty Joe Young*, the motion performer's physique was altered when he wore a gorilla suit for the capture. House of Moves president, Tom Tolles, explains that this helped the performer get into character and more closely mimic the motion that the client was seeking.

Over the years we have discovered that as highly technical as a motion capture session is, having some simple objects can really help make your job easier. We like to refer to this as "high tech meets low tech," because items like tape, chalk, cardboard, permanent markers, bean bags, and box cutters have proven to be very helpful.

One of your main goals during a capture session should not only be to capture the motions that you need, but also to capture them in a way that will help save your animators time in the post capture process. If you have ever worked with motion capture data that was captured without taking into account the game's response time and without being planned to make it easier on the animators, then you know how frustrating and time-consuming it can be to work with. Motions that are just captured without thought can double or triple the time needed in the post capture process. One of the main factors that will take the realism out of the animations in many games is when the character's feet slide or skate.

Skating feet: When a character's feet slide in a physically unnatural way on the ground whether he is moving or idle. This is also sometimes referred to as *sliding feet*.

Because of this, the motion performer's foot placement is very important, and by using some of these "low tech" items, you can have the performer's foot placement more consistent from motion to motion. Before you even begin to capture motions, get together with the motion performer and make stencils for his foot placement. Have him stand on a sheet of cardboard in the various core positions that he will need to begin and end most motions in. Make sure that his foot placement matches your needs but is also comfortable for him to be able to re-create after performing a motion. This is a good time to use those digital photos, Polaroids, or screen grab references that we talked about in Chapter 10, "Final Preparation Before the Capture Session." Trace around the performer's feet on the cardboard, and cut them out using the box cutters to create a stencil. Make sure you label the stencil so that you know what core position it is for. Once you have foot stencils for the core positions, you can use them as references during your capture. Mark the foot position on the floor using chalk or tape to give the performer and yourself reference points to start or end in. Do not leave the cardboard stencil on the ground while capturing a motion, especially if the performer is executing a motion such as stopping after a run. It is too easy to slip on a piece of cardboard while trying to stop your momentum.

All this preparation may seem like overkill, but taking these steps will help eliminate possible problems in the post capture process. Foot stencils will make the process of blending the motions together easier for the animators because they will help the motion performer be more consistent with this body position.

If you haven't already established each person's job responsibilities for the capture session, it should be done at this time. The motion studio staff already have their job responsibilities worked out, so this refers only to you (the client) and your people. In "The Preproduction Meeting or Conference Call" section of Chapter 8, GMC Studios, the motion capture studio we are using, briefly covered some of the job responsibilities for the capture.

JOB RESPONSIBILITIES DURING THE CAPTURE

It is the client's responsibility to notify the motion studio's motion capture director of any changes/additions to the capture session each morning before shooting begins.

It is the client's and the motion studio's motion capture director's responsibilities to co-direct the motion performer. The client is actively directing the performer and looking for the desired effect, while the motion studio's motion capture director is ensuring that the motion is technically sound.

It is the client's responsibility to select which take of each motion they want processed for delivery. It is also his responsibility to communicate this to the motion studio's motion capture director.

It is the motion studio's motion capture director's responsibility to keep track of all takes, selected takes, and changes to the motion list on his trial notes.

It is the client's director's and the motion studio's motion capture director's responsibility to communicate with each other to help ensure the trial notes are accurate.

It is the QA artist/editor's responsibility to check the quality of each selected take on-set.

CLIENT'S CAPTURE RESPONSIBILITIES

The best way to help assure a successful capture is for everyone to work together as a team, so job titles really aren't important. However, each person should be responsible for certain tasks. Since there aren't any formal titles given to the client's capture team, we will give them some in an attempt to define their responsibilities. We will just give them the simple titles of director, first assistant, and second assistant.

Directing a motion capture session is a lot more complicated than calling out "action" and "cut." The director's responsibilities include actively directing the performer, looking for the desired effect, and selecting which version or take of each motion he would like processed and delivered. It is also his responsibility to communicate with the motion studio's motion capture director to help ensure the trial notes are accurate. Each studio has its own terminology that it likes to use during a shoot to communicate with the client and the performer. It is important that the client, the motion studio staff, and the motion performer are all able to communicate, so the director needs to know the terminology and the order that it is used in. Here is an example of some possible terminology.

Camera: This lets the motion studio staff know when to start the cameras.

Action: This lets the motion performer know when to begin his performance.

Scale: This lets the motion performer know he needs to stop action and get into a neutral pose. Scaling is done to capture an additional calibration frame that is sometimes used if the motion was an aggressive move such as a football tackle. It is sometimes called a *Da Vinci pose* or a *T stance*.

Cut: This lets the motion studio staff and motion performer know when to stop the cameras.

The first assistant's responsibilities include helping the director communicate with the motion performer and making sure that the motions captured are the desired motions for the project. This position is best filled by the lead designer or possibly another animator or designer. The first assistant will take over for the director if he is called away from the set and will help the director co-direct the capture if needed.

The second assistant's responsibilities are to support the director and the first assistant with the capture and to learn how to best organize and conduct a motion shoot. It is best if the second assistant is an animator or designer who will one day organize and run a capture on a future project. By taking a second assistant, you can help assure that more animators get capture session experience, so future project can also be handled professionally.

It only makes sense to have one person ultimately responsible to make final decisions when questions and problems occur. The director will run the capture and the other two will assist, but we have also found it very successful to have two people co-direct if it is a complicated or multiple-day capture session. Co-directing is when two people split the director's responsibilities to help the capture run more smoothly.

Another benefit of having several people work the capture session is so that you can have several sets of eyes watching each motion. When a motion performer executes a motion, it happens quickly, so it is difficult to see everything that is happening. Having several sets of eyes watching particular areas can help. One person can watch the performer's hips, another can look to see his foot position, and a third can watch the overall performance. On certain motions, making sure the performer's hips are angled or positioned correctly can be very helpful when the animator tries to blend motions together during the post capture process. For example, let's say you have a motion where the performer is running while carrying a weapon; he turns his torso to his right while firing the weapon, and he then gets shot and is spun around, coming to rest on the ground. If the performer's hips are already turned or shifted to the right too much as he enters the capture volume, then making a seamless blend from the run cycle to the turn can be more difficult. It is natural for the performer to be thinking about what he needs to do while executing the motion; in doing so, he may sometimes start the motion early. In this case there is a little trick you can use to help the performer. Have a person or prop placed just outside the capture volume; tell the performer that when he reaches that point, turn and execute the motion. By having a reference point, the performer can focus on entering the volume with his hips square and in a solid run. Even with his hips not square, the blend may be an easy one to make, but you may need extra frames to make the blend, and extra frames can affect the user controls and response time.

Recent technological advances have helped to make your job easier during a capture session. One of the advances that have helped the client the most is the real-time or semi-real-time playback system, and you should use it to your advantage during a capture. Whether a playback system is considered real time or not depends on your definition of the term *real time*. Does it really matter if you have to wait one or two minutes after the motion is captured before being able to see it? Only a few years ago a real-time playback system was a luxury during an optical motion capture session, but now it is a necessity if you want the most effective capture possible. Watching a motion on a character mesh immediately after capturing it is very helpful because you can review the motion before moving on to another. It is best if you view it on your actual game mesh, as opposed to on a generic mesh. Having your character's mesh will help you see how much clipping is happening during certain motions and can also help the motion performer get into character. According to Matt Madden, Giant Studios' VP of production and development, with Giant Studios' motion capture system, "our clients can see the motion on their own skeleton and geometry in real time. This lets them see exactly what their motion looks like during the capture."

Clipping: When objects in a video game that are suppose to be solid pass through other solid objects. This can include a character passing through floors and walls or when body parts pass through each other, such as an arm passing through a torso. It also includes the camera passing through walls.

Viewing the playback on your game mesh will also give you a chance to see how the mesh's weighting holds up during the motions. A real-time playback system allows you to see the motion from several angles, and you can check body, hip, and feet positions. Remember not to spend too much time viewing the motion, because you want to stay on schedule. Being able to use a real-time playback system easily also allows you the luxury of taking a smaller team to the capture session if you choose; however, doing this does not give you the ability to train other animators or designers in how to conduct a capture.

Another area where you and the motion studio need to use the same terminology is when you are communicating which version, or take, of a motion you want to be processed. Some studios use the word *best* to indicate which version is to be processed, and another studio may use the word *keep* or *select*. All three of these terms describe the version of a motion you want the studio to process and deliver to you for your project.

Take: An individual version of a motion that you are capturing. You may capture several versions of a motion before you select the desired one.

Best: The version or take that the client selects to be processed by the motion capture studio. This is also sometimes called a *keep* or a *select*.

Besides organization, communication is one of the biggest issues that you need to address during the capture. As the director, it is imperative that the motion performer understand exactly what you are looking for and that you communicate to the motion studio staff. It is the motion studio's responsibility to take accurate notes during the capture; however, it is the client director's responsibility to communicate effectively to the studio. If you and the performer work well together but you don't communicate well with the studio staff, the studio may not get its trial notes correct. If there is miscommunication during the capture and the trail notes are incorrect, then getting the proper motions processed will be difficult. Figure 11.1 is an example of a motion studio's trial notes.

Trial Notes: The records taken by the motion capture studio during the capture session to be used after the capture to help process motions.

Job Number: GMC123-456	CAPTURE SESSION TRIAL NOTES

Capture Date: 02-28-04
Client Name: Quality Games Inc.
Project Name: CARRION Day 3
Tape #: 03

M#	props	Motion Name	T#	timecode	Notes
DTH_0200		Death (eaten on ground)	1	00:05:31:00	TEMP MARKER ON RIGHT HIP starting on mats; **good**
			2	00:08:32:00	starts on mats; jeff pulls him; might be okay but not sure so we are going again
			3	00:12:28:00	starting on mats; moved them in the capture volume more; **keep**
ALT_0375		Alert stance/damage shot in back	1	00:22:29:00	TEMP MARKER ON RIGHT HIP starting on mats; 1-not much action 2-same as first one 3-better; **keep 3rd**
ALT_0376		Alert stance/damage (upper body backwards)	1	00:26:11:00	TEMP MARKER ON RIGHT HIP starting on mats; 1-not much action; 2-good **keep 2nd**
ALT_0377		Alert stance/damage (upper body forwards)	1	00:27:49:00	TEMP MARKER ON RIGHT HIP starting on mats; bends forward 1-good; **keep**
ALT_0378		Alert stance/damage (shot in back-snap torso forward, arms back)	1	00:31:52:00	TEMP MARKER ON RIGHT HIP starting on mats; jeff pulls him forward to the ground; then back up to alert stance; 1-didn't get up to alert stance; 2-good **keep 2nd**
ALT_0379		Alert stance/damage (fly forward; face first. Land on chest)	1	00:35:10:00	TEMP MARKER ON RIGHT HIP starting on mats; jeff pulls him forward; then back up to alert stance; **keep**
ALT_0380		Alert stance/damage shot in back	1	00:36:59:00	TEMP MARKER ON RIGHT HIP starting on mats; good action; **keep**
ALT_0381		Alert stance/damage (upper body backwards)	1	00:40:42:00	TEMP MARKER ON RIGHT HIP starting on mats; 1-not broad action; 2-bigger action-put hand in air; 3-good **keep 3rd**

FIGURE 11.1 GMC Studios' trial notes taken during production of our game *CARRION*.

This is one of the reasons why it is highly recommended that you (the client) also take your own notes during the capture. With all the noise, confusion, and changes made on set, you can't expect the studio staff to be perfect, so if you take your own notes, they can serve as a backup for the studio's trial notes. The main reason for taking your own notes, however, is for you to use them to update your motion database before the animation process begins.

It might seem like a good idea to record your capture (or trial) notes on a laptop so that you can update your motion database as you go along, but unless your database is extremely organized and easy to access and you are a good typist and are able to change your focus quickly, then taking notes by hand is generally easier. A motion capture session is a hands-on, dynamic event, and a laptop generally does not give you the freedom you need on the set to interact with the performer, co-workers, and studio staff in an efficient manner.

The main reason for you to take good notes is because you will need to update your motion database when you finish the capture. The only way you will be able to remember all the changes you made is from your notes. It may be tempting to assign the note taking to the second assistant, but this is not recommended. If you do this, he will focus only on taking notes and not be free to help and observe all the other aspects of the capture. Remember that the second assistant's main job is to learn how to conduct an efficient and effective capture session.

In addition to good communication, staying on schedule is of the utmost importance. Reevaluate your schedule at least once every half-day. This is easy to do during the lunch break and while relaxing after the capture wraps for the day. If you are behind schedule, make sure you capture all the motions that are critical to your project, pushing the wanted motions back in case you run out of time. You can estimate that you will be able to capture 100 finished motions a day; however, this is an estimate based on the complexity of the motions and the prep time needed for each one. If you are behind schedule but you have a lot of basic motions remaining, you may not really be behind schedule, since you may be able to capture 120 or more of these kinds of motions.

As tempting as it may be to stay or get ahead of schedule, you should consider capturing at least two good takes of every motion before moving on to the next motion. Even if the first take is perfect, capture another one as a safety take. It won't cost you any additional money to capture a safety take because you only pay for processed seconds of motion, not captured seconds. A safety take's only disadvantage is that it requires more of your time and adds to the performer's fatigue. The reason for a safety take is just in case the captured data becomes corrupted or is in someway unusable. Without another acceptable version, you will be out of luck if the data is unusable.

Safety take: An extra acceptable version of a motion captured in case the desired motion data is unusable.

When capturing cycle motions, make sure the motion performer starts well outside of the capture volume so that he is moving at a constant speed when he enters the volume. You also want to make sure he does not start to decelerate before he leaves the volume. This is especially important when capturing running cycles. Have a designated stopping line outside the volume that he is trying to run past. Because of the size of most capture volumes, a motion performer generally only gets three to five steps in the capture volume before exiting, so it is important that he maintain a constant speed all the way through. After the capture you will need to make a cycling motion from this running motion, and you need to have a constant root speed for a good cycle. If the motion capture studio you are using does not have enough space for your performer to run through, there are a couple of tricks you can try to capture a running motion. You may try to capture them running on a treadmill. If you want to try this method, keep in mind that the old manual treadmills may actually work better than an electric one. With electric treadmills, the performer only has to keep up with the machine, but with a manual one the performer has to generate force, so the posture his body will take will more closely resemble the posture of someone who is actually running. Another trick you can try is to have the performer jog through the capture volume and then have an animator speed up the timing and reposition his posture to make it look more like a run. Either one of these will not give you the quality that having the performer actually run through the volume will, but sometimes you must make do with the situation.

If your project uses more than one motion performer, capture the basic cycle motions you need, in this case the walk, jog, run, and backpedal, from each of your performers. These basic cycles are not very time consuming to capture and will give you a greater variety of motions to choose from when making the frame range selections. Later you may decide you like the walk from one performer and the jog from another. Slight variations of often-seen motions are also a great way to add an additional level of realism to your game. Let's say you are making a game of baseball. If you have two or three different styles of a run cycle for the players to use, it will give the players more of an individual personality and help them seem less mechanical. Introducing some variation in a game's motion can be a simple technique you use to spice up a new version of an old game.

If you are capturing transition motions for your project, pay close attention to the transitions that will take the character from the cycle motions to the idle motions and from the idles to the cycles. Have the motion performer step with the same foot first when he is stopping. In other words, if he plants his right foot first when going from the walk to the stand, make sure he does the same when going from the jog to the stand. Have all the cycle motions go into the idle motions on the same foot. Also make sure he starts lifting the same foot first to transition from the idle to the cycle motions. In the next chapter, you will see how this will help your character stop more quickly in the game.

Conclusion

- Capture session days are long days.
- You might schedule the first half-day as prep time so that the remainder of your capture goes as smoothly as possible.
- Basic job responsibilities might be spelled out in your contract.
- The client needs to know what job responsibilities are expected from them by the motion studio. The client should also have the job responsibilities of its capture team worked out prior to the capture day.
- You need to know what terminology the motion capture studio likes to use to communicate during the capture.
- Real-time or semi–real-time playback systems are extremely helpful during a capture. They can even be considered a necessity.
- You need to communicate which version or take of each motion you select to be processed by the studio.
- Even though the motion studio takes trial notes, you should take your own notes for each motion captured. They serve as a backup and will be added to your motion database after the capture.
- Staying on schedule is very important, so budget your time wisely.
- You may want to capture a safety take for each motion before moving on to another motion.

12 POST PRODUCTION

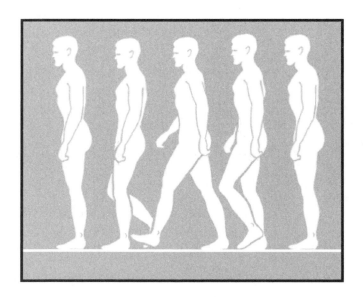

There is some terminology that is unique and can get confusing when dealing with motion capture data. The word "edit" is a generic term that refers to one or more processes performed on a motion file. Editing a motion file can include trimming of frames, pinning feet or hands, blending a motion into another, and animating the captured data. The word edit is often referred to as "animating" by some animators, while others don't think that working with motion capture data is truly animation. Regardless of what you call it, editing a motion file consists of altering the timing and look of an animation file, so animators are usually the ones to make the changes.

Editing a motion: A generic phrase that consists of one or more processes that alter the timing or appearance of a motion capture file. Editing a motion can include trimming of frames, pinning feet or hands, blending a motion into another, and animating over the top of the captured data. Editing is also sometimes referred to as animating a motion.

When an animator edits captured data, there are two different ways the animation software can deal with the data: destructive editing and non-destructive editing.

Destructive editing: A process of animation where the original keyframes are lost or destroyed when the animator alters the captured data.

Non-destructive editing: A process of animation where the changes made by the animator are made over the top of the original keyframes so that they are not lost or destroyed during editing.

Non-destructive editing occurs when the animator makes edits to the data on a different layer than the original data exists. The edit is made over the top and not directly on the original data, so it stays intact. Destructive editing occurs because the edits or changes are made directly to the captured data. Some software packages allow animators to work on layers, while others don't. Even if the software package you use does not deal with layers, your data will not be lost if you save the file using a different name. Adding rev (short for revision) and a numeric to the end of the filename after changes are made is a good way to make sure you have not truly lost keyframe information.

- Example of a filename before changes are made:

  `ALT_0100_shoulder_roll_right.amc`

- Example of a filename after a change is made:

  `ALT_0100_shoulder_roll_right_rev01.amc`

After your motion capture session is completed, it may be difficult to get motivated to work, but unfortunately your job is far from complete. If you approached your project properly, you have spent a few weeks, maybe even months, planning and organizing, followed by several long, stressful days at the capture session trying to assure all the motions are captured properly, and even though you are tired you still have a lot to do. There is still organizing, updating, scheduling, frame range selections, editing, and maintaining the database to be done before the project is complete.

FRAME RANGE SELECTIONS

One of the first and most important jobs you need to do, if you weren't able to do it during the capture session, is frame range selection. Normally, frame range selection is done after the capture session is completed, but if you are lucky enough to have a small capture session or if your capture days are fairly easy, you may be able to do the selections before leaving. The name *frame range selection* is deceiving because at this point you need to think number of seconds, not number of frames or number of motions. The frame ranges that you choose should consist of the needed motion data plus some handle frames.

Frame range selection: The process of choosing the number of seconds (or frames) of each motion captured that you would like processed and delivered.

Handle frames: The extra frames at the beginning or end of the needed motion used to blend one motion file to or from another. Handles are also sometimes referred to as *leads*, *blend frames*, or *head and tail frames*.

Depending on how your contract with the motion capture studio is handled, a large part of the cost of most motion capture sessions is based on the number of seconds processed per motion. As mentioned earlier, most motion capture studios base their contract price on an estimated or average number of seconds per motion, and any motion over that estimated number of seconds is billed at a higher price, so naturally you need to try to keep the number of seconds you select to be processed to only the needed frames plus a few handle frames. See Chapter 8, "Selecting a Motion Capture Studio," covering the motion capture contract for more information on costs.

It can't be emphasized enough how important it is to make good frame range selections. If done correctly, it can save your company a lot of money. If done poorly, it can add three times or more to the original contract price of your capture session. It is also critical that the frame range selections be done as soon as possible because the motion studio can't process and deliver your captured motions until they are done.

Let's use our game *CARRION* as an example. Our motions were captured at a capture frequency of 120 frames per second (fps), but we want the processed motions delivered at 60 fps because our game will run at that speed. When we make our frame range selections, we are viewing the raw captured data, which means it is running at 120 fps. This is important because we want to stay under or right on the average number of seconds established in our contract. Our contract states that our average number of seconds is three to five seconds, so we don't want to go over five seconds or it will cost us more money. Five seconds at 120 fps means that we can select 600 frames per motion without it costing us more than the price on the contract. Keep in mind that a motion that lasts for 600 frames when we make the frame range selections will be delivered to us as only 300 frames because the delivered motion is now running at 60 fps.

Depending on the specifics of your contract, selecting a smaller number of frames for the motion studio to process can save you a lot of money, but there is another benefit. In the past, companies have had a hard time justifying the cost of using motion capture because so much of the captured motion was not used. By making good frame range selections, you lower the percentage of wasted motion versus used motion. By saying that you used 90–95% of the motion you captured instead of 60% makes the cost seem more worthwhile to management.

It used to be standard practice for motion capture studios to process an entire motion for the client. This means that every possible frame that was captured was also processed, so the client did not need to do frame range selections. Working this way, however, was a huge waste of time and money for both the motion studio and the client. If you know that frame numbers 1 to 40 and 640 to 875 will never be used, then there is no need for the motion studio to take the time and pay someone to process them, and there is no need for you to pay for them.

How many handle frames should you include? The number of frames that you need for a handle may vary, depending on the individual motion and on how your animators are going to blend the motions. Because the transitions between motions in video games normally need to happen very quickly, you do not need a lot of extra frames to use for blends, but it is always better to have too many frames than not enough. It is common for animators to need only one good frame per handle to blend with. With that said, you may want to err on the side of caution and select anywhere from 1 to 10 frames for each handle. If you are not sure how many handle frames to include, take as many seconds (or frames) per motion as your contract allows. If the motion is coming or going to a cycle motion, you may want to select long handles so that you are sure you have enough frames to ease the root speed into the cycle. See Figure 12.1 for an example of frame range selections.

For some cycling motions such as runs, jogs, and walks, it is best to take the entire captured motion range and not worry about the handles. With cycle motions it is important to get consistent root (hip) movement and complete cycles of the legs, so by taking the entire range you have more choices to select a good cycle from. With cycle motions such as a side shuffle, you might not want to choose the entire motion if it is an excessively long take. Instead, it may be better to select a frame range that includes three or four shuffle cycles for processing. You can then choose the best cycle to make your side shuffle loop from.

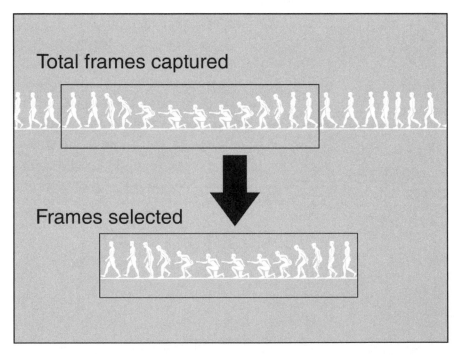

FIGURE 12.1   The total number of frames captured for a motion and the number of frames we selected, including handles, to be processed.

How to Make Frame Range Selections

How you do your frame range selections depends on the motion studio that you are working with. Frame range selections used to be done using the time-coded videotape shot during the capture session, but doing it this way poses some problems. First of all, you are at the mercy of the camera angle that the motions were video-taped from, so it may be difficult to see when the motion per-former is fully in the capture volume or when he is in the actual position you need. To counteract this, you can have the motion studio videotape the capture session from multiple angles, but like everything else this will cost you more money. It is also more time consuming for you to go through multiple tapes to find the correct camera angle you need to make a good selection.

Over the past few years it has become common to do the frame range selections using an animation viewer or an animation soft-ware package such as Kaydara's MOTIONBUILDER 5.0™ (their most recent update to FILMBOX 3.5). MOTIONBUILDER 5.0 is an all-around animation package, but many companies use it to edit and animate their motion capture files because it supports all the major motion capture formats and has a large number of motion capture-specific tools. House of Moves has its own proprietary software called DivaView™, which is a simplified motion viewer version of its motion editing software, Diva 2.0™, for their clients to use to make frame range selections. This is nice because it allows House of Moves' clients to make their frame range selections over the Internet. DivaView is a motion viewer program that allows anyone to browse and order motions from House of Moves' stock motion libraries. The big advantage to doing your frame range se-lections with a viewer or animation package versus videotape is that it allows you to view the motion from any angle and see when the performer is fully in the capture volume, thus making your frame range selections more accurate.

It may be tempting for you to do your frame range selections while on the set and immediately after each motion is captured, but this is not recommended unless your capture session is a very small one (maybe 25 to 50 motions). Stopping after each motion, evaluating it, and making the selection slows down your shoot, and you may risk running out of time to capture all your needed motions. Stopping and starting a lot also makes it difficult for the motion performer to stay focused and get into a rhythm. If for some reason you can't capture motion one day or you finish early, then you may want to get ahead and do some frame range selections at that time.

If your project requires hundreds or thousands of motions to be captured, you may need to make your frame range selections in several sections. This is why you assigned a priority to each motion in your database. You should make the frame range selections to the highest priority motions first and then work your way down the list. The motion studio also works from your priority list when processing your files.

Core motions should always be the highest priority because they will be the first motions you will need to edit. If the programming staff on your project is organized and has a plan for which motion files they are going to implement first, it is a good idea to check with the lead programmer to make sure he has not changed his mind as to which motions he will need first. If he has changed his mind, then your initial priority list may need to change accordingly. Coordinating which motions the programmers need first with the motions that are first delivered will help prevent a slowdown in your workflow, since having the programmers waiting on the animators to finish editing the motion files is not an efficient way to work.

As you submit the frame range selections to the motion capture studio, they will begin processing the motions. A schedule of delivery will be set up, but it is a good idea to check in with them every so often to see that they are still on schedule. If they fall behind schedule, it will directly affect your animator's schedule and possibly the project as a whole. One thing that could cause a motion studio to not deliver your motions on time is payment. It is common for delivery dates to be contingent on receiving payments from the client, so you need to see to it that your company meets its obligations to pay the motion studio as specified in your contract. If your company is in the habit of not paying on time, then you may be working for the wrong people. This might sound a bit extreme, but paying for services rendered is part of being a professional and can have a detrimental effect on your project.

UPDATING THE DATABASE

Another important and time-critical job that should be done upon returning from the capture session is to update your database. The sooner you do this the better, while the capture session is still fresh in your mind. Your database currently reflects the motions that you hoped to capture and not what was actually captured. It is common during a motion shoot to make changes to motions, re-name motions, add and delete motions, and so on, so your database needs to be updated with these changes. Any notes that were taken on particular motions should also be entered into the database at this time.

Use the ten-percent rule here. If you had to make changes to more than ten percent of the motions that you originally wanted to capture, then somehow you screwed up and didn't plan properly. In other words, a few changes during a capture session are acceptable and expected, but numerous changes can cause real problems later. It is difficult with everything happening during a capture session to think out changes in detail, so sometimes a change that seems correct at the time later turns out to be wrong. It is too difficult to make major changes to your motion list during a capture, which is why planning it out thoroughly beforehand is so important. Lead massive technical director for Weta Digital Ltd., John Haley, says, "advance preparation allows you more creative flexibility—you are able to concentrate on the creative performance instead of the organizational ones."

GETTING THE MOTIONS BACK FROM THE MOTION STUDIO

The first motions that you should get back from the motion studio are the core motions, along with the other highest-priority motions. When they are delivered, check them for quality. If you dealt with a quality motion capture studio, this generally isn't a problem, but sometimes there is a miscommunication, or a motion or two may slip through that wasn't processed correctly. If it isn't practical for you to check every motion delivered personally, tell the animators to check each motion all the way through for major problems before they begin to edit them. Check the Fcurves for spikes and play the motion through in slow motion.

There is a saying that we like to use when assessing the quality of motion capture data: "cosmetic not reconstructive surgery." This refers to the amount of work that you should have to do to the data once it is delivered to get it looking proper. It is not acceptable to get a motion back where the feet are skating, bones are rotated incorrectly, or there is a lot of jitter or noise in the motion. If you get motions like this back, you have a couple of choices.

Most motion editing software packages today have tools you can use to try and correct the problem yourself; however, if you are not familiar with which filters to use, you may find this a difficult procedure, and you may end up making it worse. If you do decide to correct the problems yourself, you may want to inform the motion studio that there is a problem in the quality level, depending on the types of problems you are seeing. Your other option is to send the motions back and have the motion studio correct the bad files. Sending a motion back may take some time, but it should not cost you any more money. Again, use the ten percent rule here; if ten percent or less of the motions need to be sent back or corrected, that is acceptable, however, if more than 10% of your captured motions are processed poorly, then the studio you are dealing with is not upholding an acceptable level of quality.

EDITING THE CORE MOTIONS

Your motions should be arranged in order of importance and edited accordingly. With that said, your order should be somewhat flexible to accommodate changes that occur in your project's schedule. The first stage, however, must be the core motions, and only after the core motions are edited and approved should the animators start to edit the rest of the motions. Some people may feel that, because recent animation packages such as Kaydara's MO-TIONBUILDER 5.0 and House of Moves' Diva 2.0 have made editing motion capture files so much easier than it has been in the past, it isn't necessary to have the core motion edited first. What these people are overlooking is that working on and completing the animations for a video game is a team effort that needs to be completed correctly so that others can do their jobs. By having the core motions completed first, the process becomes easier for the animators to follow. It also assures a more efficient work flow because one animator isn't waiting for another animator to finish editing a motion file that he needs to complete his work. You may be surprised how common this kind of uncoordinated work environment is at game companies.

One often overlooked detail that will make an impact on the look and quality of your project is to have well-planned core motions. Taking small details like momentum into account when planning the core motions can dramatically add to the look and flow of your game's animations. The body posture or look of your character should have been worked out prior to your capture session, but how the core motions flow and how they will blend to other motion files need to be worked out before the animators edit the remainder of the motion files. For quality control reasons and because of their importance to your game, it is best if the job of planning and editing the core motions is handled by one or two people. If you do decide to have the animators edit the core motions, have them edit the core motions first and then get together to critique the motions before they begin editing the remaining motions.

Idle Motions

When a character stops or idles in a video game, it is important that he continue to have some movement and is not completely still. It doesn't look correct to the eye to have a character go from movement to a completely stagnant pose. For most idle motions, we like to add some movement to the character's abdomen, chest, and shoulder areas to simulate breathing. Keep in mind that this breathing movement is exaggerated so that it can be seen on the screen. Humans have a diaphragm muscle, so we do not need to raise and lower our torso in an extreme way to breathe, but for the visual simulation of it in a video game we need to take some liberties and exaggerate the motion. You may even want to add some movement to the character's hips (referred to as his root). If you do add root movement, make sure it is relatively small and that it is consistent. If the character's root speeds up and slows down too extremely while idling or is not traveling on a smooth path over the course of a few frames, the movement will look awkward. A good example of an idle motion that requires some root movement would be a baseball batter waiting for the pitch. Batters tend to keep some movement so that they are ready and quicker to move when the pitch is delivered. In video games, idle motions are sometimes referred to as ready idle motions because the character is in a "ready" position and is waiting for input from the user.

> **Ready idle motion:** A looping motion that the character in a video game goes into when inactive and waiting for user input.

Depending on the type of animation (straight-ahead or pose-to-pose), many computer animators focus on the root movement first and then work their way down the chain, adding animation to the legs, torso, and arms before focusing on the secondary traits such as tail movement. Animator Alexander Omlansky, who animated the in-game motions for Acclaim Entertainment's Vexx™ character, says, "With straight-ahead animation, it is most important to get the motion on the root bone first, because most of the time your whole animation is based on it. This typically requires you to have a good imagination so that you can 'see' the whole animation even though you are only animating the root." When editing your core motions, approach them in the same way: Focus on getting a consistent, smooth root movement first and then move on to the legs and arms. Once you get the motion moving smoothly and the way you need it, then make sure the first frame of the motion is the best one to start on.

Remember that a looping motion begins and ends with the character in the exact same position, and this means that the root not only needs to move smoothly but must end up in the same position it started. Said another way, the first and last frame of a looping motion need to be identical frames. With idle motions, the character is not only in the exact same body position, but his root is located at the same world coordinates as he started in. Since cycle motions propel the character through space, when the character reaches the last frame, his body will be in the exact same position as the first frame, but his root coordinates will only be the same in two out of the three world coordinates. In our case we have our characters traveling on the z-axis, so at the end of a cycle motion, our character's root will have identical x and y coordinates, but a different z coordinate.

To create a loop, select a section of motion that has smooth root movement and then duplicate a frame and blend it into another frame in that section that it best corresponds with. This means that you find the next frame where the character's body position best matches the frame you are duplicating, and then you blend in the duplicated frame so that there are two identical frames. Once you've done this, check the root movement again to make sure it has not been altered too much. If the root is moving smoothly, check the rest of the body and make corrections if they are needed. Make sure the character's feet are not sliding, arms are not cutting into the torso or legs, and so on. You can also scale the timing of the loop to get the speed and look you desire. Let the loop play over and over and look for hitches in the movement or parts that move out of sync with the motion. Once you get the loop completed, the last remaining task is to select which frame the loop will begin with.

In addition to the consistency of the root, another factor that affects the smoothness of a core motion is the duration, or number of frames that it takes to complete the loop. For the most part, idle motions for video games are relatively short in duration; however, if there isn't a large range of motion, the idle can be longer and still respond well for the user. An idle motion that takes five seconds to complete its loop is probably too long if you are considering the user response time. No matter how long your idle motions are, however, there will be times when it is necessary to skip to or "pop" out of a core motion and to another motion file.

Pop: When one motion file needs to begin before the previous motion file has had time to complete its loop, or when a game does not have transition motion files and skips from one motion to another. This commonly happens in an attempt to speed up the response time, and when it does the character appears to skip or pop into a new position.

A pop or skip in a character's movement takes away from the feeling of realism, but there is something you can do to help minimize it when it does occur. Frame order will have an effect on how well your core motions will look, so if you choose the first frame wisely, your motions will pop less. It is beneficial if the first frame of an idle is when the character is in the middle of his range of motion. Doing this will help prevent a large pop when the motion file needs to cut directly to another motion file. If the user gives input to the character before an idle motion has completed its loop, a game often will cut directly to the end of the idle so that it can then transition smoothly to the next file. By skipping to the end of the motion, however, a pop will occur in the motion; on the other hand, it will be smaller and less noticeable because no matter what frame the idle is on, it only pops half the distance instead of the entire distance of the range of motion. Figure 12.2 illustrates the range of motion a character travels while breathing.

In Figure 12.2, we see that the character is in the standing, breathing idle motion. Our game, *CARRION*, runs at 60 fps, and we want the character to breathe casually, so our idle will be 120 frames in length. This allows the character one second to inhale and one second to exhale. If we want the character to appear out

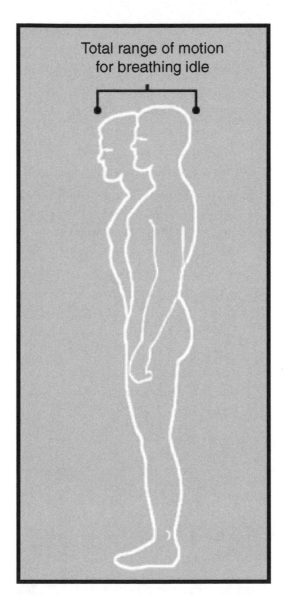

Total range of motion
for breathing idle

FIGURE 12.2 The range of motion the character travels while in the standing, breathing idle motion.

of breath, we could either shorten the number of frames, increase his range of motion while inhaling and exhaling, or both, to make him look like he is breathing heavier.

Another way to help reduce the severity of a pop is to take the character's momentum into account when deciding which frame will be the first frame of your idle motion. Although you are dealing with an idle motion, one of your goals as an animator is to make sure that the idle motions will transition into and out of the cycling motions seamlessly, so you need to consider the momentum of the character and make sure the movement of the idle motions flows in the same direction.

In our example game, *CARRION*, we have three basic cycle motions—the walk, jog, and run—that propel the character forward and only one cycle motion—the backpedal—moving the character backward. Because more motions propel the character forward, it will be smoother if the first frame of our idle motion is when the character is exhaling. When exhaling, the character's torso will move forward; this is the same direction that his momentum is going in the majority of the cycle motions. See Figure 12.3.

If the first frame of your idle motion is when the character is inhaling and therefore his torso is moving backward, then there will be a hitch or pop in the motion when the character's momentum changes direction abruptly. See Figure 12.4.

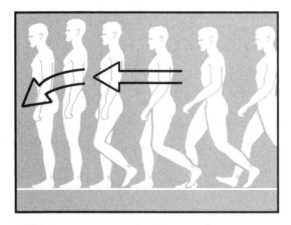

FIGURE 12.3 The direction of his momentum while exhaling is moving the same direction as his momentum while walking.

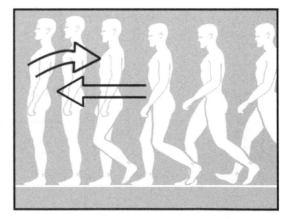

FIGURE 12.4 The direction of his momentum while inhaling is moving the opposite direction as his momentum while walking, which will create a pop when the motions transition together.

Cycle Motions

In Chapter 11, "The Motion Capture Session," we mentioned that it is extremely important during the capture session to make sure the motion performer tries to maintain a constant speed as he goes through the capture volume for looping motions. Just as with idle motions, one of the most important issues when making cycling motions is to have a consistent, smooth root movement. If a motion that you captured for a cycle motion has extreme accelerations or decelerations in it, your game character will appear to limp when it is looped over and over. See Figures 12.5 and 12.6.

FIGURE 12.5   A run motion with consistent root movement.

FIGURE 12.6   A run with inconsistent root movement.

When making frame range selections for a walk or jog cycle, you may want to select a certain range of frames to be processed. When selecting your run cycle motion, however, it is best just to take the entire range of captured frames, unless you have time to study the root movement and are confident that the root is consistent and that you have a full two steps (each foot contacting the ground at least once). Because of the size of most capture volumes, it is common with fast running motions for the performer to only get four steps (each foot contacting the ground twice) captured while in the volume. This means that by taking the entire range of frames you only get two chances to get a consistent cycle that you like. Since producing good idles and cycle motions is so important, it is worth the extra expense to take the entire captured range and not worry about selecting a certain frame range. A good generic rule of thumb is to select the entire range of motion on motions that need to loop.

Just as with the idle motions, the cycle motions need to be thought out if you want them to be user friendly for the animators and function effectively in the game. Once the cycle motions are edited, make sure the first frame of each cycle is the passing position. Generally, the passing position is considered the midway point between the two contact positions; the body is balanced, and the rear foot is passing by the planted foot. In traditional animation, the passing position is sometimes referred to as the middle position or the breakdown position. See Figure 12.7.

The main reason for making the passing position the first frame of the cycle is the same reason we made the first frame the middle position on the breathing idles: to help minimize the pop in the motion when the user breaks out of the motion before it has completed its loop. Of all of the basic cycle motions—walk, jog, run, and backpedal—the largest pop will be seen during the run, but this is to be expected because the legs and arms extend away from the body more while running.

Once you have consistent root movement and have chosen which frame is to be the first frame, you can complete the loop. Copy the frames or duplicate them so that you have two complete

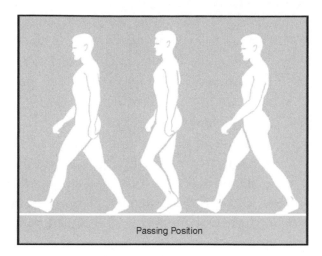

Passing Position

FIGURE 12.7   An example of the passing position and two contact positions.

loops of the motion. How you duplicate the motion will depend on the software package you are using. With some packages you then need to translate the second looping section so that it lines up with the end of the first looping section, but other software packages will line them up for you automatically. The next step also depends on the software you are using. Some packages duplicate the entire range of frames that you want, and others automatically drop out the first frame. If the software that you use duplicates the entire range, then you will have two identical frames right next to each other where the first looping section ends and the second looping section begins. Remember that the first and last frames are the same, so when butted up against each other there will be two identical frames in a row. You should delete one of these two frames, and it doesn't matter which one. After the identical frame is deleted, you simply select the frame range that begins with the first frame that you selected; the frames before and after this section will be either deleted or not saved when you save the file. This again depends on the software you are using to edit.

In Chapter 11 we also talked about making sure the motion performer is consistent with which foot he stops on when transitioning from the cycle motions to the idle motions. This is an issue only if you are capturing transition motions for your game. When the performer comes to a stop from the walk, jog, or run cycle, make sure he plants the same foot first, followed by the other foot. Keep in mind that from a full run it may take him several steps to come to a stop. For example, if the motion performer planted his right foot first, followed by his left foot, then you want the first frame of your cycle motion to be the passing position when his right foot is coming forward. By doing this, you can make your game character come to a stop in half a step instead of a full step. Obviously it will take more than one step for the motion performer to stop from a hard run, and it may be difficult to get the transition to look good in a step or two because of how long it may take the performer to slow his momentum to a stop. In video games we are usually forced to make a transition from a hard run to a stop in fewer steps than is humanly possible, but you need to try to slow the root in a way that does not look too abrupt. Figure 12.8 depicts a quick stop.

Pinned Motions

Some games may require the locomotive motions such as the cycles and any motion that moves the character through space to be

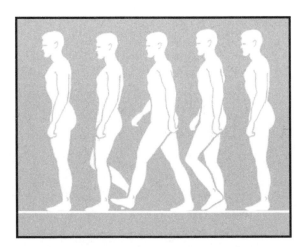

FIGURE 12.8 A character coming to a stop in one-half a step.

"pinned" in place when given to the programmers. In other words, pinned motions require you to take the translation out of the motions. The game engine will then control the distance and speed the motion file is played in the game. If this is the case with your project, here are a few things you need to keep in mind:

- Edit the motions with the translational data in them; only after the motion is finished should you take it out.
- The speed and distance at which the programmers play back the motion will make a big difference in the look of the motion. If motions that require the character's feet to touch the ground are translated a greater distance than they were originally captured, the feet will appear to skate or slide on the ground. Skating feet take away from the realism and believability of the motions.
- If the character is being propelled through the air, for example during an explosion that propels the character, skating is not an issue.

Having your core motions arranged in a user friendly way is also highly recommended. Have all of them facing the same world axis (in our case, the positive z). The axis will vary, depending on the software you are using; most software packages used to edit motion capture files have the positive y-axis facing up, the positive z-axis facing forward, and the positive x-axis as the lateral axis. This should not be too much of an issue; actually, most motion capture studios will deliver all of your motion files facing the direction you specify. Also, have all the core motion files translated to the same world coordinates (0.00 on the z-axis and 0.00 on the x-axis). Having all the core motions consistent will make the next few months of motion editing easier on the animators because it can be time consuming and frustrating to open motion files edited by different animators, and because of the need to locate the character within the software's world space.

AFTER THE CORE MOTIONS ARE EDITED

After the core motions are completed, a meeting should be called to review the motions. The animators, project manager, designers, lead artist, and anyone else who will have a final say in the look, design, and playability of the game should attend. The purpose of this meeting is to get all to agree with the look of the motions and to approve them. Only by getting them to sign off on the motions can full editing begin. Hundreds of motions may blend either into or out of a core motion, so if you have to go back to one later in the project and change the look of it, it could severely affect your schedule or cause you to miss a deadline. Having everyone approve their look initially will lessen the likelihood that a major change will be needed later. Minor changes to core motions might occur with minimal impact on the project, and I will discuss how these can happen later in this chapter.

It is important to note that the core motions need to be completed motions, not just one-frame poses (once referred to as a master transition position). A single frame can show only the basic pose of the character but not his movement, so it tells only half the story. Everyone needs to view the speed and range of motion in order to get an accurate feel for how the motions will look in the game.

The Animation Meeting

Once the core motions are approved, there is only one more step to complete before the animators can start to edit the bulk of the motions. Call an animation meeting, gather the animators together, and talk about the quality level expected from them and the goals you hope to achieve on the project. Doing this lets everyone knows what is expected of them and in what direction the project is going. An actual meeting is more desirable than an e-mail because a meeting gives everyone a chance to contribute their ideas and also adds to the feeling of working as a team. E-mail is too one sided and does not allow for give and take or add to a team environment. Teamwork needs to be emphasized if you hope to achieve the highest level of quality possible for your game.

During this meeting you can also hand out a sheet explaining the directory structure, where working motions are to be saved, and where the finished motion files need to be saved. If your animators are not familiar with your database sheet or directory structure, go through it and make sure everyone understands. As the motion coordinator and leader of the animators, it is important that you communicate well and that you have a written structure for them to follow. Keep in mind that leaders who do not take responsibility for their decisions tend not to put things in writing. This gives them an out later if a problem should occur. This is not meant to suggest that every decision you make must be correct, but you should have a clear direction in mind.

The major benefit to putting everything in writing is that it empowers the animators to work efficiently and independently. Even though it is best to have a team atmosphere, you do not want animators dependent on others; instead, give them all the information they will need in a clear, concise manner so that they can work freely. If they choose to work on weekends or after hours and they have a question or problem, they just need to refer to their sheet, and it won't hinder them from completing their work. Working this way allows them to focus on upholding a high level of quality while meeting their deadlines.

Some companies focus too much on the animators meeting individual daily quotas of edited animations instead of on working as a team to achieve a goal. When daily quotes are focused on, the team camaraderie breaks down, and there is no longer pride in the quality level of the animation. Animators will focus more on meeting their daily number than on doing a good job or helping a co-worker who is for one reason or another behind schedule. As a way to try to prove their value, some animators may even compete to see how many motion files they can edit in a day. When this happens, quality is sacrificed. It is better to have an animator who can complete 10 motion files at a high quality level that won't need to be re-edited than to have an animator complete 20 motion files that will need to be touched up or reworked later in the project.

The following is information to cover in the animation meeting:

- Describe the directory structure of the project.
- All edited motions should have the character facing the same direction. In our case the character will face the positive z-axis.
- All edited motions should start at world coordinates 0.00 on the x-axis and 0.00 on the z-axis.
- For motions with multiple motion performers, designate a naming convention for each character and have him always facing the same direction; in other words, have a character always facing the positive z-axis and translated to world coordinates 0.00 x and 0.00 z. This is very helpful if your project has offensive and defensive characters interacting.
- When blending into or out of an idle motion, *always* use the first frame of the idle to blend with. It cannot be emphasized enough how important this is. You have already set up your idle motions so that the first frame helps to minimize the amount of pop that will occur and to maximize flow to and from the cycling motions. There is another reason to use only the first frame when blending idle motions. If later in your project it is decided that you need to change an idle motion—maybe the speed or range of movement does not look quite right—then you will need to re-edit all the motions that the animators have already completed using that idle. Depending on your game and when this change is discovered, that could mean hundreds of motion files would need to be redone. However, if the animators used only the first frame to blend with, then you can change the speed and range of motion without affecting the first frame and not causing any re-edits to be necessary. Although you have tried to minimize this by having a meeting so that others can view the idle motions before the animators begin the main editing, changes are sometimes required. Using the first frame of an idle to make the blends gives you more options for changes if

they need to occur. Unfortunately, due to the user response time, it isn't possible to use this same approach with cycle motions. If you use the first frame of a cycle motion for all your blends, it may add too much lag time to a motion before there is a response from the controls. However, if you know that the motions will be used only for computer-controlled characters, you may be able to use this approach.

Starting to Edit

When making up a schedule for the animators, keep in mind that editing motion capture files can be challenging, frustrating, and boring. Animators who first work with motion files usually find it exciting, but after editing a few hundred files, it quickly loses its mystique. Knowing this may help you better gauge what reasonable deadlines are and how many motion files can be edited in a set amount of time. Motions with a lot of prop interaction or files that contain multiple performers interacting are usually more complex and take longer to edit, so you may want to assign the majority of these difficult motions to your best animators. However, you should assign some of them to the less-experienced animators also. If you assign only the basic motions to junior or less-experienced animators, they will quickly become bored, because every animator likes a bit of a challenge. It is a good idea to have the less-experienced animators edit some of the fluff motions first so that they can get used to editing motion files or learn the software. As we stated in Chapter 3, fluff motions are a luxury as far as game play is concerned, but they are quickly becoming a necessity in many games. The little subtleties in motion, such as when a base coach moves, claps, and gets out of the way of foul balls, or in an action game when guards investigate the area when they hear a noise or get a cup of coffee when they're tired, add the level of realism needed if you want to be able to compete in today's market.

The first motions, after the core motions, that need to be assigned and edited depend more on the programmers than anything else. Talk to the lead programmer to find out which motions the programmers will implement first. Make sure that these motions are assigned and edited first so that the programmers are not waiting on the animators to finish before they begin. As your project progresses, there may be times when you need to switch priorities and put more importance on motions that were lower on the list. Good communication here is again the key. Make sure you are clear about which motion files need to be edited and when, as the motion coordinator, you should be staying in contact with the lead programmer and project manager to make sure all the motion file needs are met.

Hopefully, from here the animators are editing the motions faster than the programmers can implement them. As the motion coordinator, you should be editing motions, too. As a leader it is important that you do not assign all the high profile or more fun motions to yourself. You should edit the boring motions just like everyone else. Never ask someone to do work that you are not prepared to do yourself. Since you are overseeing the animators as they edit and communicating with the programmers, do not expect to edit as many motions as the animators do. Give yourself time in your schedule for managerial responsibilities; otherwise, things will be neglected and get out of hand.

RE-EDITS AND DIRECTORY MAINTENANCE

You also need to have a plan for how to handle the re-edits that need to be done on the motion files. Without a set plan, it is hard to stay current on which file is the most recent version and who has worked on each file. This might sound like common sense, but it is surprising how many people don't believe that having a system will help prevent a lot of the confusion and miscommunication that often occurs during a video game project. The more times a file is handled, or if numerous people handle a particular file, the greater the likelihood that the file will be misplaced or altered incorrectly or that there will be a miscommunication about the location it has been saved to.

Motion files for video games are often lumped together in groups of motions that are similar, so if one of the files needs to be re-edited, then often other files will also need to be reworked the same way. The best example of this would be in a baseball video game. A good baseball game will have several different types of batter swings, depending on where the pitch crosses the plate. If one of these motion files has the bat reaching the contact point in 20 frames and needs to be re-edited so that the bat reaches the contact point is 15 frames, then all the other batter swing files should also be resized so that they too have the bat reaching the contact point in 15 frames. Another smaller but often overlooked grouping is in action games. If a shoulder roll motion to the character's right side is resized, the shoulder roll to his left side should also be resized so that the two motions happen in the same number of frames; this will give the user a consistent user feedback response.

Because groups of motions need to be considered when re-edits are asked for, it is best to have a system for how to handle them and not just re-edit each motion when a problem is discovered. Whatever plan you decide to implement for handling the animation files that need to be re-edited, you need to make sure that your plan does not create a bottleneck in the workflow. If in an attempt to be better organized your plan slows down the programmers, you may risk missing deadlines, which could affect bonuses or just cause others to have to work longer hours. Since creating a bottleneck is not an option, you need to have a simple plan that each person on your team follows. A simple plan can make the re-edit process effective and efficient.

A simple plan for re-edits is to have one animator, most likely the motion coordinator, in charge of all re-edits. This means that as changes are needed in the motions, they are reported to the person in charge. From there that person either makes the changes himself or, if there is a large group of motions that need to be reworked, gets other animators to assist. Having the motion coordinator oversee the re-edits is generally best because his schedule should be lighter by that point in the project than the other animators, it frees the other animators up to work on other things, it helps him stay in the loop as to what is actually happening with the game's animations, and it helps maintain a level of consistency and quality in the game's animations. Having any animator re-edit any motion file whenever there is a problem creates an organizational nightmare and often leads to wasted time, lost files, and confusion.

Maintaining your project's directories is also an important job that needs to be monitored constantly. Even with a plan for handling re-edits, it is common as a project progresses over the months for the directories to become cluttered with files. Files that are no longer needed or revisions of files in progress tend to build up, lead to confusion, and make finding the most recent files difficult to locate. Your programmers may even pull the wrong files to use in the game if they can't locate the correct ones quickly and easily. Think of maintaining your project's directory structure as keeping your body in shape. It is always easier to maintain a level of fitness than it is to try to get back into shape after having neglected it. Again, this job is best handled by the motion coordinator.

ACKNOWLEDGMENTS AND CREDITS

To maintain good working relations with the motion capture studio and its staff, it is a good idea following your capture to send thank you e-mails or notes to all the people at the motion studio who helped make your motion shoot successful. If your capture lasts for several days, it gives you time to learn a little personal information about each person, so it is easier to personalize each e-mail as opposed to sending a generic one. This might sound trivial, but everyone likes to be acknowledged for their hard work. Also keep in mind that these people may one day leave that particular motion capture studio and go to work for another, so keeping good contacts can benefit you in the future.

Along with personally thanking the individuals, your company may be obligated to give credit to the motion studio that captured your motions for you. Our example studio, GMC Studios, even mentioned studio credits in their preproduction conference call in Chapter 8:

Studio Credit

Screen credits for the motion studio's personnel are required. Immediately after completion or distribution, the client will provide the motion studio with suitable materials to be used for promotional purposes and press releases. These materials will include, but are not limited to, one broadcast quality copy of any rendered footage, imagery rendered to at least 300 dpi for print, and if it is a video game at least five copies of the finished game.

If you worked with a major motion capture studio, your company my also be contractually obligated to give credit to the motion capture studio. There is most likely a paragraph in your contract that states that you must mention the motion capture studio, and its staff who worked on your capture, in the game's credits. Our example contract in Chapter 8 states:

GMC Studios reserves all right, title and interest in the technology created or developed by GMC Studios in producing the project. GMC Studios will have the right to use and permit others to see recorded excerpts or still photographs for GMC Studios' internal use and promotion of GMC Studios' business, provided that GMC Studios' obtains QGI's written consent which shall not be unreasonably withheld or delayed. In addition, GMC Studios will receive a motion capture credit in the published game credits.

It is equally as important to thank the motion performers who help bring your animation to life. A simple thank you e-mail can help maintain good working relationships with good performers, and this is very important if you hope to work with them again. Make sure the performers are also mentioned in the game credits for the work they did; sending them a complimentary copy of the game when it is released is also a good idea. Even if you decide to use a different motion studio, having proven motion performers is of the utmost importance.

CONCLUSION

A lot of work needs to have gone into organizing and preparing if you want the editing process to go as smoothly as possible. Regardless of the size of your team or the company that you work for, you need to be prepared and work together if you want to achieve your goals. Here are a few things to keep in mind:

- It is important to make your frame range selections as soon after your capture as possible.
- Your frame range selections need to include handle frames for blending purposes.
- In order to make smart frame range selections, you need to know the average number of seconds that your contract is based on.
- Update your motion database as soon as you return from the capture while it is still fresh in your mind.
- When getting motion files back from the motion studio, check the quality level. Remember "cosmetic not reconstructive surgery" is best.
- Get the core motions edited first, then have them approved before beginning to edit the remainder of the motions.
- When editing looping motions, focus on getting the root movement correct first.
- When editing idling motions, take the character's momentum into account when selecting the beginning frame.
- Consider what frame is best to begin a looping motion on in order to minimize pops in the motion.

13 THE *CARRION* PROJECT

I n this book we have given what we believe to be the ideal way to handle a project using motion capture as the source of its animations. Every company and every project have unique circumstances that affect the decisions that are made, so it might not be possible to handle your project in the most ideal way. As you will see, we had some less-than-ideal circumstances to work with, and some poor decisions were made while developing CARRION. Some areas we were able to handle very well, and some were less than ideal, but realistically this is to be expected.

Background Information

Since projects vary drastically on their specs, we will start by giving you a little of the basic background information laid out by lead designer Matt Warchola for the game CARRION:

Project Name: CARRION. In nature the word "carrion" refers to animals that feed upon the dead; in our game it will be the dead that feed upon the diseased living.

Project Concept: Players return from the dead and have a single night to avenge a misdeed. In the game world, players will arise at midnight and will progress through the game until dawn, which occurs in real-time six hours later.

Genre: 3D Action/Adventure—Third Person Viewpoint.

Target Platforms: Sony PSX2, Microsoft Xbox.

Development Time: Eighteen months for initial product, nine months for each future sequel.

Handling the Animation

One of the first questions we needed to answer was how to handle our animations. Do we use motion capture or do we keyframe the animations? We had a meeting to discuss the pros and cons of both keyframing and motion capture, and we ultimately chose to use motion capture for several reasons. First, from a business point of view we had the money in our budget for it, and from an artistic point of view we were seeking realistic human motion. Second, we had a limited time frame to complete the animations and we had a small animation staff. Originally we were slated to have three animators and a motion coordinator; however, due to a hiring freeze at Quality Games, Inc., we were given only three people total. The two animators were also given additional responsibilities other than animating, and the motion coordinator also had the managerial responsibilities of setting up the capture session, setting up the animation pipeline, directing the capture, scheduling and training the animators, overseeing the quality level of the animations, solving problems, and making sure the animations were completed on time. There was one other factor that also influenced our decision to use motion capture: Our project had an experienced motion capture animator to be the motion coordinator.

We then needed a tentative schedule for when we thought the motion capture sessions would take place. Our total development time for the game was 18 months, and management was pushing to have the capture as soon as possible, so they gave us three months before the capture session. This might sound like a lot of time, but keep in mind that there was a tremendous amount of work that needed to be done by the design staff, art staff, and motion coordinator before the capture session could happen. We weren't able to determine how many days of capturing we would need at this time because we did not know how many motions we would need to capture. In addition to giving us very little time to prepare for the capture, QGI management created less than ideal working conditions for us by allowing us to have only one capture session. QGI is a large company, so this decision was made by someone in upper management who probably did not understand how scheduling this way can really hurt the success of the project. When we questioned them about it, the answer was "too bad, deal with it." This meant that we had one shot at capturing everything we needed, so if we missed or captured motions incorrectly, we would either be stuck or have to find another way to get the job done. This is one of the main arguments for having a systematic approach to planning a capture session and why a system is needed. Without a system of organization and planning, the likelihood of not getting it correct increases drastically.

STAGE 1: PREPARING FOR THE CAPTURE SESSION

Once it was decided that we were going to use motion capture, a lot of prep work was needed because we were developing the first generation of *CARRION*. If the motion coordinator does his job properly the percentage of work he does at the beginning of the project will be the opposite from all the other animators. In the video game industry, an animator's schedule is usually slow during the beginning of the project and then gets very busy at the end, with long hours of overtime required in order to finish the project. The motion coordinator, on the other hand, should be very busy at the beginning of the project preparing everything so that months later the capture and post capture stages go smoothly and efficiently. The motion coordinator will do 70–80% of his work during this preparation stage. This can be deceiving and create some problems later, when others don't remember or see all the preparation work done at the beginning of the project and wonder why he isn't as crazy busy as the other animators. Developing a first-generation game means that the entire game, and in our case this included the game engine, would be built from the ground up. As the design staff was developing the design document, the motion coordinator met with the lead designer and the lead programmer to talk about the desired look and feel of the game. We already talked about how important it is for the motion coordinator to know what the designers envisioned the game to be. One of the first questions the motion coordinator needed answered was how the transitions between the core motions were going to be handled. Were they going to be created in the game engine, or did they need to be captured? The motion coordinator hoped to capture them because captured transitions tend to look better, but this really depends on the type and speed of the transition. With advances in software, quick and easy transitions are fairly easy to create, but the lead programmer agreed that the transitions should be captured. This meeting also provided the motion coordinator with additional absolutes and gave him enough information to flowchart the game's greater states. During this meeting we also set up several meetings to go over the motion list. We decided to have several short meetings once a week to talk about the motion list. We divided the motion list into sections and covered one section per meeting. During one meeting we discussed the casual motions, another meeting the death motions, and so on until we covered all the game states.

The Motion List

In Chapter 3, "The Motion List," we said that the most ideal way to develop a motion list is to create a wish list of every possible motion and then reduce it to the minimum number of motions to make the type of game you want. We used this approach even though our company hindered us from being able to capitalize fully on it. Before we finished our initial motion list, upper management at QGI made another bad decision and put a limit on the number of motions we could capture. They allowed us to capture only 700 in-game motions and 50 cinematic motions. It is completely counterproductive to put a number on the amount of motions for cinematic sequences before they are even storyboarded, but this is a good example of when a business decision made by management affects the creative aspects of a project. We decided to ignore their number and create our in-game wish list and cinematic sequences the way we needed to and then worry about making their number when we reduced the lists. We continued to develop our wish list but knew we would eventually have to reduce it to only 700 motions; this is where the experience of our motion coordinator really helped. Seven hundred motions wouldn't be enough motion for the kind of game we wanted to make, so as we met to reduce our wish list, our motion coordinator also combined motions together and saved even more room on our list. Combining two or three motions together allowed us to capture far more than the allotted 700 motions, even though our list reflected that we captured only 700.

The one positive to having a set number of motions is that it let us know how many days in the studio we would need for our capture session. Depending on the complexity of the motions, a generic rule of thumb is that you can capture 100 finished motions a day. We had seven 750 motions to capture, so that is seven and a half days of capture. We do, however, like to pad our capture schedule, so we allocated eight and a half days in the studio to capture our 750 motions.

Flowcharts

As the motion list was being developed, the motion coordinator and lead designer worked together to flowchart the motion sets as a way of double-checking the design and make sure the motion list included all the needed motions.

Contacting and Selecting a Motion Capture Studio

To select the best motion capture studio for *CARRION*, our motion coordinator contacted three motion studios to bid on it. One of the studios was a small local studio, while the other two were large, experienced studios. Because we didn't have a finalized motion list (shot list) for them, our motion coordinator gave them as much information as he had. He knew the total number of motions we were going to capture, approximately what percentage of them were basic motions, what percentage of them were complex motions, and how many involve stunts. QGI already had an existing working relationship with GMC Studios; however, we still wanted to get other bids to make sure we selected the studio that would best suit our needs and was the most cost effective for our project. This does not mean, however, that we used the studio that gave us the cheapest bid, because all three bids were close to the same amount. Whichever studio we chose, we needed to feel comfortable that they would be able to giving us good quality motion data and the service we needed and meet the deadlines we had for the processed motions. We had a meeting to go over each bid. The motion coordinator was the contact person with each studio, and he knew the most about motion capture, so after reviewing each bid the other project members took his recommendation of which studio to use. It was decided to use Generic Motion Capture Studios. We contacted GMC Studios about our decision, and they began to draw up the contract to finalize the deal. The motion coordinator also contacted the other studios to let them know that we decided to use another studio, but he also let them know that he would contact them about bids on future projects.

GMC Studios scheduled a conference call meeting with us to make sure that they understood the specifics about our project and to make sure that we understood what they needed from us and when and what we should expect to happen during the capture session. All the necessary questions were answered, and everything was in line. One area that they really emphasized was that they needed to see our motion list, so a copy was sent to them when it was finalized. They also needed a copy of our skeleton *before* our capture session so that they could make sure that everything was in order. Our game skeleton was already set, so the motion coordinator made arrangement to have it sent to them.

GMC Studios then sent their contract to us. Because it is a deal involving a lot of money, upper management at QGI said they would handle the contract. Our motion coordinator let management know that he would like to look it over before it was signed. Initially there was some resistance by QGI's management to having him involved with the contract because they considered contract negotiations to be an upper management job. Our motion coordinator had to explain that he wanted to help them make sure the contract reflected the needs of their project, and if they weren't careful and fully understood certain areas, the capture price could double or triple, depending on how it was worded. Management finally agreed and allowed him to look over the contract. He paid particular attention to the number of seconds allotted per motion before additional charges incurred and also made note of how much those charges were. This information would help the motion coordinator make smarter decisions on how to combine motions together, make smarter decisions at the capture session, and make his selects after the motion capture session was complete. Knowing this, it seems obvious that the motion coordinator needs to know the specifics of the contract.

The Motion Database

In addition to the motion list and flowcharts, the motion coordinator also had to create the motion database we used on *CARRION*. None of the other projects using motion capture at QGI used this checks and balances system, so like everything else on *CARRION*, it needed to be created from the ground up. Our database was created using FileMaker Pro, and it took some initial thought to generate one that included all the necessary information; we covered this information in detail in Chapter 5, "The Motion Database." Inputting all the motions from our final motion list into the database took a lot of time, so the motion coordinator, one of the animators, and one of the junior designers all pitched in to help get it done.

Selecting Motion Performers and a Stunt Coordinator

Ideally it is best if you audition motion performers yourself or in conjunction with the motion studio you are using, but on *CARRION* this wasn't the case. GMC Studios and QGI are in different cities, and we couldn't get approval to travel for auditions, so we had to do the next best thing. We sent GMC Studios a list of motions and scenes that we would like to see the performers do. GMC Studios contacted performers and then directed and videotaped them performing the moves and scenes we sent. The videotape was then sent to us for our review. We needed to select several performers, and their abilities would dictate how many performers we needed. For example, we might find a performer who moved very well for our in-game character but wouldn't be able to perform the stunt motions, or we may find a stuntman who could also act, so he could do the stunt moves and also be one of the characters in our cinematic scenes. This means we would need one, possibly two, performers for our in-game motions and at least four performers for our cinematic sequences. Unfortunately, the auditions didn't find us anyone for our stunt and in-game motions, but it did produce two guys we could use for the cinematic sequences. We contacted GMC Studios and had them schedule the two performers for our capture. We didn't have time to schedule another audition, so we would somehow need to find an in-game performer, stunt performer, and two more people for the cinematic sequences on our own. Our motion coordinator also realized we should have a stunt coordinator to supervise the stunt motions, so he called Jeff, a stunt coordinator, with whom he had worked before to see if he was available to work our capture. He also told Jeff that we were still looking for a stunt performer, along with some other performers. Jeff said he knew a stunt performer named Steve that he recommended and that in addition to being a stuntman he was also a good actor. Jeff sent a videotape of Steve from an old capture session to our motion coordinator, and after seeing it we knew we had found our stunt and in-game performer. We then contacted Steve to see if he was interested and available to work our capture. Along with being our in-game performer and stunt performer, Steve would also act as one of the characters in our cinematic sequences. This left us with only one performer spot in the cinematics to fill. Jeff, our stunt coordinator, has also been a performer for many captures and suggested that he could also be our last performer. We thought it was a good idea and had all of our performers and stunt coordinator selected. When it was finished, our motion coordinator sent a copy of our finalized motion list to both Jeff and Steve for them to review.

Coordinating and Making Props

We had several issues concerning the props we needed to use on *CARRION*. We purchased a fake hard rubber pistol to use for our single-handed weapon motions, and one of our designers made a large two-handed rifle-like prop out of wood to use on the motions requiring a two-handed weapon. For safety reasons, he made sure the prop didn't have any sharp edges on it. The week prior to our capture session, we sent the props to GMC Studios so that they could see the props and fix markers on them. We also needed to have a prop made to simulate a character riding on a horse-like creature. Instead of making it ourselves and shipping it to the capture session, we had GMC Studios make it for us. We explained to them what type of motions we needed to use it for and let them design it. After our capture session, they would keep the prop for future use. The design they came up with was perfect. They suspended a 50-gallon drum by bungee cords from a wooden support frame. It was easy to move onset and gave us the right amount of movement.

Assembling the Capture Team

We also needed to assemble the team of people to go to the capture session. This can be tricky because a motion capture shoot is seen by a lot of people as something cool, so everyone wants to go. The best way to select who should go is to take only people who will be helpful during the capture. QGI's creative director and our art lead both expressed an interest in attending, but neither one of them would have been helpful to the capture; instead, they just wanted to observe. Having people go just to observe didn't fit into our budget, so we selected three people who would actually work and contribute to the success of the capture. The people making up our team were the motion coordinator, the lead designer, and an additional animator. We wanted to include an additional animator to given us some additional help during the capture and to give him some experience working a capture session so that he would have the experience to one day be the motion coordinator on a project.

Preparing the Reference Material

Another thing we needed to do before our capture was to prepare some reference material for our in-game and cinematic performers. The reference for our in-game performer was simple and easy. We had one of the artists on our project pose in the core positions while we took profile and head-on Polaroid photographs of him. These photos would later be used to show to our performer so that he could mimic them, and we could make stencils of his foot positions. As the capture session progressed, we could also use these pictures to make sure our performer was closely matching his body position day after day. Having the performer closely match the same body position makes blending motions together easier for the animators during the post capture stage. Our cinematic sequences on the other hand weren't handled as well as they should have been. The reason for this was due to the fact that we only were allowed one capture session, and it was scheduled early in our project's timeline. We didn't have the time to work out the cinematic sequences fully and record the audio track prior to capture, so we had to make do just to get some motions captured. The designers hurriedly worked out the cinematic sequences and the dialogue. Then together with an artist the sequences were storyboarded. We videotaped artists acting out the sequences, but we didn't have the camera set up from the rendering camera's angle. We mainly videotaped the artist to get a feeling on timing and a loose idea of the blocking of the characters. Once the cinematic sequences were flushed out, a copy of the dialogue, storyboards, and video tape were sent to each motion performer so that they could see what we were looking for, develop ideas of their own, and rehearse.

Travel Arrangements

The travel arrangements for our capture session were made by QGI's secretary. She arranged airfare and accommodations for our capture team, stunt coordinator, and our main performer. Two of our cinematic performers were local to the capture studio area, so they did not require travel arrangements. QGI didn't want to pay for a rental car for the capture team; instead they wanted us to pay for cabs out of our own pocket and then submit the receipts after returning from the capture for reimbursement. Being a large company, QGI had gotten into the bad habit of taking months to reimburse employees for expenses, so our motion coordinator made other arrangements. QGI was willing to pay for a rental car for the stunt coordinator and performer we were using, so he made sure that we all stayed at the same hotel and that they got a large rental vehicle. This way we could all ride together to and from the capture session. Because we had only one capture session scheduled, the success of the capture hinged on everyone being there, so a few days before the capture our motion coordinator double checked the travel arrangements to make sure everything was booked properly and everyone knew when and where they needed to be.

STAGE 2: THE CAPTURE SESSION

Overall, the capture session for *CARRION* went very well. The capture had been well organized, and the motion performer we selected was experienced and the perfect choice to help us capture the motions we needed. Selecting an experienced performer was crucial for the success of our capture because we weren't able to have a rehearsal with him prior to our capture. Earlier we talked about the importance of rehearsals, and despite our recommendation, QGI wouldn't allow it because it would involve travel expenses. We started the first day of our capture with a half-day of preparations, making sure the performer was comfortable with each core position. We showed him the Polaroids and made stencils of his foot positions, taking care to label them so that we knew which ones were which.

Another excellent decision we made that helped our capture tremendously was to hire an experienced motion capture stunt coordinator. His job was to make sure all stunts were done under safe conditions and to help us achieve the look we were seeking. Since our motion performer, Steve, and our stunt coordinator, Jeff, knew each other and had worked on past motion capture projects before, they trusted each other and communicated very well. Hiring Jeff really proved valuable when we had a slight setback prior to capturing some stunt motions. Many of our stunt motions required the use of a pulley to drop, hoist, or pull the performer around, and the pulley that GMC Studios purchased for the job was not approved to be used for humans; it was a pulley for cargo. This obstacle was quickly overcome when Jeff made a few phone calls, found the correct type of pulley, and during lunch break went with one of GMC Studio's employees to pick it up, along with some better ropes. The cost of the pulley and ropes were paid for by GMC Studios because they would keep them after our capture session for use on other captures. Jeff also brought his own rappelling harnesses for us to use during our capture because his were better than the ones the studio had. He was able to think ahead and do this because of his experience and because we had sent him a copy of our motion list prior to our capture for him to review.

The combination of using a quality motion capture studio, an organized motion coordinator, and an experienced stunt coordinator, along with the experience of the motion performer, helped us from the first day of capture get and stay ahead of our capture schedule. Even though it was a complicated capture due to the stunts and limited prep time, the stress was minimal because we were ahead of schedule and all worked together. A lot of credit should be given to Steve because his ability to give us the performance we were looking for, hour after hour, day after day kept the capture moving along at a good pace. The second night of our capture, the staff at GMC Studios took our capture team, Jeff, and Steve out to dinner. This was a very nice gesture on GMC Studios' part because they didn't have to do it, and it did help build more of a relationship between us. In reality, our company, QGI, paid for the dinner because the cost was worked into the padding of our contract, but GMC Studios didn't have to use it to take us out; they could have just as easily kept the money as profit. On the last day of our capture, we shot our cinematic sequences, and they turned out as good as could be expected. Even with the extra half day of prep the first day and the extra setup time needed for the stunt motions, we were able to finish our capture one day early. Although we used seven and a half days instead of eight and a half, our contract with GMC Studios required us to pay them for the unused stage time. We also paid Steve for the extra day. These weren't extra expenses because they were originally calculated into our cost from the beginning. Steve gave us exactly the motions we needed, so he should not be penalized because he finished earlier than we had calculated. We made sure that Steve, along with our other motion performers, were paid in full on the last day of the capture. That night we all went out for drinks to celebrate a successful capture. Figure 13.1 shows stunt performer Steve Pope and stunt coordinator Jeff Gibson.

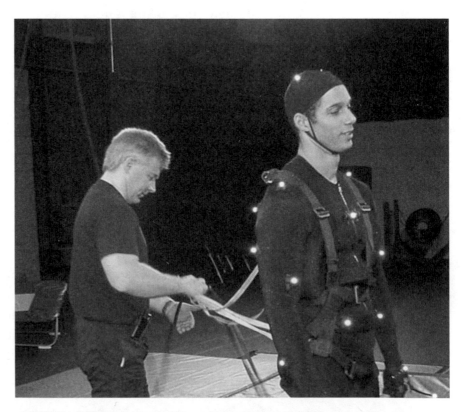

FIGURE 13.1 Jeff Gibson and Steve Pope preparing for a stunt at a motion capture session. © 2003. Reprinted with permission from Michael Mann.

STAGE 3: THE POST CAPTURE SESSION

The post capture stage on *CARRION* was made easy because of all the preparations that were done before the capture session. We had set up a system that covered the directory structure and file-naming convention that we were going to use. Our system also addressed what our animation pipeline would be, where the motion files would be located, where they were to be placed once they were edited, and where the programmers could retrieve them to implement them into the game.

Upon returning from the capture session, the motion coordinator began updating the motion database with the notes he had taken during the capture. At this time, he also began making the selects for the motions to be processed and trained the other animators on the software that we used to edit the motion data with. Before GMC Studios began sending us the processed motions, they sent a few motions so that we could check the quality level of the processing. The motion coordinator liked the quality of processing; he edited the few motions, called the art lead and lead designer together to show them the motions, and got their approval. Once we gave GMC Studios the OK, they began processing the bulk of the motions per our priority level and sent motions to us on a weekly basis.

The first motions to be edited were the core motions and were edited by the motion coordinator and one of the animators. This was done for quality control reasons because all the other motions would begin or end in them. Before the bulk editing began, the core motions were again shown to the lead artist and lead designer for approval. This approval is of the utmost importance. Every motion hinges on the look of the core motions, so it is important that everyone agree on their look. Without this approval, the likelihood that someone may want a core motion changed later in the project increases.

Before we began editing the bulk of the motions, the motion coordinator called a meeting of the animators to discuss the quality level expected. He created a sheet of instructions and hints and called a meeting of the animators to discuss what was needed. The meeting went well, and all the animators understood the quality level expected and were excited and eager to begin editing. On some projects the prevailing way of thinking is, "just get the motions done; there will be time to make changes or tweak them later." We wanted to get away from this "hurry and throw the motions into the game to make it look like we are further along then we really are and then work overtime later to make it look good" way of working. Instead, we let the animators know that we wanted the motions edited correctly and fully from the outset. There are several reasons why editing the motions this way is the better approach.

Sample rate. Sometimes the game engine or the programmers need to resample how many frames of an animation is played in order to get them to execute in the timeframe they need. This is a bad thing from a creative point of view because resampling the speed or distance a motion travels can make the motions look artificial. If the motions are edited and the props are not in the character's hand on every frame, this may become more apparent, depending on which frames are dropped during the resampling process. To avoid this, we wanted the animators to make sure that prop interaction and the timing of a character's movements were smooth and accurate on every single frame.

Screen shots. The screen shots taken for magazine or online advertising can make a game look bad if the character isn't holding onto a prop correctly, if his arm is cutting into his leg, and so on. A truly finished motion will look good no matter which frame a screen shot is taken from.

Close-ups and cinematic sequences. Close-up shots and cinematic shots lose their realism if an arm passes through a torso or environmental object, or if a handshake doesn't line up properly.

Slow motion instant replay. If your game has (or will have in future versions) a slow motion or instant replay mode and you didn't take the time to make sure the character's gun is actually in his hand on every frame, the illusion of reality will be lost if it floats during the instant replay.

Alternate camera angles. The motions may be seen from a different camera angle than originally thought, and a truly finished motion will also look good no matter what angle it is viewed from.

Tweak time. There is never enough time at the end of a project to tweak everything that you want to, and since you are dealing with a large number of motions, inevitably some will be overlooked.

Burnout factor. People are burned out at the end of the project, so their attention to detail isn't as good. Because of this, it is foolish to expect a burned out person to concentrate on small details and perform as well as he would if he were fresher. When people are burned out, it takes them longer to perform simple tasks. It is a fine line, but once people are overworked, they actually take longer to do simple tasks than they would if they worked less.

Handling the file. The more times a file is handled, the greater the likelihood that it can be misplaced or forgotten about. Basically, if communication between the animators and the programmers isn't exceptional, then the new, tweaked file won't even make it into the game.

One motion affects other motions. One motion can affect multiple other motions, so if it is reworked late in the project, other motions also may need to be reworked.

The only argument against this way of working (usually given by people who do not directly deal with motion) is that this approach creates a bottleneck and slows down the work of the programmers, and deadlines will be missed. This might be true if the motion is not organized, planned, and supervised properly, but on *CARRION*, all deadlines were met without an excessive amount of overtime, and the programmers never waited on the animators to finish editing motions, so a bottleneck was not created.

As the editing stage continued, the motion coordinator and the lead programmer stayed in contact regarding which motions the programmers were going to implement next. A couple of times the priority changed, so the animators would stop editing the motions they were working on and finish the ones the programmers needed.

Even though at the beginning of the project we flowcharted the motion sets, later during the post capture stage we decided that we didn't like how a particular area of the motions flowed together. The motion coordinator called a meeting with the lead programmer, lead artist and lead designer. They all agreed that if it was possible the flow should be changed, but that posed a problem. All our motions were already captured, so that meant that new motions would need to be created, and there was some concern to how good these new created motions would look when they were seen together with the captured motions. The motion coordinator created one of the new motions and showed it to them as an example of the quality level. The created motion did not look as good as the captured motions, but it was better to use it than to go back to our original design. It was decided to have the animators create the rest of the needed motions. Creating these motions would add more work to the animator's schedule; the motion coordinator took this into consideration and assured them that the amount of new work needed could be easily added and not affect their deadline.

The animators and motion coordinator edited the bulk of the motions. The two animators edited more motions than the motion coordinator because he had other responsibilities. He checked the quality of their work, made corrections to the motions that the programmers needed, solved problems that came up regarding the animations, and kept the motion database updated. All the motions were edited on schedule and, despite all the setbacks, *CARRION* finished on time and on budget.

Conclusion

As you can see, there are many obstacles to handling a motion capture project in the ideal way, but this does not mean you should not try to set up your project in a way that best addresses all the possible obstacles and gives you the best chance of success. Many times the obstacles are created by people within your own company or because the person in charge did not plan with the entire scope of the project in mind. With that said, people do make mistakes, and some mistakes are minimal, while others are more severe. If you are inexperienced, you may consider hiring an independent experienced motion coordinator as a consultant on your project, or you may decide it is better just to use the people you have in-house. Even if mistakes are made, learn from them and refine your system so that your company or project can operate in the most effective and efficient way possible the next time around.

CONCLUSION

The concept of capturing motion is not a new one. As technology advanced, however, so did our capability to take the capturing of motion from its primitive two-dimensional roots into what we consider present day motion capture. Present day motion capture, like its ancestors, has been used as an aid for medical research and for entertainment purposes. As motion capture advanced, several different types of capture systems were developed, each with distinct advantages and disadvantages. Motion capture is still a fairly new technology in a commercial sense and is still struggling to find a place in the animation community.

An animator's main goal is to create the best-looking motion possible for his character. As a video game animator, however, this goal needs to change slightly. Video game animators need to try to balance the look of their motions with a good response time for the end user. This means making some artistic sacrifices in order to do what is best for the project. If an animator is seeking realistic human or animal motion, motion capture is without a doubt the best tool to use. This does not mean, however, that motion capture is the best for every project. A number of considerations should be thought through in order to choose what is right for each particular project. If you decide to use motion capture as the source of your animations, organizing and planning thoroughly before the capture session and surrounding yourself with the best people possible is your best bet for success.

Since there are so many things to consider when using motion capture, there is no substitute for planning and organizing thoroughly. This means that you try to take all possible problems into account and come up with ways to deal with them to lessen the likelihood that they will occur. In other words, you help to assure your success. Another way to help assure success is to surround yourself with quality people. Choosing a quality motion capture studio and choosing the best people as your motion performers are just as crucial as planning and having good animators to edit the captured data. If you were going on an adventure or needed to complete a project, would you feel more comfortable with a "Scott" or an "Amundsen" type of person? Nothing sums up dealing with motion capture better than the old adage, "Failing to plan is planning to fail."

I hope you found the information in this book helpful and wish you the best of luck in dealing with your future projects. Hopefully, this book has given you some good tips and tricks so that nobody can ever say to you that "you know one tenth of what everyone else knows."

A MOTION CAPTURE STUDIOS

Auvis Studios (formerly
   Acclaim Entertainment
   Motion Studio)
70 Glen Street
Glen Cove, NY 11542
(Ph) 516-759-3800
(Fx) 516-759-3888
www.auvisstudios.com

Elemental Motion
Troy McFarland
Seattle, WA
206-782-8167
www.elementalmotion.com

Giant Studios
2160 Hills Ave., Suite A
Atlanta, GA 30318
404-367-1999
www.giantstudios.com

House of Moves
5318 McConnell Ave.
Los Angeles, CA 90066
310-306-6131
www.moves.com

Kinetic Impulse
87 Hadlow Rd.
Tonbridge
Kent
TN9 1QD
UK
011-447-788-710-481
   (from the U.S.)
www.Kinetic-impulse.com

LocoMotion Studios
108 S. Valley View Dr.
Wimberley, TX 78676
512-847-7277
www.locomotionstudios.com

Madcap Studios
P.O. Box 862
Bondi Junction
NSW 2022
Australia
+61 2 8338 0173
www.Madcapstudios.com

Mantis Motion Productions
352 W.
12300 S.
Sandy, Utah
801-330-4615
www.mantismotion.com

Motion Analysis Studios
8611 Hayden Place
Culver City, CA 90232
310-204-4794
www.motionanalysisstudios.com

Perspective Studios
3200 Expressway Drive South
Long Island, NY 11749
631-232-1499
www.perspectivestudios.com

Pyros Pictures, Inc.
3197 Airport Loop Drive
Building A
Costa Mesa, CA 92626
714-708-3400
www.pyros.com

Red Eye Studio
2155 Stonington Ave., Suite 122
Hoffman Estates, IL 60195
847-843-2438
www.redeye-studio.com

Z-UP Productions
106 Crafton Dr.
O'Fallon, MO 63366
636-379-0880
www.Z-UP-productions.com

B MOTION CAPTURE CONSULTANTS, PERFORMERS, AND COORDINATORS

Jeff Gibson
Stunt Coordinator, Stunt
    Performer, Second Unit
    Director
SAG Stuntman
jlgstunts@hotmail.com

Cosmo Hom
Stunt/Character Performer
www.cosmoproductions.com
cosmo@cosmoproductions.com

Matt Liverman
Motion Capture
    Consultant/Coordinator
512-797-6615
mocap_matt@hotmail.com

Troy McFarland
Motion Capture Consultant
206-782-8167
www.elementalmotion.com

Steve Pope
Stunt/Character Performer
SAG Stuntman
spope14@aol.com

Smashcut
Stunt Performers/Stunt
    Coordination
310-202-6566
www.Smashcut.com
smashcut@smashcut.com

Alan Noel Vega
Stunt Coordinator
310-428-8585
noel@makeyourfilm.org

Richard Widgery
Studio Design, Mocap
    Consultant, Production
    Management
www.kinetic-impulse.com
richardw@kinetic-impulse.com

C OPTICAL MOTION CAPTURE SYSTEM MANUFACTURERS

**Motion Analysis
   Corporation**
3617 Westwind Blvd.
Santa Rosa, CA
95403
707-526-0629
www.Motionanalysis.com

Vicon Motion Systems, Inc.
9 Spectrum Pointe
Lake Forest, CA
92630
949-472-9140
www.vicon.com

Vicon Motion Systems Ltd.
14 Minns Business Park
West Way Oxford
OX2 OJB
U.K.
+44 1865 261800
www.vicon.com

GLOSSARY

A

absolute: A commitment by the design staff about the design or flow of the motions in the game.

acoustic motion capture: Consists of transmitters attached to a subject that emit a sound. Audio receivers surrounding the subject then measure the time it takes for the sound emitted from the transmitters to reach the receivers, and from this they can triangulate the location in space of each transmitter. The transmitters are commonly placed on a person at his joints to capture his body movement.

anticipation: An animation principle that refers to movement in the opposite direction before the main action starts. The more simple the movement, generally the more simple the anticipation will be. An example of anticipation is when a human shifts backward, sinking his weight into his back foot before pushing forward to run.

arcs of motion: An animation principle that refers to objects traveling on an arc through space as opposed to traveling on a straight line. For example, your hand does not move straight from front to back, but rather it travels on an arc as it swings.

asymmetrical markers: Markers that are added to the marker configuration or whose position in the configuration is changed to help identify a performer's orientation or distinguish one performer from another. These are also referred to as *offset markers*.

B

base motions: Motions that all the other motions begin or end with and whose beginning and end frames are identical. This is sometimes referred to as *root position, base position, in/out motion,* or *core motion.*

base position: *See* base motions.

behavior: A character's response to either an internal or external stimulus. A character's response to a stimulus is dictated by the game state he is in. For example, if your game character is walking down a sidewalk casually and gets shot, what does he do? Does he run away? Does he attack?

best: The version or take that the client selects to be processed by the motion capture studio. This is also sometimes called a *keep* or a *select.*

blend frames: The extra frames at the beginning or end of the needed motion used to blend one motion file to or from another. Sometimes referred to as *leads, handle frames,* or *head and tail frames.*

C

capture session: The time spent on location capturing the performer's motion. It is also referred to as a *motion shoot.*

capture space: The total space available in the motion capture studio.

capture volume: The actual three-dimensional area in which the motion data is able to be captured.

captured seconds: The actual number of seconds of motion that are captured per motion. Sometimes called *raw seconds.*

cleaning: A generic phrase that includes several processes to get rid of irregularities in the motion capture data in order to improve its quality. Sometimes referred to as *processing.*

clipping: When objects in a video game that are supposed to be solid pass through other solid objects. This can include a character passing through floors and walls or when body parts pass through each other, such as an arm passing through a torso. Also includes a camera passing through walls.

cloud data: The position information of unlabeled markers in the motion capture software as they travel through time and space. Sometimes called *marker data*.

combination approach: A method of animating in which the animator uses keyframes as guidelines to block out or get a rough estimation of the animation and then goes back and animates the motion using the straight ahead method. Many traditional animators feel that this gives them the best result even though it is more time consuming.

combination motions: Motions that are captured together during the capture session as one move and then broken apart into individual motions after the capture by the animators.

core motions: *See* base motions.

cycle motions: Looping motions that are used to propel the character through space.

D

daily shot list: A record containing the names of the motions and the order in which you want them captured on a given day.

data rate: The amount of data captured per second. If you capture at 120Hz, you will get 120 frames per second. Sometimes referred to as *frame rate* or *sample rate*.

destructive editing: A process of animation where the original keyframes are lost or destroyed when the animator alters the captured data.

digital armature devices: Devices that consist of a series of rigid modules connected by joint sensors whose rotations are digitally recorded. The most common type of armatures are keyframe armatures.

digital puppetry: A live action performance that uses several processes to create an animation and where the performer's controls do not necessarily correspond directly to the character's action. For example, a performer may use a joystick to drive the character's facial expression. Some of the processes a performer can use include but are not limited to real-time animation, performance animation, joysticks, sliders, digital gloves, pedals, and touch pads. Several performers also may act in unison during the performance, each controlling different parts of a single character.

directory structure: A series of folders and subfolders arranged for the purpose of organizing files.

dummy markers: Markers that are added to the marker configuration in order to help rebuild the position of markers occluded from the cameras during the capture. These are also called *redundant markers*.

E

ease-in and ease-out: An animation principle that refers to the change in speed as objects move. Most objects start slow, accelerate to a constant speed, and then slow to a stop. When an object accelerates until it reaches a constant speed, this is called ease-in. When an object decelerates until it stops, this is called ease-out. Heavier objects need more time to ease-in and ease-out. Sometimes referred to as *slow-in* and *slow-out*.

editing a motion: A generic phrase that consists of one or more processes that alter the timing or appearance of a motion capture file. Editing a motion can include trimming frames, pinning feet or hands, blending a motion into another, and animating over the top of the captured data. The words *editing* and *animating* are used interchangeably when dealing with motion capture.

eight-dot-three filename: A file that has eight characters in the filename followed by a three-character file extension.

exaggeration: An animation principle that refers to dramatizing a character's motions by pushing them past the extreme of natural movement. Generally, the more cartoon-like the character is, the more extreme the exaggeration can be and not look out of place for the character.

F

fluff motions: Any motion not critical for game play and used to enhance the visual look or feel of the game.

follow through: An animation principle that is the opposite of anticipation; it occurs when the main action comes to a stop. Follow through, in character animation, is the secondary movement, such as limbs that stop after the source of the movement, usually the hips, has stopped. Often, secondary movements move past the stopping point of the source and then settle back before coming to a rest. An example is when your arms continue to swing after your body has come to a stop after running. Also referred to as *overlapping action*.

frame range selections: The process of choosing the number of seconds (or frames) of each motion captured that you would like processed and delivered. The frame ranges that you choose should consist of the needed motion data plus some handle frames.

frame rate: *See* data rate.

G

game response time: Refers to the amount of time it takes a video game character to react after the user has given the character input. In other words, it is the amount of time it takes the character to react after a button is pressed.

greater states: Refers to the different emotional or mental states that the character is influenced by. An example would be if your game character is walking around casually, he is in a "relaxed" or "casual" state as opposed to an "agitated" or "attack" state. In a sports game, the different positions the players occupy can be the states; pitcher, kicker, goalie, etc.

H

handle frames: *See* blend frames.

head and tail frames: *See* blend frames.

I

idle motions: Looping motions that do not propel the character through space; rather; he remains almost stationary.

in/out motions: *See* base motions.

J

jitter: Random variation or disturbance in the timing of a signal that obscures or lessens the quality of the signal. Jitter can be caused by several things, including the wiggling of a loose marker or when one camera sees a marker flickering in and out of view, while other cameras see it constantly. Also called *noise*.

K

keep: *See* best.

keyframe animating: A method of animating where key poses showing extreme or important moments in time are done first. The space between the keyframes is then broken down further into smaller and smaller increments of time until the animation is complete. Also called *pose planning* or *pose to pose*.

L

layered animating: A method of animation that allows an animator to work on separate levels or "layers," which are independent of each other, but when composited together blend to create a unique, new animation. For example, layer one contains a walk cycle, layer two is a raised arm and hand wave. When composited, the character will walk and raise his arm to wave.

leads: *See* blend frames.

linear motions: Motions that do not require any input from a user in order to be executed. These motions have a predetermined outcome.

linear project: A project that does not require any user input and where the animations have a predetermined outcome. An example of a linear project is a movie, TV commercial, or cinematic sequence in a video game.

looping motions: Motions that have identical beginning and end frames. They are sometimes also called *tile motions*.

M

magnetic motion capture: A series of sensors that magnetically measure their relationship in space to a nearby transmitter. As with acoustic, these magnetic sensors are placed at the joints in order to capture the person's movement.

marker: A retro-reflective sphere or hemisphere whose location is tracked by the cameras and is attached to the object that you wish to capture.

marker configuration: The arrangement of the markers on the performer or object being captured. Sometimes called *marker placement*.

marker data: *See* cloud data.

marker placement: *See* marker configuration.

motion capture: The process of obtaining and recording a three-dimensional representation of a live action performance or event by capturing an object's position and/or orientation in physical space. Also called *performance capture*.

motion database: A file that contains detailed information about every motion to be captured, edited, or created.

motion diagram: A visual aid other than flowcharts and graphs that is used to help visually represent the greater states or motion sets.

motion list: A record noting and breaking down all motions that will be captured during the capture session and the positions that each motion begins and ends in. It can also contain descriptions of each motion if needed.

motion performer: Any person or animal whose performance is going to be captured, sometimes referred to as *motion talent*.

motion set: A group of movements made up of all the individual motions applied to a character or characters in a game.

motion shoot: *See* capture session.

motion talent: *See* motion performer.

moves list: A record noting all motions that will be captured during the capture session, along with a description of each motion. Also called a *shot list*.

N

noise: *See* jitter.

non-destructive editing: A process of animation where the changes made by the animator are made over the top of the original keyframes so that they are not lost or destroyed during editing.

non-linear animating: A method of animation that allows an animator to alter an animation or several animations from separate sources to create a new animation. The animator can blend, edit, scale, or reposition portions of an animation or several animations when creating the new one.

non-linear motions: Motions that require input from the user in order to be executed. Also called *user-controlled motions*.

non-linear project: A project whose motions respond to commands from user input. A video game is an example of a non-linear project.

O

offset markers: *See* asymmetrical markers.

optical motion capture: A series of reflective markers whose position in space is tracked by a number of digital cameras. In the case of human and animal captures, the markers are generally placed near the joints.

overlapping action: *See* follow through.

P

performance animation: The motion performer's live action performance that is viewed as it is generated. The performer gets feedback to his performance as it happens, so it can be modified as it occurs.

performance capture: *See* motion capture.

personality: An animation principle that refers to an intangible quality that makes a person or character unique.

physical marker: *See* marker.

pop: When one motion file needs to begin before the previous motion file has had time to complete its loop, or when a game does not have transition motion files and skips from one motion to another. This commonly happens in an attempt to speed up the response time. When this occurs, the character appears to skip or *pop* into a new position.

pose planning animating: *See* keyframe animating.

pose to pose animating: *See* keyframe animating.

primary capture session: The main motion capture shoot scheduled for capturing the bulk of the motions needed on a project.

procedural animating: A method of animating where the laws of physics or mathematics take over and dictate the look of the animation.

processed seconds: The number of seconds of motion that are cleaned and delivered after the capture session.

processing: *See* cleaning.

prop: An inanimate object that serves as a means of support or assistance during a motion capture session.

prosthetic motion capture: An external structure attached to a limb or part of the body. Included in this structure is a series of encoders that measure the rotation and position of the performer's body as he moves so that his motion can be analyzed. There are several different types of prosthetic motion capture input systems. Waldos, gloves, and some electromechanical suits can be included in this group.

R

raw seconds: *See* captured seconds.

ready idle motion: A looping motion that the character in a video game goes into when inactive and waiting for user input.

real marker: *See* marker.

real-time animation: A live action performance that is presented on a character in real time. This includes animations that are performed, captured, and rendered in real time.

redundant markers: *See* dummy markers.

root position: *See* base motion.

S

safety take: An extra acceptable version of a motion captured in case the desired motion data is unusable.

sample rate: *See* data rate.

secondary capture session: A supplemental motion capture shoot scheduled to capture any missed, changed or cinematic motions needed on a project.

select: *See* best.

shot list: *See* moves list.

skating feet: When a character's feet slide in a physically unnatural way on the ground, whether the character is moving or idle. This is also sometimes referred to as *sliding feet*.

skeletal data: The movement of a skeleton as it travels through time and space after the marker data has been applied to it.

skeleton: An articulated kinematics hierarchy that consists of several ridged links connected by joints.

sliding feet: *See* skating feet.

slow-in and slow-out: *See* ease-in and ease-out.

squash and stretch: An animation principle that is used to create a feeling of weight. A good example would be a bouncing ball. As it descends, the ball should stretch out to more of an oval shape, as it hits the ground it squashes, and then as it leaves the ground it stretches into an oval again before returning to a more round shape near the apex of the bounce.

staging: An animation principle that refers to presenting an idea or action clearly. How characters relate to each other, how a character moves, when actions happen in relation to other events, and how the scene is viewed all play a part in how clearly it is understood. Scenes that are too busy often overwhelm the viewer, and the idea is lost.

states: *See* greater states.

straight ahead animating: A method of animating where the action is built in an evolving sequence of events one frame at a time. The animator starts at the beginning and moves one frame at a time until the animation is complete.

T

take: An individual version of a motion that you are capturing. You may capture several takes of a motion before you select the desired one.

talent: *See* motion performer.

three-in-one motion: A motion that is captured as a single move during the capture session and broken into three separate motions by the animators in the post capture phase.

tile motions: *See* looping motions.

timing: An animation principle that refers to the pace in which actions occur. The character's personality and body type need to be taken into account when an animator is considering timing. Primary movement and secondary movements all need to be paced properly. Timing also refers to the pace at which interaction between characters and props occurs.

transition motions: Motions that take the game character from one core motion to another.

trial notes: The records taken by the motion capture studio during the capture session to be used after the capture to help process motions.

two-in-one motions: A motion that is captured as a single move during the capture session that will be broken into two separate motions by the animators in the post capture phase.

V

virtual marker: A mathematical equation usually used to find the location of an imaginary point. This calculated point is often used to find the actual center of a joint.

virtual point: *See* virtual marker.

W

weight and balance: An animation principle that refers to having a character's weight balanced, disturbed properly, and shifting correctly as the character moves. When a person moves, his weight is shifted over the planted leg and the passing leg is moved forward, finally hitting the ground in front of the character. A character's center of balance will also tip forward in the direction it is moving. The amount it tips depends on the speed of the movement (the character should tip more the faster he is moving).

Z

zooba-dooba: A word made up by the author to see if you read this book to the very end.

BIBLIOGRAPHY

Chiarella, Tom. *Writing Dialogue*. Story Press, 1998.

deGraf, Brad. Quoted in "The Great Debate," by Wendy Jackson. *Animation Magazine* (August 1999).

Gleicher, Michael and Nicola Ferrier. "Evaluating Video-Based Motion Capture." © 2003 IEEE.

Jackson, Wendy. "The Great Debate." *Animation Magazine* (August 1999).

Lindsay, Alex. "Thinking Inside the Box: Kaydara's Filmbox 2.0." *3D Magazine*, © CMP Media LLC, (April 2000): pp. 45–47.

Menache, Alberto. *Understanding Motion Capture for Computer Animation and Video Games*. Morgan Kaufmann (Academic Press), 2000.

Muybridge, Eadweard. *The Human Figure In Motion*. Dover Publications, Inc., 1955.

Rubin, Jeff. *Antarctica, 2/E*. Lonely Planet Publications Pty Ltd, 2000.

Sito, Tom. Quoted in "The Great Debate," by Wendy Jackson. *Animation Magazine* (August 1999).

Sturman, David J. "A Brief History of Motion Capture for Computer Character Animation." © 2003 IEEE.

Sturman, David J. "Computer Puppetry," *Computer Graphics & Applications*. (January/February 1998): pp. 38–45. © 2003 IEEE.

Trager, Wes. *A Practical Approach to Motion Capture: Acclaim's optical motion capture system*. Available online at *http://www.siggraph.org/ education/materials/HyperGraph/animation/character_animation/ motion_capture/motion_optical.htm*

White, Tony. *The Animator's Workbook*. Billboard Publications, Inc. (Watson-Guptill Publications), 1986.

Williams, Richard. *The Animator's Survival Kit*. Faber and Faber Limited, 2001.

INDEX

percentage of wasted, 227
three-in-one motions, 57, 292
two-in-one motions, 57, 292
See also Capture sessions; Core motions;
Motion list; Motion database
Moves list, 43, 288. *See also* Motion list
Muybridge, Eadweard, 2–3

N
Names, motion, 58, 89–90, 96
Neck markers, 129
Nelvanna/Medialab, 4
Nike commercials, xv
Noise and unacceptable motion files, 232, 286
Non-disclosure and contract, 165–166
Non-linear animating. 10–11, 288
Non-linear motions
described, 41, 288
response time, 41–42, 285
user-controlled motions, 15–16, 54
Non-linear project, 22–23, 288
Notes
in motion database, 92, 93, 96, 218–219
trial, 292

O
Offset markers, 134, 281
Olsen, Chris, 137
Omlansky, Alexander, 234
Optical motion capture
described, 8, 289
development of, 3
markers for, 128
system manufacturers, 279
using, 9, 22
Orientation of characters, and world coordinates,
235, 243, 246
Overlapping actions, 285. *See also* Follow through

P
Passing position, 240, 241
Payment schedule for motion capture session,
153, 160–161, 230
Pedals and digital puppetry, 7, 284
Performance animation, described, 7, 289
Performance capture, 6–7. *See also* Motion
capture
Performers. *See* Motion performers

Per-second bid, 146–147, 148–149
Personality
described, 13–14, 289
post capture considerations, 18
preparing for motion capture, 15–16
Perspective Studios, 132, 175, 276
Pinned motions, 242–243
Platforms, game, 24
Playback systems during capture sessions,
144–145, 196, 199–200, 216–217
Playstation 2 (Sony), 24
Pop or skip to new position, 236, 240, 289
Pope, Steve, 181–182, 261, 265–266, 277
Popeye, 2
Pose planning animating, 9–10, 286
Pose to pose animating, 9–10, 286
Posing armatures, 8
Post production
blends and cycle motions, 227–228
considerations during capture, 17–18, 32,
211–212
frame range selections, 225–230
handle frames, 226–228, 282
processed vs. captured seconds, 170, 226–227,
282, 290
*Practical Approach to Motion Capture: Acclaim's
Optical Motion Capture System, A* (Trager),
7
Priority, processing, 90, 92–93, 96, 202, 230
Procedural animating, 10–11, 289
Processed seconds, 170, 226–227, 290
Processing motion files
best takes, 92, 94, 96, 157, 217, 282
cleaning data, 25–26, 282
data processing, 158–159
priority of, 90, 92–93, 96, 202, 230
See also Editing
Programmers
finished motion files for, 115, 124, 230
pinned motions for, 242–243
priority for finished files, 247–248, 270
Projects
coordinated approach to, 35–37
new project and motion list, 49–50
patchwork project and motion list, 49
re-shoot project and motion list, 49–50
suitability of motion capture for, 22–30
See also Capture session; Schedule for projects